30[00]

WHEN RACE, RELIGION, AND SPORT COLLIDE

Black Athletes at BYU and Beyond

Darron T. Smith

ROWMAN & LITTLEFIELD
Lanham • Boulder • New York • London

EL CAMINO COLLEGE LIBRARY

Published by Rowman & Littlefield
A wholly owned subsidiary of
The Rowman & Littlefield Publishing Group, Inc.
4501 Forbes Boulevard, Suite 200, Lanham, Maryland 20706
www.rowman.com

Unit A, Whitacre Mews, 26-34 Stannary Street, London SE11 4AB,
United Kingdom

Copyright © 2016 by Rowman & Littlefield
First paperback edition 2017

All rights reserved. No part of this book may be reproduced in any form or by any electronic or mechanical means, including information storage and retrieval systems, without written permission from the publisher, except by a reviewer who may quote passages in a review.

British Library Cataloguing in Publication Information Available

Library of Congress Cataloging-in-Publication Data
Names: Smith, Darron T., 1965–
Title: When race, religion, and sport collide : Black athletes at BYU and beyond / Darron T. Smith.
Description: Lanham, Maryland : Rowman & Littlefield, [2016] | Series: Perspectives on a multiracial America | Includes bibliographical references and index.
Identifiers: LCCN 2015034699| ISBN 9781442217881 (cloth : alk. paper) | ISBN 9781442217898 (pbk. : alk. paper) | ISBN 9781442217904 (electronic)
Subjects: LCSH: Brigham Young University—Sports. | African American athletes—Utah—Provo. | African American Mormons. | Racism in sports—Utah—Provo. | Race relations—Religious aspects—Church of Jesus Christ of Latter-day Saints. | Race relations—Religious aspects—Mormon Church. | Sports—Social aspects—United States. | African American athletes. | African American athletes—Social conditions. | United States—Race relations.
Classification: LCC GV691.B74 S65 2016 | DDC 796.04309792/24—dc23
LC record available at https://lccn.loc.gov/2015034699

∞ ™ The paper used in this publication meets the minimum requirements of American National Standard for Information Sciences Permanence of Paper for Printed Library Materials, ANSI/NISO Z39.48-1992.

Printed in the United States of America

school. This book is a welcome voice to the growing body of literature on Mormon race relations. It is a superb achievement."

—Matthew L. Harris, Colorado State University–Pueblo; coauthor of *The Mormon Church and Blacks: A Documentary History*

"Darron Smith's study of institutionalized racism as informed by religious doctrine is an important, thought-provoking work. Smith asks hard questions and does not settle for easy answers. Whether readers agree or disagree with his analysis, observations, and conclusions, they will not leave his stimulating book unchanged."

—Gary James Bergera, coauthor of *Brigham Young University: A House of Faith*

"*When Race, Religion, and Sport Collide* is a thoughtful and unique examination of the sociocultural issues at play within intercollegiate athletics. Dr. Smith's work sheds light on larger social and structural issues by focusing on a truly interesting case study that will benefit students, administrators, faculty, and other personnel in both athletics and education."

—Mark Vermillion, chair, Department of Sport Management; executive director of Partnership for the Advancement of Sport Management, Wichita State University

"In *When Race, Religion, and Sport Collide*, Darron Smith has the keen insight to examine the intersection of race and religion and how these categories intersect sports. This book should be added to the corpus for scholars who are interested in the murky terrain of collegiate sports scholarship and to the growing work in Mormon studies, race studies, and sports."

—Stephen C. Finley, Louisiana State University

Praise for
When Race, Religion, and Sport Collide

"This book is a revealing examination of race in sports and religion with a unique focus—the treatment of black athletes at BYU. Darron Smith uses football, basketball, and other sports to explain a deep-seated prejudice at the heart of Mormonism. Anyone surprised to learn that Brigham Young was a racist should read this book."

—Luke O'Brien, Politico

"This is a story of young black men used, abused, and too easily discarded under the guise of amateurism and faith. As he explores the crushing subtleties of racism in a respected college athletics program, Darron Smith reminds us that conscience is no defense for the indefensible. An important read."

—Chad Nielsen, sportswriter

"In this book, Darron T. Smith demands that we move beyond box scores, beyond wins and losses, beyond March Madness and bowl season, and beyond the cheers to reflect on the intersecting histories of religion, race, and sport. Offering a powerful discussion of college sports, blackness, and whiteness, Smith chronicles the story of black students at BYU. Using sports as a staging ground, despite claims of postraciality and colorblindness, Smith offers a powerful discussion of race within and beyond the sporting fields. Interdisciplinary at its core, *When Race, Religion, and Sport Collide* brings together discussions of race and Mormonism, the revolt of the black athlete, contemporary college sports, and new racism. An important work for scholars of religion, sports, and race, this work is timely."

—David J. Leonard, Washington State University

"I want to highlight this amazing book. . . . [It] is a really fascinating read . . . I can't plug this book enough and tell everybody they need to read it."

—Mormon Stories

"In this provocative new study, Darron T. Smith examines the connection between blackness and Mormonism using Brigham Young University's honor code as a case study. His book bristles with new insights, demonstrating the ways in which Mormon racial theology has affected the lives of black athletes at the church-owned and -operated

Perspectives on a Multiracial America Series
Joe R. Feagin, Texas A&M University, Series Editor

Melanie Bush, *Breaking the Code of Good Intentions: Everyday Forms of Whiteness*
Amir Mavasti and Karyn McKinney, *Middle Eastern Lives in America*
Katheryn Russell-Brown, *Protecting Our Own: Race, Crime, and African Americans*
Victoria Kaplan, *Structural Inequality: Black Architects in the United States*
Elizabeth M. Aranda, *Emotional Bridges to Puerto Rico: Migration, Return Migration, and the Struggles of Incorporation*
Richard Rees, *Shades of Difference: A History of Ethnicity in America*
Pamela Anne Quiroz, *Adoption in a Color-Blind Society*
Adia Harvey Wingfield, *Doing Business with Beauty: Black Women, Hair Salons, and the Racial Enclave Economy*
Angela J. Hattery, David G. Embrick, and Earl Smith, *Globalization and America: Race, Human Rights, and Inequality*
Erica Chito Childs, *Fade to Black and White: Interracial Images in Popular Culture*
Jessie Daniels, *Cyber Racism: White Supremacy Online and the New Attack on Civil Rights*
Teun A. van Dijk, *Racism and Discourse in Latin America*
C. Richard King, Carmen R. Lugo-Lugo, and Mary K. Bloodsworth-Lugo, *Animating Difference: Race, Gender, and Sexuality in Contemporary Films for Children*
Melanie E. L. Bush, *Everyday Forms of Whiteness: Understanding Race in a "Post-Racial" World, 2nd edition*
David J. Leonard and C. Richard King, *Commodified and Criminalized: New Racism and African Americans in Contemporary Sports*
Maria Chávez, *Everyday Injustice: Latino Professionals and Racism*
Benjamin Fleury-Steiner, *Disposable Heroes: The Betrayal of African American Veterans*
Noel A. Cazenave, *The Urban Racial State: Managing Race Relations in American Cities*
Cherise A. Harris, *The Cosby Cohort: Race, Class, and Identity among Second Generation Middle Class Blacks*
Louwanda Evans, *Cabin Pressure: African American Pilots, Flight Attendants, and Emotional Labor*
Kristen M. Lavelle, *Whitewashing the South: White Memories of Segregation and Civil Rights*
Ruth Thompson-Miller, Joe R. Feagin, and Leslie H. Picca, *Jim Crow's Legacy: The Lasting Impact of Segregation*
Mary K. Bloodsworth-Lugo and Carmen R. Lugo-Lugo, *Projecting 9/11: Race, Gender, and Citizenship in Recent Hollywood Films*

CONTENTS

ACKNOWLEDGMENTS

I always ask for forgiveness when writing acknowledgments in fear that I may overlook those who have made significant contributions to this book. I have benefitted from the camaraderie of many instructors, friends, colleagues, mentors, librarians, archivists, and strangers. I hope these forthcoming words adequately represent my deepest appreciation for your individual efforts and contributions in time and advice.

First, I would like to thank many of the former players at BYU who bravely shared their stories. I can only imagine that revisiting such a painful period would bring up feelings of loss, anger, and remorse. Thank you for allowing me the intrusion into your personal lives. I hope this book adequately gives voice to the struggles you faced during your ordeal on campus and to how the events shaped your lives thereafter.

The journey of this book was sparked in the wake of the Brandon Davies dismissal with the intent to bring to light the complicated history of race and religion in the Mormon Church and the hypocrisy illuminated through the medium of sport. A few years earlier during the Gary Crowton coaching era, freelance writer Chad Nielsen was working on a story for *Salt Lake City Magazine* about the high expulsion rate of black athletes at BYU. Chad sought out my thoughts on the situation, as an adjunct member in the sociology department at BYU. His courageous reporting on a number of important, probing, and insightful pieces set the stage for this book, and I thank him for that.

Additionally, I would like to thank Chad for linking me up with journalist Luke O'Brien. The piece I coauthored with Luke for *Dead-*

spin jumpstarted the idea for this manuscript. Thank you, Luke, for your support, encouragement and inspiration for this book and, most of all, for giving me a platform to write.

As I mulled over the concept and direction of the manuscript, my partner and confidant, Tasha Sabino, was there as a sounding board and collaborator from the initial stages. She was instrumental in the creative direction of the book, editing and rewriting alongside me every step of the way. Her keen eye and attention to detail brought what seemed at times a garbled mess into form, providing a clear pathway for its eventual publication. Thank you, Tasha, for your unyielding support through countless delays and life struggles, which makes this accomplishment all the more rewarding.

I would like to thank Joe Feagin for his continual mentorship and guidance and for the work he continues to do in the cause of justice for African Americans and other Americans of color. I very much appreciate my good friend, Robert Foster, not only for his time and wisdom but also for blazing the trail for future young brothers and sisters finding their way through the austerities of BYU life. Your story is next. Paul Mogren offered a wealth of knowledge and time in aiding our research at the University of Utah Marriot Library, Brian Webber gathered invaluable data as the resident "research assistant" for the book, and Nicholas Hartlep shared his insight on the myth of the model minority. I thank you all. Additionally, I would like to thank Sarah Stanton, Karie Simpson, and Alden Perkins with Rowman & Littlefield Publishers for working really hard and fast to bring this book into existence.

There are those who spent much time reading various drafts of this manuscript and offer critical insight to improve and strengthen the narrative. A heartfelt thank you to Brenda Juarez, Matt Harris, Cardell Jacobson, and Cleveland Hayes. I am additionally grateful to those who took time out of their day and allowed me to either interview them or pick their brains: Ronney Jenkins, Hassan McCollough, Mel Hamilton, Rashaun Broadus, Marcus Whalen and his mother, Christian Parker, Marlon Terrell, D. Michael Quinn, Gary Bergera, and Sandra Tanner. My good friends, Edmond Washington, Adelwale Sogunro, and Prince Achime, posed as a much forgiving audience when I needed to bounce around ideas. And a special gratitude goes out to Earl Smith, Mark Vermillion, David Leonard, Stephen Finley, Susan Harris O'Connor,

W. Paul Reeve, and Shaun Harper for providing strong reviews and support for this book.

Most importantly, I thank my family, including my beautiful girls, for their unconditional love and inspiring strength despite the many challenges they face daily; I love you.

INTRODUCTION

In the wake of the Donald Sterling fiasco in which the white Los Angeles Clippers owner was recorded (by his biracial mistress) making off-color racial commentary regarding black athletes—Magic Johnson principally—NBA executives were scrambling. The reason being that, although the American public was able to wave Sterling off as a curmudgeon and old-fashioned racist, it is not hard to imagine that other corporate executives had likely said similar things about their African American players or fan base in private settings with like-minded friends. This is, of course, pure speculation, but one grounded in evidence-based research that shows that most white Americans cognitively refrain from outwardly speaking about race in public spaces while engaging in racially charged conversations behind closed doors. This is known in the literature as "backstage" racism, a pattern of behavior in which white people use offensive racist language behind the scenes with family and/or close friends, but out of the earshot of the general populace.[1]

Among those scrambling NBA execs, Atlanta Hawks majority owner Bruce Levenson combed back through two years' worth of e-mails to find any link to racialized language. Once such evidence was found, he turned himself (and the suspicious text) in to the NBA.[2] In that correspondence, Levenson sought to solve the mystery of declining profit. Some of the material that he wrote (his "theories") was racially misguided, insensitive, and typical of what many white people think about African Americans. But some of what he wrote merely underscored the cold, hard facts about the sad state of American race relations and the seemingly colossal failure of Dr. Martin Luther King Jr.'s vision of a society where one day the burden of race would be less salient for his children.

Found in the words of Levenson's e-mail was the reality of systemic racism at the core of American capitalism. While investigating the cause of low season-ticket sales, Levenson found a lack of thirty-five- to fifty-five-year-old white males (who predominate in the NBA market as season-ticket holders) in his audience. Instead, the Hawks' typical crowd was 40 to 70 percent black in any given year. In his e-mail, he discusses ways to attract a bigger white fan base, such as adding more white cheerleaders to the team, ensuring the "kiss cam" focuses on white fans, and including music that is "familiar to a 40-year-old white guy."[3] The reasons why Levenson is so focused on this change are market driven, motivated by capitalist tendencies toward the bottom line. For Levenson and other professional sports team owners and managers, the forty-year-old white male is the demographic that guarantees profitability, demonstrating the crucial role that race plays in consumerism.[4] This is just one example of the racialization of people of African descent within a popular American institution.

White racism is an everyday reality for African Americans and other Americans of color and, therefore, must be understood as systemic and overarching, something very different from individual acts of meanness. It is the total domination and exploitation of African Americans and other Americans of color by whites in the economic, political, and sociocultural spheres of U.S. society. The system was produced by white hegemonic antidemocratic forces determined to stymie black progress for personal gain by unjustly uprooting future kings and queens who were captains of industry in their own right. Africa became the European prize for its precious human resources—involuntary gang labor forced to build up the coffers of an emerging white, patriarchal, Western empire. European Americans accomplished this task by weaponizing racial difference, politicizing its meaning, and placing value judgments on the bodies of black people. Hence, skin color became the locus of control and impetus for group marginalization, as blacks were considered three-fifths of a human being and subsequently barred from full participation on equal terms with whites from 1619 until the last civil rights law was passed in 1969.

For almost 90 percent of U.S. history, powerful and elite white men laid the foundation for a stratified society (i.e., by race, class, and gender) established on an expansive and malignant ideology that negatively informed the worldview of generations of Americans. These inheritances are repeated and passed along to ensuing generations of white Americans and their descendants for centuries to come. Systemic racism relied on racial identity politics that established psychic barriers meant to derail the black freedom movement at both the structural and ideological levels of society, often with harsh consequences to black initiative, black progress, and ultimately black success. One institution that has been particularly unforgiving on black Americans is higher education.

In 1984, Jacqueline Fleming noted that the state of black men in America was grim.[5] She came to this conclusion after studying this population in both historically black and predominately white institutions. Based on the comprehensive variables she once used to measure how well students adjusted, not much has changed today. This book seeks to analyze the fate of black men just as Fleming did, but through the Church of Jesus Christ of Latter-day Saints (LDS or Mormon) and its academic flagship institution, Brigham Young University (BYU), whose journey squarely intersects with America's troubling history of black denigration. The LDS church is the most prolific (at home and abroad) religious sect born in nineteenth-century America, which means that it is as quintessentially American as apple pie. The principles of the Mormon Church are based upon white-centered values and traditions that drove American idealism. Thus, the Church shares with other white organizations the same dominant narrative of the so-called protestant work ethic embodied within the framework of individualism. And just as U.S. history is rooted in white supremacy, so is the history and theology of the Mormon faith shaped by this convergence. The two are bound together. In other words, the Christian faith of Mormonism stands as a litmus test for the American experience.

To be fair, the LDS church is not the only white North American religious movement that relied on racist ideology as part of its teachings. However, the Roman Catholic Church and other Protestant-based sects—the Episcopal Church, the United Methodist Church, the Southern Baptists and Lutherans—have since made peace with their racist past and issued public apologies for their role in slavery and Jim

Crow racism and their participation in the oppression of African Americans at the hands of misguided Christians.[6] Mormonism is the only one of these faiths to not fully reconcile their past with an *official* apology.[7] They are the lone holdout.

The LDS church has a long, sordid past of denying people of African lineage full access to the Church. And not coincidentally, BYU has an extended history of a disproportionately high expulsion rate of black men over the past twenty-five years, since the recruitment of black athletes became increasingly more commonplace at BYU. Analyzed within the covers of this book are religious teachings and theological folklore within the private Church-owned institution and the subsequent implications for black men on campus. This initiative will be conducted using theories derived from sociology and the cognitive sciences on framing.[8,9,10]

Frames, which are discussed along with their central components in great detail in chapter 2, have significant consequences for communities of color, especially for lower-class black men and boys, who are more vulnerable to severe and adult-like treatment than their white peers in the criminal and juvenile justice system.[11] The ways in which white people permissibly marginalize and disrespect black people would be considered morally objectionable to a same-race peer. But frames provide the kindling, thereby allowing white racial prejudice and bigotry to flourish systemically through implicit bias and explicit behavior in a country that sees itself as "post-racial."

One enduring aspect of the white racial frame is the tendency for white people to associate black Americans with nonhuman primates and stereotype them accordingly.[12] The specific portrayal of blacks as bestial and more ape-like (e.g., President Obama was recently referred to as a chimpanzee in circulating racist e-mails by the Ferguson Police Department[13]) than other populations of humans is not new in Western culture. The underlying belief or frame of African Americans as closer to nature leads to the old racist image of blacks as more dangerous. Levenson eloquently exposed this in his e-mail. He wrote:

> On fan sites I would read comments about how dangerous it is around Philips yet in our 9 years, I don't know of a mugging or even a pickpocket incident. This was just racist garbage. When I hear some

> people saying the arena is in the wrong place I think it is code for there are too many blacks at the games.[14]

Levenson was referring to the racially coded language that whites use in their attempt at being "colorblind" and its effects on certain institutions, in this case the genre of sport. In reality, this frame of blacks as dangerous and animal-like leads to the misguided notion that blacks are in need of white surveillance, subordination, and control. With that comes widespread social acceptance for disciplinary tactics and even sanctioned violence on the black body. Take, for example, research conducted by Goff and associates in which white participants were subliminally exposed to images of apes before watching a video of law enforcement thrashing a black man. They were found to be more likely to condone the behavior as appropriate, notwithstanding the violent nature of the scene, than were others who did not receive the hidden message.[15] Racial frames such as these influence white racial attitudes, beliefs, and practices at both the macro and micro levels of society.

One can, therefore, hypothesize the results of the retrospective study by Wolfers and Price in which they found, over a thirteen-year period in the NBA (National Basketball Association), that white referees called fouls on black players more frequently than on their white teammates.[16] This signifies the way in which color distinction informs white consciousness, shaping our perception of reality and powerfully influencing our action. Another study in the National Hockey League (NHL) found that even players wearing dark-colored jerseys (particularly black jerseys) acquired more penalty time than those wearing white or light colored jerseys.[17] If a black jersey can elicit such strong anti-black sentiment, one can only imagine what the black body does to the white psyche.

This bias is deeply ingrained and largely unconscious but provides a necessary rationale for exclusion, punishment, and sanctioned violence used against blacks that we see in a number of white controlled institutions, such as education, religion, employment, and sports, to name a few. Each entity has its own particular racial genesis, which dictates white habits and dealings with blacks. The most salient example of this today is noted in the excessive discipline of black children in public education, which coupled with lack of quality instruction in the urban schools has led to the school-to-prison pipeline with an overrepresentation of black and brown folks winding up in the penal system.

The positioning of African Americans as on the wrong side of evolution enables many, if not most, whites to sleep well at night despite the brutal and persistent treatment that blacks withstand at all levels of society. Research conducted on racism and empathy, the ability to understand and feel another individual's pain, found that when correlated with implicit racial bias, whites reacted less to the pain of black people compared to same-race participants in a series of experiments. According to Feagin, "Psychiatrists use the term 'alexithymia' to describe persons who are unable to understand the emotions of, and thus empathize with, other people."[18] Taking this concept beyond the clinical diagnosis of the individual, he further describes "social alexithymia" as a group-based dynamic, such as the inability to feel the pain and suffering of those communities that are targets of systemic white racism. This notion describes a collective state of white delusion. Most white Americans politely ignore, and in fact work very hard to deny, that blacks bear differential treatment in life. This failure to acknowledge the ways in which white racism inflicts trauma upon and exacts energy from its victims is something akin to the mental disorder of "psychosis."[19] Hence, it becomes evident that racism requires from the oppressor a detachment of emotion, a loss of the capacity to feel the depths of human suffering and misery. In fact, a lack of empathy in people has been linked to abuse, violence, and interpersonal and intergroup decline in relationships.[20] This may explain the relentless police brutality against black Americans and even the degree to which black student-athletes have been removed from a religious school professing universalism, such as BYU.

How whites are conditioned to understand the racial order has a modulating effect on their degree of pro-social empathic behavior.[21] Alexithymia is one way in which systemic white racism prevails in American society, chiefly targeting African Americans and distorting the reality of their conditions and circumstances. It has robbed most white Americans of full humanity by desensitizing them to the travails of the oppressed and blinding them to racial privilege they unjustly earned. People of European descent in North America have been overtly primed to see the world through the standpoint of a white lens. This myopic disposition has consequences for subaltern peoples in various institutions. The white racial frame, hence, has become the instrument to subdue black Americans.

This book will take a journey through the intersecting histories of sport, race, and religion. Utilizing systemic racism theory and its correlate, the white racial frame,[22] it will analyze the various dimensions of race and race-based practices within American institutions. As this book delves into the realm of the sacred through the examination of Mormonism, a faith born out of the American experience, it unpacks the religious production of white racial knowledge and meaning making within the framework of sport. Chapter 2 will outline the history of blacks in sport while chapter 3 discusses the history of race in Christianity, with specific focus given to white racial framing in the Church of Jesus Christ of Latter-day Saints. Paying particular attention to black male student-athletes, chapter 4 deconstructs the widespread revolts in the sporting world over injustices they faced both on and off the field of competitive play. In chapter 5, this book details the response to these revolts by LDS church authorities and how matters of race are produced through ethereal stories, images, and commentary under the aegis of God. The LDS church has a sordid past in its dealings with people of African descent. By exploring the cross-connection of the entities of sport and religion, chapter 6 aims to thoroughly dissect and understand modern forms of everyday racism reflected within the LDS church and at BYU. Chapter 7 examines the harmful effects of colorblindness leading to the poor state of higher education for many black collegiate athletes. And chapter 8 will discuss the importance of robust and meaningful measures that must be instituted at BYU and throughout America's predominately white colleges and universities as transparent policy designed to prevent the failings of the next generation of black Americans. It will further investigate the way contemporary athletes, black student-athletes in particular, are standing up to decades of exploitation and taking some measure of their power back. The Mormon church must take this opportunity to positively transform the fate of many black men and women without repercussions to their self-concept and identity as people of color. Only then can the status of black people in the LDS church and in the United States as a whole be altered on its present course and ultimately rectified.

I

THE MEANING OF SPORT IN THE POPULAR IMAGINATION

The Collision of Race, Religion, and Sport

> White is the symbol of Divinity or God; Black is the symbol of the evil spirit or the demon. White is the symbol of light; Black is the symbol of darkness and darkness expresses all evils.—Jacques Nicolas Paillot de Montabert[1,2]

America loves sports. And most Americans are crazy about competition no matter the type or arena.[3] Whether it is college or the professional ranks, both institutions generate millions of dollars per year for their respective schools and franchises. The lucrative character of sports in the United States says a great deal about the American psyche and the extent to which competitive play captivates, entertains, and thrills fans. More importantly, the power of sports to generate huge profits provides insight into how and why athletes are venerated in U.S. society and often placed on a public pedestal for their talents, especially in the high-revenue-producing sports like football, basketball, and even baseball.

One reason why sports are so appealing is that at the basic level of competition it is presumed that socioeconomic status and racial group affiliation are of no consequence; to win, talent and hard work matter, not social differences. Put simply, sports are supposed to be blind to differences of race, socioeconomic class, religion, and more. In fact, a

2013 Rasmussen Report states, "Most Americans (53%) believe professional sports have *improved* race relations in the United States" (emphasis added).[4] Hence, athletic competition is considered to take place on an "even playing field." And if that terrain is indeed level, then success is warranted to the one that put forth the greatest effort. This focus on victory earned among rival competitors with an equal opportunity to succeed is what sport represents in principle to fans and the broader society.[5]

Interestingly, sport captivates fans from all walks of life, even as it reflects and typifies dominant (Eurocentric) ideas about merit and meritocracy—that is to say, effort-based achievement through individual initiative and labor. But is it possible that athletic competition in America has escaped being tainted by the difference-based hierarchies of inequity that are still reproduced in society's other key domains such as healthcare, employment, education, and other institutions? According to Mary Jo Kane, the industry of sport actually mirrors society. "Sport has become such a bedrock of our national psyche that sport figures often come to symbolize larger pressing concerns."[6,7] For example, the love/hate relationship between American football fans and former NFL quarterback Tim Tebow stands as an emblem of the religious tug-of-war in our society. Additionally, the rise of the black quarterback who personifies black stereotypes through dreadlocks or tattoos, such as Robert Griffin III or Colin Kaepernick, is representative of black men struggling on the fault lines of race in search of full personhood and an equal seat at the proverbial table. Sport, then, "consists of a set of ideological beliefs and practices that are closely tied to traditional power structures."[8] Through the prism of sport, this book will explore the complex nature of race and racial meaning making within religious practices. As the narrative unfolds, this book uncovers contextual evidence regarding the unjust wielding of power and privilege within white controlled institutions of academia and religion. It further illuminates the marking of black bodies as "Other" through America's most cherished national pastimes.

CONSIDERING RACIAL DIFFERENCES IN SPORTS: "LINSANITY" AND THE MODEL MINORITY MYTH

For those constructed as the "Other," sport "is a contradictory space, for while it is an area where black athletic achievement and success are apparent and visible, the physicality of sport performance simultaneously reinscribes beliefs that blacks are inherently superior athletes."[9] Because the belief in black athletic prowess is so deeply engrained in mainstream thinking, there is little room for "boundary crossing," even by other groups whose bodies have not been marked in the same way. Take, for example, the electrifying nature of the "Linsanity" craze. Jeremy Lin is an Asian American basketball player who played collegiate hoops at Harvard University before joining the NBA in 2010.[10] Despite playing sparse minutes in his rookie season, he broke out on the sports scene the following year as a national and world sensation when he started as point guard for the injured Baron Davis and the struggling New York Knicks during the shortened lockout season of 2011–2012.

The addition of Lin to the starting lineup, taking charge on the basketball court, infused new life into the deflated Knicks team, propelling them to a 6–0 winning streak.[11] The nation's sports fans, in response, went bananas over Lin. Linsanity, Linsational, Lincredible, Linspiring; these were only a sample of words and phrases that developed during this time. Lin puns continued for three consecutive weeks, all while the world fanatically followed Jeremy Lin. To be sure, Lin is a very good basketball player and an incredible athlete. But what sparked the sensationalism surrounding his success?

Jeremy Lin did spend some time in the NBA's Developmental league (D-league) so one might assume that his underdog story is what catapulted his stunning rise to public adoration.[12] However, there are a handful of other NBA stars including Aaron Brooks, Ramon Sessions, and even NBA championship players, such as Jose Barea, Shannon Brown, and Jordan Farmar, who similarly spent some of their early career in the D-league before transitioning to NBA starter. Yet all of these players received minimal attention compared to Lin.[13]

When it was Lin's time to display his talents on the basketball court, he did not just have the average sports fan excited over an energetic, yet brief, ESPN highlight. The world was truly riveted by him, to the point that *Time* magazine declared him one of the "Top 100 Most Influential

People in the World."[14] Jeremy Lin garnered a magnitude of public attention that was unparalleled by other talented players. What was it that made him stand out among the world's top athletes as an object of attention and fascination?

When we consider Jeremy Lin's rise to fame in the NBA, his race as an Asian American man becomes an important factor. Because of the minoritized status of Asians in the United States, discursive stereotypes abound on what it means to be Asian, both physically and culturally. Race scholar Joe Feagin attests that stereotypes act as "filters, straining out information inconsistent with the dominant racial frame."[15] (*Framing* will be discussed in the following chapter.) Following Feagin then, most Americans do not conceptualize Asians as premier NBA basketball players, certainly not someone who attended an Ivy League school such as Harvard and majored in economics.[16,17] It is true that there are very few Asian Americans in the league. But what is also correct is that Jeremy Lin's athletic feats were often overlooked due to society's racial expectations and stereotypes of him.[18] Lin was a star high school player in California, named to California first team all-state and earning the title of regional Player of the Year in his division and California-Hawaii Sports Scholar Athlete of the Year in his senior year, but he was not highly recruited.[19] In fact, he did not receive a single scholarship offer from any Division I school, mid-major or otherwise. Further, he was one of the best players to ever come out of Harvard, setting multiple Ivy League records, but he was not drafted into the NBA.[20] Both Lin himself and his high school coach have acknowledged the fact that race seemingly played a major role in his recruitment, or the lack thereof.[21,22]

Hartlep writes that Lin embodies the academic model minority.[23] He is a stereotype as articulated in Petersen's "Success Story: Japanese American Style" in the *New York Times Magazine*. Constructing the notion that Asians are docile, unassuming, smart, and self-reliant, Petersen maintains that the Japanese are model citizens and other minorities should follow their lead.[24] His piece, however, was racially divisive in that it exceptionalizes Asians and their experiences as the "model" in how a racially marked person should be or behave in a white dominated milieu. Similarly, ESPN analysts often revere Lin, personifying him as the model minority when they describe him as selfless, hardworking, humble and intelligent. This "intelligence" was further magnified during an interview with former CNN correspondent TJ Holmes. The special segment entitled *From Harvard to the NBA* emphasized Lin's academic accomplishments.[25] It additionally mystified his rise to the professional sports arena, as the Asian stereotype does not classify Asians as athletic. Having said that, embedded within the essentialized framework of a race-based stereotype exists an exception clause to the stereotypic "rule." Lin often hears references that describe him as that exception. In an interview with Rachel Nichols, he recounts hearing the description "deceptively athletic" attributed to him despite his 6-foot 3-inch, two hundred pound build.[26]

The model minority myth assumes that Asian Americans do not experience race-based discrimination, and if they do, it is not akin to the discrimination experienced by black Americans. But while Asian Americans are often mythologized in the racist formulations of white Western thinking in apparently positive ways as highly intelligent, they are also marginalized. Some discrimination is more overt than others, such as the staggeringly offensive epithet atop a headline story about Jeremy Lin entitled, "Chink in the Armor."[27] Moreover, Lin describes hearing racial taunts and slurs from fans and players alike during his high school and college days playing around the country.[28,29] But even while they are being mocked and ridiculed, Asians are positioned and propped up as an example of how a racially marked person should behave. Just as Petersen's piece illustrated, the myth of the model minority is racially divisive in exceptionalizing the Asian experience as the "model" for black Americans if only they would "followed the rules" on racial etiquette regarding how to appropriately conduct oneself as prescribed by the white power structure.

SPORTS, RACE, CLASS, AND ACCESS

The unequal representation of Asians in differing sports has little to do with pseudoscientific arguments that particular racial groups are genetically more or less likely to excel in a certain type of physical activity over another.[30] This is true as well for blacks, whites, and all other groups distinguished by ethnicity or race. Instead, stereotypical racial expectations contribute to and fuel these dramatic depictions. Accordingly, there is an overabundance of African Americans in football, basketball, and track and field, while Asians are underrepresented in these high-profile American sports.[31,32]

Additionally, sport participation has much to do with how families and communities socialize children, adolescents and early adults around certain sports. Harry Edwards, a leading authority on the sociology of sport, has argued that pushing athletics in the black American community hinders the social and cognitive growth of black youth.[33] When physicality is the most highly valued commodity that blacks possess in a racist society, then school becomes a means to an end, while the professional leagues pose as a viable and accessible option to propel not only themselves, but also the entire family, out of the cycle of economic uncertainty. This is what sport has come to signify for scores of black families, many of them low-income, living paycheck to paycheck and seeing their children's talents as a possible gateway to better days ahead.

With limited economic resources available to participate in sports within black communities,[34,35] games like football and basketball, which are generally inexpensive and publically supported by local school districts and various community and church leagues, become staples, even outlets. When all that is needed is a ball to practice (and, possibly, a make-shift hoop), the talent pool is large. Any young child has the potential to practice hours on end to become a star. But when an ice rink or an aquatic arena is added to the mix, the potential sports stars are limited to those who have access and means to such facilities. The abundance of African Americans in the high-revenue, high-profile sports has maintained the racial myth that blacks are genetically superior in physicality to their white counterparts, which has contributed to a pernicious self-fulfilling prophecy when it comes to recruitment efforts.[36] But the relative nonexistence of blacks in the so-called highbrow sports like golf, tennis, and swimming rebuffs this myth. Save a handful of prominent professional athletes like Tiger Woods or the emblematic tennis super stars the Williams sisters, expensive private coaching and burdensome court fees, green fees, and country club and tournament fees, not to mention the price of travel and equipment, are cost prohibitive for many African American families, a significant number of whom are living in penurious areas below the official government poverty line.[37] It becomes clear that these divisions are more about access than biology.

And the same can be said for a quality education. To put it nicely, schooling in low-income areas is subpar throughout the country. In a time and place where over 75% of NBA players are black,[38] two-thirds of NFL players are black[39] and yet only 3.8% of all doctors are black,[40] this well-orchestrated effort to derail black academic achievement through the use of sport becomes apparent. When value is placed on sport over academic excellence, youth are unprepared to become global citizens in a steadily changing context, displacing their precious energy into physical prowess while compromising their academic potential.[41] This malignant underdevelopment in black youth derails the social and economic mobility that is necessary to drive them forward into important career paths such as medicine, law, engineering, and other technical fields where a critical mass of African Americans is absent.[42,43] Yet the truth is, black bodies are tied to systems of white knowledge production and domination created centuries ago through European and European-American imperialism and colonialism. By design, whites are kept at the top of the power structure[44,45] through a long-standing history of unjust, repressive, and often violent means (i.e., subjugation of African, Native American, and other subaltern peoples), and that hierarchy is interconnected in a complex matrix of sustained economic and racial inequality felt presently in contemporary society.[46,47,48,49,50]

TEBOWMANIA AND RELIGIOUS EXHIBITIONISM IN SPORT

Inasmuch as social-class position and race play a significant role in American sports, as we have seen in the case of Jeremy Lin, so does the practice of religious faith. In a country where over 90 percent of its population claims to believe in God (and over 80 percent polled believed that religion is an important factor in their life), faith cannot help but inform what we think and do in our everyday lives.[51] With the lionization of both sport and God, America is bound to fuse the two.

From YMCA youth sports leagues to the influence of religion-based academies on our budding junior high and high school sports stars, the early influence is unmistakable. In fact, religion has become so commonplace that athletes on every level are routinely seen and encouraged to pray before and after an event, and many are even shown performing some aspect of prayer following touchdowns, homeruns, and post-celebratory victories (though great irony is found in praying to God for victory over the defeat of one's opponent).[52] These religious rituals, according to Womack, "make [the athletes] feel as if they have some control over what happens to them. The uncertainty that exists in highly competitive sports is so great that many athletes use rituals. The use of rituals among athletes has become so widespread that it has been described by journalists and voted by many spectators."[53]

What is particularly compelling about religion in sports, however, is not necessarily the source behind the athletes' motivations, but how the two factions converge at various times on the field of play and how society reacts to the intersections of religion and sport in regard to our favorite athletes and sporting contests. Because of this strong pull toward religiosity in the United States, Christianity in particular, we are drawn to an athlete who is seen openly expressing his or her own devotion to faith around the contested battlefield of sports. It moves us on some level, while at the same time reinforcing the age-old debate, still very much alive, of what kind of nation we wish to become, religious or secular. Despite the fact that many American youth participated in some religion-sponsored sporting event, church league, or faith-based school growing up, religiosity in an elite athletic arena still seems foreign to the causal observer. And when these players offer their grace to God, sports fans and enthusiasts, fascinated by anything that humanizes the athlete, tend to enshroud them in glory for doing so. Once again, they are placed on a pedestal, yet this one is raised even higher for their theological beliefs (despite the paradox that idolatry is frowned upon in most religions). This was evidenced by the national phenomenon of Tebowing.

Tim Tebow's stardom is mind-boggling. He came out of Florida deemed one of the best college quarterbacks to lead a team at that level.[54] Those same pundits, however, also highly questioned his ability to be an effective quarterback in the NFL.[55,56] Yet Tebow stunned everyone by going in the first round of the 2010 draft ahead of Jimmy Clausen and Colt McCoy, two other college standouts and, arguably, higher ranked professional prospects at the time.[57] While no one doubted his athletic ability, his work ethic, and will to win, many questioned his quarterbacking skills and his capability to direct an NFL offense.[58,59] Tim Tebow, importantly, did not doubt it, and behind him was a huge fan base.

But Tebow does not just have a typical fan base, he has a crazed following of millions of devotees who had gone so far as to place billboards up in Denver appealing for his starting role.[60] His jersey ranked number one in NFL merchandise sales in his rookie year, which was unlikely given his role as a backup quarterback.[61] He became the national symbol of prayer and was the source and inspiration of Tebowmania.

There is not just one thing that made Tim Tebow the national sensation that he was. It is not just his work ethic, desire, or even athletic ability, because there are professional athletes of similar character, heart, desire, and, many sports analysts would argue, better football mechanics than Tebow himself. Maybe it is his unsuspecting rise to stardom that captured the world's attention. But then we encounter the likes of Arian Foster and Victor Cruz, both undrafted free agents out of college with stellar, breakout performances when most NFL fans had never heard their names.[62] These were not just walk-on performances worthy of a little praise; these are athletes who burst onto the NFL scene with play that shocked everyone. For example, Arian Foster led the league in rushing yards in 2010, and fantasy footballers everywhere were pining to get him on their team.[63] Fans were equally excited to see both of these stars play week in and week out, itching to follow their fantasy football stats. And akin to Tebow, they both had a signature move following a touchdown.[64] Yet the world has never heard of "Fostering" or "Vic-sational."

In reality, much of Tebow's sensationalism came from his Christian faith. It is true that his fan base certainly helped contribute to his rise to stardom. In fact, Tebow would likely not have gotten on the field as a starter had it not been for his popularity, which undoubtedly stems from nearby Colorado Springs. As the "mecca" of evangelism, legions of conservative Christian followers in Colorado Springs, the headquarters of Ted Haggard and James Dobson,[65] are known for their outward expression of faith.[66] Accordingly, it is no surprise that they would act favorably toward a fellow practitioner, a *symbol* of their faith. (It does raise the question that if Tebow started his career in a place more like his second home in New York City, the "bastion" of sarcasm, liberalism, and in-your-face confrontation, would that city have easily been beguiled to jump on his bandwagon from the beginning like Denver did?[67]) The evangelical fan base coupled with many avid Tebow sports fans spawned Tebowmania as the rest of the sporting world watched and longed to be a part of the movement, this new Christian "revolution."

It is not just the sports fans who latched on to Tebow's moment, but even the coaches and front office personnel saw, among other things, an opportunity to capitalize on his fame and status. Nothing was more obvious than when the Broncos starting quarterback, Kyle Orton, faltered while under the intense microscope of the Tim Tebow era, and the coaches, who in any other situation would have deferred to their previously named backup, Brady Quinn, instead passed Quinn on the depth chart for the fan-crazed, third-string Tebow.[68] And in the off-season of 2012 when, after his release from the Broncos in favor of incoming pro-bowler Payton Manning,[69] the teams vying for Tebow's affection were not necessarily teams that needed a quarterback, but ones that needed an image makeover or a boost of fan support and revenue. Tebowmania is one salient and prime example of how religious attitudes inform the world of college and/or professional sports, which has everything to do with image branding in the service of financial gains.

This, however, is not the entire story that shaped Tebowmania. Just as Tim's athletic capacities alone did not earn him his star-studded acclaim, it did not come from him merely being Christian, either, as there are and have been many outspoken Christians in the league (Kurt Warner, Shaun Alexander, Steve Young, and Tony Dungy to name a few).[70] Hundreds of NFL players are Christian, and you can find them in the center of the field after a game, heads bowed in prayer. Time after time, you see a player point to the heavens or drop to a knee in prayer after a touchdown, but not one has spawned a media commotion quite in the same manner as Tim Tebow.

Tebow emerged on the scene during a time of Tea Party politics and congressional gridlock in the course of President Obama's bid for a second term in the White House. Hence, Tebow stood as the antithesis to what many on the conservative right deemed liberal politics and the rise of a repressive socialist welfare state. Actually, Tebow unwittingly embraced the political contentiousness during the 2010 Super Bowl with his anti-abortion advertisement for Dobson's nonprofit organization, Focus on the Family.[71] It is difficult to ignore the conflation of faith and racial politics in the context of the sporting world. Thus, from the cross section of athletic talent, determination, and youthfulness united with Christianity and whiteness, Tebowing arose and largely catered to a conservative audience.

CONFLATING RACE AND RELIGION IN SPORTS

Because we are a highly racialized society that views the world in relationship to contrasting skin pigmentation, race remains a noticeable marker and expression of difference for less powerful groups singled out for disparate treatment. This makes the concept of race impossible to block from our filter. Race remains the elephant in the room, the unspoken signifier, which represents Eurocentric modes of thought, reified anew with each succeeding generation. It is not just that we hold in awe the Christian athlete (who gets more love than the Jewish athlete or Muslim athlete), but more praise is generated specifically to the *white* and Christian athlete. It is as though they become the spokesperson for the largely Christian and white viewing world.

Recall Jeremy Lin and Tim Tebow. As pundits tried to compare the two, both being devout and open Christians, they were unsuccessful in branding Lin as the next Christian leader of the sporting world because his "Asian-ness" is his most significant marker. The difference in these two athletes' appraisals based upon their "unique factor" is that Lin cannot hide his appearance, his "Asian-ness." Whereas Christianity is only known if a person openly expresses their faith by "wearing it on their sleeve," race, on the other hand, is an unmistakable sign. It is what we see first, despite claims of "colorblindness." Thus, sportscasters continued with the prevailing stereotypes about Asians, and Tebow remained the pillar of Christianity while Lin remained the pillar of the model minority.

Though sport is more a racially contested terrain than a religiously contested one, race *and* religion are both paramount issues in sports. The idea that sport can transcend racial differences reigns supreme in American culture. This conceptual idea is shared by a substantial number of Americans, particularly those who are white and conservative, as are many of the students and faculty who make up BYU. However, sport iconography is rooted, in part, on unequal power relationships between whites and non-whites. The construction of these differences gives rise to the production of racial ideology by white elite stakeholders, which is grounded and framed in centuries of white racial knowledge production usually at the expense of nonwhites. The confines of the sporting arena might be the only place where athletes are given a license to contest the "isms" that vex them. But the belief that race does not play a larger role in the sports-industrial complex is a troubling and naïve assertion, especially given the historic experiences of systemic terror of the practice of white supremacy.

The abundance of white racial attitudes and beliefs about black Americans persists in contemporary society and engulfs not only competitive sports but other disciplines and traditions as well. Western religious epistemologies of the human condition have a protracted history of reinforcing and maintaining deep racial and cultural divisions. White Christian theorizing has been used as a means to justify the brutality of African slavery and European colonization of Native peoples.[72,73,74,75] To this day, Sunday church hour still remains the most segregated hour of the week. So then, how does Brigham Young University (BYU), the flagship school of the Church of Jesus Christ of Latter-day Saints (the LDS Church or Mormon Church), which in some ways is the epitome of a Christian institution, portray and protect its image (as a genteel organization) in the minds of many Americans while the interplay of race and religion unfolds all around?

EXAMINING THE HISTORY OF RACE IN MORMONISM THROUGH AMERICAN SPORTS

The LDS church is no exception in its early exposure to prevailing racist beliefs; however, Mormonism is unique in that it is purely Americana. That is, it is the only world-recognized religion to have been born in the United States during the modern age (e.g., the age of the printing press, etc.). The Church is the incarnation of the American experience in that they both espouse similar elements, such as the concept and belief in industry, a hard-work ethic, and education/literacy as well as patriarchy,[76] faith in God, and family values—the "American dream" metaphor wrapped up in the American experiment.

Born out of the colonial struggle with British tyranny, oppression, and various kinds of persecution including religious,[77] from the rise of industrialization to the hostile takeover of global capitalism, the LDS church exemplifies the history of this nation. With it come the twin evils of slavery and the invention/extension of white racism in various forms maintained and reinforced by a predominately white, male order.[78] For much of its 185-year history, the LDS church imposed doctrinal understandings on black people, which led to a forced policy restriction that lasted until 1978. The Church upheld this racist policy for 80 percent of its history, which is codified within its theology, practices, policy, messages, and ways of knowing, doing, and thinking.

Because it is a uniquely American church, the Mormon faith will certainly have conflicts such as those found within the polemics of race, class, and gender, for example. If we have not yet reconciled these festering issues in our nation's history, why would we assume the LDS church, which to some extent is a microcosm of white American culture, to have already reconciled these same issues? These ideas do not die easily by simply changing the rhetoric or ignoring the past. Such thinking places too much faith in the hands of organized religion. Mormonism is no exception, as it continues to have difficulties in purging itself of the stigma of racism.

This book will investigate the LDS Church and its peculiar dominant white framing of people of African descent with a special focus on black athletes who participated in NCAA (National Collegiate Athlete Association) sports at Brigham Young University. The objective is to provide a comprehensive and thorough analysis of the Mormon faith in respects to its history, institutional norms and contemporary practices. Moreover, it is the intent to bring to light the circumstances of Mormon theology and its ostensible indifference toward blackness by highlighting encounters with racialized events within the sporting public through the later part of the Church's history to include recent events over the last few years.

Enshrined in the notion of freedom, justice, and equality is the idea that sports are colorblind and fair. Yet, tensions lie in the contradictions to those principles. Few researchers have considered the intersection of religion, race, and sport despite all three constructs being substantially important in the formation and maintenance of race-based ideas directed principally at African American males. The athletic department at BYU is a perfect setting to observe the crossroads of these three social conventions. Utilizing the white racial frame to analyze the history of blacks in the Mormon Church and the circumstances around BYU's revolving door of black student-athletes, this book will explore the touchy and sensitive nature of this triumvirate at Brigham Young University with the hopes of gaining insights into the continuing collision between race and religion in American sports.

2

THE ORIGINS OF RACISM AND FRAMING

Setting the Stage for the History of Blacks in Sport

> Black athletic culture, like the rest of African American culture, evolved under the pressure of oppression.—William Rhoden, *Forty Million Dollar Slaves*[1]

When European nations began expanding their power and scope of influence beyond their borders, much of Africa—mainly the western regions of the continent—was among the first of the non-European nations marauded for its priceless natural resources.[2] According to Walter Rodney, "At a certain point in time, there also arose the exploitation of man by man, in that a few people grew rich and lived well through the labor of others."[3] As a result of this initial contact with imperial rule, Africa was severely underdeveloped—its human and material resources stripped by colonial powers during the rise of Western capitalism.

In their quest for wealth and wealth-generating opportunities, European whites invented the concept of race predicated on "pseudoscientific principles," which suggested that nonwhites were stuck in the evolutionary holding pattern that made them appear more childlike in their constitution.[4,5] Whites, on the other hand, were believed to be moral and developing in congruence with the laws of nature that conveniently manifested with advancing asymmetrical relationships of power over non-European peoples. Whites were thus enabled to further their interests, both as individuals and in groups.[6,7] Progress, then, for whites meant the repression and devaluation of the "Other" (by force if necessary) as demonstrated in the faulty and racist science of the measuring of skulls, heads, genitalia, and other anatomical markers between races.[8,9]

Northern Europeans and later European Americans created distinctions based on skin color and other phenotypical characteristics (e.g., bone, hair, eye shape) to differentiate and alienate themselves from oppressed groups including Eastern and Southern Europeans and, especially, Africans.[10,11] The eminent historian Winthrop D. Jordan writes extensively about the first contact thesis as the impetus of the white racializing process: "For Englishmen, the most arresting characteristic of the newly discovered African was his color."[12] Jordan mentions that few European travelers failed to comment on the blackness of Africans, a finding that was important in constructing them as abnormal. Prior to New World conquests, no other color but black conveyed so much emotional impression. According to Jordan, before the sixteenth century, the *Oxford English Dictionary* included black as foul, atrocious, horrible, wicked, sinister, and baneful, to name a few negative denotations.[13] These racialized social constructions were then transported across the Atlantic Ocean with the exploration of the New World. European whites brought this ideology with them, expanding these constructions through the trans-Atlantic slave trade to authorize and legitimize the unequal misallocation of valued economic, political, and social resources in a society that claimed a democratic ethos.[14]

These temporal aspects of systemic racism firmly established a racial hierarchy (the great chain of being) by coercive power and control over the lives and livelihood of black Americans through the pretense of Western science.[15] European contact resulted in unjust white enrichment and African American misery since twenty Africans first set foot in North America in 1619 as indentured servants. As the peculiar institution of chattel slavery evolved in the latter half of the 1600s, elite white men were in charge of the development of the country, producing truth claims that glorified restrictive forms of freedom, progress, equality, and other highly cherished enlightenment principles not intended for women or people of color, specifically blacks and Native Americans.[16,17]

By marking the Africans' blackness and cultural habits as abnormal and therefore deficient, white America endorsed and legitimized stolen labor and land theft during the trans-Atlantic slave trade and beyond. Dark skin as perceived by whites, though truly differentiated only in appearance, helped to establish and lay the foundation that blackness would remain a badge of inferiority that exists presently. And as it later became the United States, white America would unify around the marginalization of black Americans.

Black as anathema became enshrined in the foundational architecture of U.S. society's major institutions, which positioned black Americans as unimportant and incompetent, singling them out for group relegation. As a system of control and domination, race and racism often functioned discursively while informing the national psyche and re-inscribing negative representations of African Americans that were important in disqualifying them as members of the human family. As the distinguished philosopher Charles Mills put it, "European humanism usually meant that only Europeans were human."[18] This skewed sense of nationhood came about through "[t]he racialism of the West, slavery, imperialism, [and] the destruction of indigenous cultures."[19]

White oppression and terror were unleashed on scores of blacks for generations to follow. By gaining unequal economic footing in the land, white Americans were able to codify "an unjust system for creating and extending the impoverishment of large groups of people, such as African Americans, to the profit of other large groups of people, principally white Americans."[20] In virtually every domain in society, this unjust white enrichment came by way of blood, sweat, and tears of the innocents, through the redefinition of deity and the cosmos, in the destruction and near annihilation of minoritized peoples along with their language and culture.[21,22] This well-calculated and well-orchestrated, race-based scheme heard around the world would forever transform people of color through the incandescent, blinding coerciveness of white supremacy.[23] It was behind this veil that an extensive white racial frame emerged—a frame created in the minds of whites and materialized in their racist practices through centuries of slavery and group disenfranchisement that only *legally* ended less than fifty years ago following the baby boom era.

COGNITIVE FRAMES, LANGUAGE, AND KNOWLEDGE PRODUCTION

Cognitive frames (i.e., mental models) are not necessarily truths, but instead are half-conscious understandings based on visual images or abstractions that trigger internal thought processes about one's external perceptibility, whether real or imagined.[24] Frames are mental structures, conceptual systems constituting our intuitive interpretations of the social world that are produced by historical circumstances and shaped by dominant, societal understandings.[25] They provide orienting structure and explanatory justification for socially based phenomena while creating a mental impression about anything and anyone from those who do not own a TV to those who watch reality TV, from those who do not go to church to those who are devout Christians or devout Muslims. Though frames can vary within individuals, many are based upon societal stereotypes and, thus, become universal among a community of people. In other words, frames are mental shortcuts that exist for the purpose of making sense of how we see the world and the concepts, groups of people, and images in them. We invoke these cognitive frames continuously in our daily lives in a typical prejudicial manner in effort to deliver order out of chaos based on limited information.[26]

Conceptually speaking, a mental frame represents a predictable path of thinking and reasoning about people and their place in society. An image is seen, a language is heard, or an idea/concept is encountered that invokes a thought process that triggers impressions and attitudes about that person or group and subsequently prompts "appropriate behaviors" about how to best relate with them through our perceived understanding of reality. Interestingly, human thoughts are not just free-floating cephalic instantiations, but serve to maintain our unconscious inclinations and collective habits. The very identity and allegiance to those emotion-laden memories and histories we hold sacred activate neural, sensorimotor, motivational, and cognitive systems that are chemically linked in our brain.[27] Thus, human beings have investments in cognitive frames that are not just mental processes but are value systems reinforced through a bio-psycho reaction in our brain attached to social beliefs.[28]

Each cognitive frame is seductively hardwired to neural circuits in our central nervous system that enjoin our most deeply held convictions with emotional arousal.[29] This neurochemical process can further confirm our unconscious beliefs in a number of unproductive ways. Neurochemicals are activated during times of stressful events, even occurring during an event as incidental as a discussion on a controversial issue. In situations like this, we feel the urge to defend our particular framing of an issue, not really knowing why we cling so tightly to it in the first place. But in actuality, many of the presumptive behaviors we cling to are tethered to emotion, making unlearning destructive attitudes and beliefs quite difficult, more than a rhetorical exercise.

Think of cognition as an iceberg, both heavy and buoyant, exposing only a small portion of its mass on the visible surface of human awareness. Beneath the surface lies the large expanse of the collective unconsciousness comprising much of human thought. According to Lakoff and Johnson, "It is the rule of thumb among cognitive scientists that unconscious thought is 95 percent of all thought . . . moreover, the 95 percent below the surface of conscious awareness shapes and structures all conscious thought."[30] In other words, this hidden portion of the iceberg provides the bulk of our understanding outside the realm of conscious awareness. This proves especially onerous at the macro level of society where the collective power of whiteness reinforces our subconscious beliefs through social manipulation, typically in the form of media representations of difference, which, in turn, impacts upon our micro or individual lived realities.[31]

The duality of micro and macro understandings of the human experience are intertwined and affect the various identity constructions (such as woman, African American, Christian, etc.) that we recruit at different times to make sense of reality in a deep and complex manner. Each social construction like race, gender, religion, or even the role of athlete effortlessly engages the other,[32] providing greater attention to whatever master narrative is at stake at the time. These constructs, thus, inform how we perceive the intricacies of difference and the inequalities that exist in society, and they particularly influence how we discern our place in them. These experiences happen automatically, shaping consciousness that is not evident or apparent. Wars have been fought and empires decimated over a solitary frame with overarching social or political ramifications.

THE WHITE RACIAL FRAMING OF BLACK INFERIORITY

The white racial frame represents a grand narrative derived from a particularized historical vantage point of white Americans.[33] Generally passed down over generations and passed off as commonsense thinking, the white racial frame refers to "an organized set of racialized ideas, stereotypes, emotions, and inclinations to discriminate."[34] Put differently, Americans are routinely socialized to view the world through the prism of an interpretive white frame, which lends to unconscious or half-conscious beliefs and assumptions about the overall superiority of white culture, achievement, and Christian privilege.[35]

White frames, therefore, contain a large array of dominant white rules and knowledge about people of color, in general, and African Americans, in particular. These ideas are often inscribed through the use of metaphor, which provide structure and meaning to the world.[36] For example, the concept that originated during the Gilded Age of bootstraps individualism, or the meritocratic time-honored notion that anyone can succeed if they "pull themselves up by their bootstraps," is a type of overarching grand narrative (a frame), especially applicable for white Americans, that working-class youth can rise to middle-class respectability and "success" with enough effort.[37,38,39,40] A metaphor based on Horatio Alger's stories, this frame neglects the cast of characters—whether big or small—that aid any one person's "success"; family, friends, strangers, even politically motivated circumstance and especially race all contribute to one's achievement. The novels of Horatio Alger gave life to the "Old World meets the New World" perspective of the early Puritans and other Protestant settlers. This frame was further reinscribed through periods in American history, such as the boom of the middle class following World War II with the introduction of the GI Bill and VA loans for returning veterans, making it possible for the first time for the average (white) American to afford a home and attend college.[41]

The strength behind this Euro-Christian ethic of "hard work" is a political frame grounded in durable ideas of liberty and justice (i.e., liberalism) that the colonists are said to have brought with them in establishing the United States. Goldberg noted that "liberalism is committed to individualism, for it takes as basic the moral, political, and legal claims of the individual over and against those of the collective."[42]

For this reason, individualism is the locus of white America's attitudes about ability and work captured in the human-centered, "bootstraps" metaphor. But the concept of "hard work" is often misinterpreted as individual merit or the "go it alone" attitude consistent with contemporary white views that blacks only have themselves to blame for their struggles. In other words, their place in society is directly attributable to their moral failings and flaws, which are reduced in our minds to stereotypes of blackness as a racialized, geopolitical space of individual delinquency.

Individualism, as an indispensable tenet of liberalism, is the most common reason that whites believe that people of color are not doing well in an otherwise egalitarian society. When coupled with white racial understandings, it conceals history and the way in which wealth accumulated over time to position whites where they are today in the racial order. The modern version of racism draws from white attitudes similar to those that President Ronald Reagan captured in his "tough-on-crime" campaign in the 1990s. Reagan stated, "Choosing a career in crime is not the result of poverty or of an unhappy childhood or of a misunderstood adolescence; it is the result of a conscious willful choice."[43] This disguises the unjust structural race-based implications of crime—both existential and resource inequality—that lead to the school-to-prison pipeline, fueling the disproportionate incarceration rates among black and brown men.[44] These early narratives helped to buttress the standpoint that black bodies were believed to be on a lower evolutionary scale[45] than the more enlightened Anglo-Saxon stock and, therefore, must be controlled (legally or otherwise) in efforts to protect the virtues and moral goodness of white society.[46] The philosophical justification of black marginalization employed by white, privileged decision makers has been coined the "white racial frame."

Race, viewed from this reading as a socially constructed conceptual frame developed and passed down by whites over twenty generations, serves as an interpretive lens deeply held and routinely applied by whites to the surrounding social milieu as a way to make sense of or understand information and experiences in daily life. Frames link the unknown characteristics, whether true or not, to the limited information with which individuals are in contact. For example, arbitrary attributes of an individual are deduced based upon their physical markers of clothing or skin color or gender, even though the presumed attributes are completely unrelated to physicality, such as the assumption that any person wearing a turban is a terrorist. It is not difficult to see then how mental frames result in snapshot judgments on the basis of skin color and other physical markers of difference singled out by white society for marginalization and exclusion.[47] In the United States, the hypodescent, or so-called one-drop, rule of assigning the race of the child to the "socially subordinate parent" (i.e., nonwhite parent) still occupies the popular imagination and is based largely on this paradigm of stereotyping. These formulations, then, develop into grand schemas, which undergird prejudice and bias such as the Western ideals of superhumanizing blacks as better athletes and impervious to pain.[48]

Given the long-held white racial beliefs that African Americans were brutes, lazy, oversexed, dimwitted, and dangerous, these particular European American understandings about black people emerged throughout much of the seventeenth and eighteenth centuries during New World conquests.[49,50] European civilization devised a way to racialize the human bodies on the basis of differences in physical characteristic related to head circumference, the contours of the eye, and other factors that ran counter to the image of the blue-eyed, blond Aryan thought to be a superior form of *Homo sapiens* in every way imaginable. These ideas gained currency over time through the authority and claims of "science." Moreover, the physical features linked with racial difference supposedly determined and predicted all types of behavior from criminal tendency, sexuality, intelligence, and physical capability.[51,52] These corporeal markers, in addition to social class indicators like a brand of clothes and patterns of speech, have been used to assess what "truth" it yields about the black experience in the white mind. These enduring frames provide unifying meaning making for whites in simplistic ways to appear perfectly reasonable, even commonsense.

Furthermore, these white-centered frames provide the bulwark of historically patterned and ritualized outcomes of white racial priming—that is to say, the ways in which white people systematically internalize racist beliefs, attitudes, stereotypes, assumptions, and fictitious racial scripts that fit into a dominant white paradigm.[53,54] At times serving as a generic meaning system and other times as a comprehensive conceptual theme, white racial frames "tell" whites how to reasonably see and act within a racialized society.[55] Examples of these include locking the door when driving through a black neighborhood, clutching one's purse or crossing the street when black youth are approaching, acknowledging one individual as the spokesperson for their entire race, or neglecting to notice that the vast majority (if not all) of one's circle of friends are from a background racially homogeneous in appearance to oneself.[56] "Not all whites use the dominant frame to the same extent, and in everyday practice there are multiple variations."[57] But even when these thoughts are openly disputed, they play out in the form of racialized unconscious motives and actions such as what church you attend, whom you marry, in what neighborhood you reside, and where your children attend school.

These dimensions of the white racial frame become major sources of white knowledge production, influencing individual and group-based collective memories. In actuality, societal assumptions about various groups of people are informed by politically and religiously influential white men who "viewed themselves as powerful 'white' fathers controlling not only their families but also their communities and society more generally."[58] By focusing on the transferal of race-based lessons within the everyday social networks of whites, "[w]e see here how the larger system of societal racism is built up from smaller social units."[59] White racial frames, then, are recursive structures limiting us to think and act out of ignorance and prejudice because we have failed as a society to teach children not only our successes as a nation, but our failures as well, while encouraging differing viewpoints and well-informed opinions.

White racial knowledge about people of African descent is woven into the tapestry of the American experience. Replete with its brutal and violent history of European conquest, American expansionism culminated in the formation of the trans-Atlantic slave trade and genocide of indigenous peoples. While most whites have recognized that the brutality of slavery was morally reprehensible, most do not fully understand how the legacy of slavery gave rise to the industrial revolution, which created much of the wealth of this nation and further informed the thoughts of its citizens to this day.

SYSTEMIC RACISM: UNDERSTANDING HOW THE WHITE RACIAL FRAME INFORMS COLLECTIVE WHITE RACIAL KNOWLEDGE

The white racial frame is born out of the systemic racism theory, a useful paradigm posited by Feagin that is comprised of a wide range of key dimensions and aspects that can best be applied to U.S. society in the illumination of systemic racism.[60] This allows an examination of racism in a way that deals justly with race-based inequalities in its multiple forms. This theory accounts for (1) a dominant racial hierarchy, (2) individual and collective discrimination, (3) the social reproduction of race-based inequalities, and (4) racist institutions, which uphold white domination in sports, religion, and other key domains in American society. Ultimately, this theory utilizes (5) a comprehensive white racial frame, involving the transmission of white collective knowledge—racist images, attitudes, ideology, emotions, habits, and actions—to succeeding generations of whites.

The multiple racial assumptions and ideas we hold in our minds about various groups of people were imported from Europe. These impressions were originally etched in our centuries-old racist society, resulting in the early framing of colonial America by the seventeenth-century Protestant colonizers. These influential white men used their superior status in the emerging society to inform the politico-economy of slavery, which guided the subsequent debates on the morality of enslaving fellow human beings. What developed was a uniquely American racialist framing of society that was foundational in shaping our understandings and beliefs about the human condition in mostly nonegalitarian ways.

Today, as in the past, white racism blights the life chances of generations of black Americans in significant ways, robbing the black community of its youth, strength, and vitality. To discern the vastness and its significance requires powerful conceptual tools of analysis, allowing for a realistic assessment of America's racist past and contemporary realities. For example, racism in its institutionalized form is more than individual acts of meanness of one race against another but instead is a "predication of decisions and policies on considerations of race for the purpose of subordinating a racial group."[61] Systemic racism is structural and requires a network of generational and coordinated support from individuals and groups working to maintain ideological supremacy over institutions and major organizations. The reality of black suffering is evident given the number of minoritized peoples (particularly blacks) living in abject poverty, languishing in underperforming schools, and caught up in the prison-industrial complex. Additionally, black disenfranchisement is manifested in the sheer dearth of black Americans in higher education, medicine, and law, in CEO positions of Fortune 500 companies, and in the top 1 percent.[62] This can only be explained in one of two ways. Either blacks are inferior in morality, intellect, motivation, drive, and execution, or it must be recognized that a systemic process is in place that gives rise to these grave numbers.

The social reproduction and transmission of race is fundamentally shaped by connecting abstract concepts—frames—of human differences uncritically applied to skin color. We view these frames that materialize in our lives as sacrosanct, thus fueling our indignant sense of rightness, and, unfortunately, this often results in dire consequences as seen in the recent rash of police killings of unarmed, black men in America.[63,64] This perfunctory thinking, in turn, obscures true reasoning for xenophobic tendencies that are commonplace in the history of American society. But with its emotion-laden and action-oriented inclinations, the white racial frame is more than a deep-seated tool historically used by whites to interpret the world. Historical framing of the white experience, or the discourses surrounding the circumstances that shaped white thinking about the black body, remains firmly entrenched within the recesses of the unconscious and informs systemic racist patterns that go well beyond a concept of individual racial bias disconnected from institutional power and unequal privilege. High-powered, white decision makers played a major role in establishing and maintaining racialized institutions through an extensive and elaborate framing of African Americans and other groups targeted by whites. By drawing on the white racial frame, whites perpetuate and obscure matters of racial discrimination, which limits the opportunities of African Americans while promoting their own continued race-based advantages and control over key societal domains, including education, health care, and certainly the sports-industrial complex.

African Americans and other Americans of color have not been idle participants in their own marginalization. African peoples have worked tirelessly in the cause of freedom, evoking counter-frames that call into question white ways of knowing and being. The major ways in which blacks contend with the white racial frame include accenting the strength and accomplishments of black Americans, calls to revolutionary action, a prophetic analysis of the unjust enrichment of whites, and a critique of institutions and social structures they occupy and govern.

THE RACIALIZATION OF BLACKS IN SPORT

Conventional thinking (or framing) regarding the black athlete evolved from the encounters and unequal relationships of power that blacks had with whites. The white racial framing of black folk as less than human situated their bodies as a source of entertainment, amusement, and spectacle. Beasts of burden, black bodies were used as labor power—not just in the cotton field, but also in competitive play—in what later became the sport-industrial complex. Sport was formalizing itself into an industry, starting with horse racing, and later track and field, boxing, and basketball. Black muscle was essential in white-imposed athletic contests during the antebellum period, and as a result, laid the future groundwork for a highly profitable and exploitative enterprise.[65]

The rise of the black athlete in the United States began with black African slavery. In British colonial America, white elites built up the coffers of their wealth on the backs of enslaved African Americans. Those battered and bruised bodies would later rise up and become the symbol of hope and pride for a people amid the harsh and vicious realities of North American bondage. But until that time, blacks had to find alternative ways to survive their ordeal. In the hot and steamy region of the American South, black slaves worked from sunup to sundown in the subtropical conditions. Ruled by white fear and control, slavery was sustained by the constant threat of humiliation, death and separation from family and community. Too much work, too little food, and poor medical care deprived the physical body of the energy it needed for a well planned escape, yet slaves would still find the resolve to engage in the play of athletic games and sporting activities. And the plantation owner often encouraged it as a way to mollify the slaves while in captivity.[66]

Some slaves could escape the extremes of the backbreaking gang labor with other types of conformable work in the service of white people, including the roles of the seamstress, cook, and blacksmith, to mention a few. Still, ever vigilant, blacks waited for new opportunities to improve their conditions in life. Most slaves faced routinized and mind-numbing fieldwork, but in rare instances, some were additionally tasked to participate in sport-related contests at the behest of their masters. These particular blacks possessed a variety of mental and physical abilities well suited for sport labor outside the drudgery of plantation work. It is against the backdrop of slavery in which the black athlete emerged.

Using their bodies as instruments in the pursuit of freedom's dream, early black athletes counter-framed[67] white racist thought by serving in a variety of athletic roles as oarsmen, hunting assistants, cyclists, horse trainers, jockeys, runners, wrestlers, and boxers, all while entertaining the white masses in black-on-black competition.[68] The winners were generally more trusted and rewarded with greater autonomy and flexibility than their fellow bondmen on the plantation. Few also gained the status level of a local celebrity when competing across the region in many high-profile events and even earning considerable wages for their time. And on rare occasions, athletic victory resulted in freedom. Such coercive attraction enticed talented individuals cut out for the rigors of competition.

Beginning in the mid-seventeenth century, the first American sport of horse racing was gaining in popularity along the border of the southern states of North Carolina and Virginia. African American jockeys were among the first athletes to race in what was then an integrated sport of both white and black riders.[69,70,71] A major event, horse racing drew huge crowds at a time when black jockeys dominated the racing industry from the 1850s through the 1890s. Though black jockeys were highly regarded among their peers, the work of jockeying itself was considered low by the southern gentry standards of the day, permitting whites to tolerate blacks in the sport. So despite the prevailing racist attitudes of the day, blacks were allowed to participate, providing a window of opportunity to make their presence known as "race riders" in the lucrative horse racing business. In addition to racing in one of the oldest sports in North America, these pioneering black athletes were occasionally given additional responsibility to train the horses.[72] The work was arduous and intense, but the reward was that it provided a small prospect of respectability in the inexorable life of a slave (or free black for that matter) in a racist society. Once organized, owners converted the talent of these black athletes into capital in what became the institution of sport. Like other white-controlled institutions, sport largely profited from the sweat and labor of black people.[73,74]

But there were a number of accomplished black jockeys who used the sport in an attempt to rid themselves of all vestiges of slavery, poverty, and the circumstances of skin color. For some fortunate riders, this served a conduit to rare fame and fortune, procuring enough earnings to buy their freedom. The remaining riders, however, experienced a short-lived feeling of triumph. It did afford them some semblance of freedom to the point where a small number were convinced that they actually had rights similar to those of whites. In reality, they were still black. And as soon as the black jockey ended his career and the prize money dried up along with his prominent status, he quickly reverted back to his relegated position in a deeply racist society. Interestingly, some were able to escape this regression in status by relocating abroad.[75]

After the Emancipation Proclamation issued by President Abraham Lincoln in 1863, blacks increased their presence in other sports as well. Where America was deeply divided and segregated, sport was one area where blacks and whites comingled. American sports were, in fact, truly integrated during this time. Though white-imposed racism still occurred on a daily basis on all levels of society, blacks were actually competing in the same leagues with whites. This integrated activity brought new heights as well as incipient trials for black Americans.[76]

THE NEW NEGRO MOVEMENT AND THE TENSIONS OF RACE MIXING

It was not until the nation began moving toward the doctrine of "separate but equal," undoing the Civil Rights Act of 1875 with the institution of Jim Crow laws in the late 1890s, when blacks were formally pushed out and barred from partaking in white American sports.[77] During this period, hundreds of thousands of blacks migrated to the industrial Northeast and Midwest in search of better jobs and reprieve from southern bigotry. These same blacks and their posterity faced an equally compelling, yet less organized, color line in cities like Chicago, Pittsburgh, New York City, Milwaukee, Detroit, and other urban centers.

The mass movement of black Americans to the industrial North brought about an amalgamation and explosion of powerful and creative forms of black expression in religion, literature, art, music, and sport. The melding of black people (rich in history) brought together under the banner of community and culture likewise produced black intellectuals, musicians, philosophers, playwrights, and poets who wrote, spoke, and played their truth about black life. This, in turn, gave meaning and purpose to a people not too far removed from slavery. These cogent narratives of black life underscore the meaning of struggle in the margins of a nation in which equality of opportunity was never meant for nonwhites, all the while maintaining the illusion of equality as a figment of societal imagination.

Through it all, black people found a way to subsist and transcend the circumstances of white supremacy by forging a movement, a cultural revolution of purpose, in the shadows of a racist society. This "New Negro Movement," the Harlem Renaissance, marked the prominence of black achievement in art, literature, and sport, along with a greater freedom of cultural and recreational leisure for African Americans. For many black Americans, sport and athletic competition signified an existential place where black folk as a group could take out their frustrations without fear of white reprisal. The black athlete stood as an emblem of hope and a symbol of racial pride each and every time their brawny feats and achievements were reported in the popular press.

Segregation, however, did not come without tribulations. The 1900s to the 1930s saw an increase of violence and intimidation against blacks involving angry white mobs unleashing their unrestrained hatred on black people, killing many in a number of race riots that erupted throughout America. The most notable of these riots transpired during the occasional integrated sporting event. Despite the de jure separation between races, black and white athletes/teams would occasionally come together during this period and compete against one another. And nothing sparked tension more than a disturbance of the racist customs of the day (segregation), leading to unwanted interaction (athletic or not) between blacks and whites.

In 1910, during one of these integrated events, Jack Johnson became the first African American world heavyweight boxing champion by defeating a white Jeff Jefferies. Johnson's victory over Jefferies triggered race riots in fifty cities across the country that underscored the revulsion that most whites had for black Americans.[78] It did not matter what the setting or circumstance was surrounding their success, white racial framing was dismissive of black achievement. Blacks were positioned in opposition to whites—a threat to white ways of being. Thus, blacks turned to each other for comfort, using entertainment in efforts to lift the group out of white-imposed deprivation.[79]

RE-INTEGRATING THE BLACK ATHLETE IN MAINSTREAM SPORT FOR WHITE GAIN

It was during this period when black entrepreneurs and other stakeholders would capitalize on Jim Crow laws by organizing black talent for the Negro Leagues of baseball. The Negro Leagues flourished and provided black baseball players with a venue where they could cultivate and showcase their "unique" style of play before a large receptive black fan base and press corps eager to promote black initiative. Because black ball players were excluded and forbidden to access white sports, they did not have the same access to "formal" instruction on the various aspects of the white man's game. Innovation and creativity would nevertheless allow black ball players to hone their skills on the backyard lots of urban America, developing skills that would later contribute to the advancement of the game, such as base stealing, as they unknowingly ushered in a new era of baseball.[80,81]

Before the collapse of Jim Crow in 1954 (*Brown v. Board of Education*), Major League Baseball (MLB) needed "reinvigorating" and looked to the Negro Leagues in search of the perfect black athlete to heed the call—one that would be acceptable to white sensibilities. Many black players were understandably eager to answer this call, and with the help of Brooklyn Dodgers president and general manager Branch Rickey, MLB got its wish by pushing toward desegregation (on a national level). This started with the signing of Jackie Robinson with the National League's Dodgers in the 1946 season and was followed by the signing of Larry Doby in 1947 with the American League's Cleveland Indians.[82] This began a long and arduous relationship between the black athlete and white baseball. Both seminal moments in the history of white baseball would ironically spell the end of the Negro Leagues as well as their control over their own highly regarded labor power in the burgeoning sports enterprise. Football and basketball would soon follow with similar trajectories that culminated in the eventual desegregation of the sports.

Last to change was the recalcitrant South. The South had long resisted recruiting black players, instead relying on the banality of white-only athleticism. But suddenly the black competitor was in popular demand, especially after Paul "Bear" Bryant discovered the value of the black athlete in college football following Alabama Crimson Tide's 1970 defeat by a mixed-race USC Trojan team. The University of Southern California had broken the color barrier with black quarterback Jimmy Jones, but most significantly, black running back Sam Cunningham ran for over a hundred yards and two touchdowns in the rout against Alabama. Coach Bryant was impressed enough with Cunningham's performance to congratulate him on it following the game. As the myth goes, Cunningham is "said to have done more to integrate Alabama in 60 minutes than Martin Luther King Jr. did in 20 years."[83] This reaction by Bryant set in motion an uptick in recruitment efforts for black players to big-time white college athletic programs across the country, especially in the South. Interestingly, many of the predominately white university players around the nation were from the South. But black males were recruited to these institutions solely for their athletic prowess—the same institutions that denied them full inclusion in the first place. To this day, white universities and colleges still rely on black bodies to fill their coffers and to further the interests of whiteness through a coordinated method of black exploitation.

That black bodies only exist to thrill and entertain a disaffected white populace is the story of America and its racial commodification of blacks. The white racial frame that black bodies are closer to nature and possess superior, genetically predetermined characteristics is still pervasive and very much alive in mainstream society today. Even people of color fall prey to dubious stereotypes that athletic ability is a matter of genetic inheritance, as these stereotypes play out in popular culture through multiple forms of media. For example, in the film, *White Men Can't Jump*, Woody Harrelson's character mocks the continued impression that race has given African Americans a competitive edge over whites when it comes to the game of street basketball by hustling black players with his ruse.[84] The (mis)representation of black bodies by centuries-old white racism remains a salient factor in the United States. Reflected mainly in macro-societal arrangements such as the media, these racial notions can be viewed through the window of sports. Hence, sports are a kind of microcosm into what particular instantiations of troubles afflict U.S. society.

Intractable white racial frames continue to inform discriminatory practices in society, which contribute to the existential inequities[85] experienced on a broad scale almost exclusively by blacks.[86] Black suffering that begins with the deliberate scourge of race-based economic inequality, community divestment, joblessness, and underemployment also includes white-orchestrated schemes to promote sports participation over academic achievement among blacks, contributing to the relegation of black Americans. The impact carries over to present-day black student-athletes who remain prodigiously abused for their physicality with little regard for their intellectual development beyond the lifespan of their collegiate career.

3

THE WHITE RACIAL FRAMING OF BLACKS IN MORMON THEOLOGY

> If the white man who belongs to the chosen seed mixes his blood with the seed of Cain, the penalty, under the law of God, is death on the spot. This will always be so.—Brigham Young[1]

As seen in Chapter 1 with the examples of Jeremy Lin and Tim Tebow, sports in the United States is infused with racial dynamics and socially constructed understandings of the bio-racist framing of people of color despite the commonly held inference that athletic competition is colorblind and victory is based solely on merit. As history has taught us, success in the form of the "American Dream" is an illusion predicated chiefly upon race as the salient construct. This chapter will trace the roots of systemic racism in religion, specifically examining the race-based practices and theological traditions of the LDS Church. Further, this chapter will investigate the nascency of Mormon-specific frames of blacks and blackness and how those views mirrored the conventional wisdom (i.e., social science research, general attitudes toward race) that racism is mainly a matter of *individual* prejudice, stereotyping, and bias, instead of something much more structural in magnitude, deeply-woven within the everyday fabric of life.[2,3,4]

CHRISTIANITY AND OBEDIENCE TO THE WORD OF GOD

Religious institutions were important places during colonial America, not only for worship and devotion to God among colonists but also for civic activities and social gatherings. The church was the center of daily life for Protestant Americans, but they were not democratic establishments where the ideas and practices of liberty and freedom flourished. Instead, they were strict authoritarian communities of worship that revolved around conformity and compliance to the dictates of the clergy who governed thought and action. Churches thus played a key role in shaping the lived experiences of English Puritans and their Anglo-immigrant counterparts with regard to how to behave in America as devoted followers of Christ.[5]

The rules were typically confining, often haphazard, and extraordinarily unequal for most churchgoers. Within most congregations, there was a clear distinction between the gendered bodies of men and women and what was expected of them. Additionally, the emerging significance of color distinction highlighted the racialized discordances between blacks and whites and the democratic discordances between the bound and the free. The clergy often set limits on the pursuit of freedom and liberty, which generally meant more liberty for "Us" and less freedom for "Them" in antidemocratic ways. Thomas Jefferson, a slaveholder himself, underscored the profound religious intolerance of early Americans, stating,

> The first settlers in this country were emigrants from England, of the English church, just at a point of time when it was flushed with complete victory over the religious of all other persuasions. Possessed, as they became, of the powers of making, administering, and executing the laws, they showed equal intolerance in this country with their Presbyterian brethren, who had emigrated to the northern government. The poor Quakers were flying from persecution in England. They cast their eyes on these new countries as asylums of civil and religious freedom; but they found them free only for the reigning sect.[6]

The Mormon church, essentially authoritarian in nature and structure, shares with early Christian Protestant traditions the devout following and loyalty of the purportedly omniscient church leadership. The

First Presidency, historically, has been the final authority on matters of church doctrine.[7] And as a consequence, its word was (and generally still is) taken by the general membership as the literal Word of God. Former LDS church president Ezra Taft Benson applied certainty to any lingering doubt when he declared, "Doctrinal interpretation is the province of the First Presidency. The Lord has given that stewardship to them by revelation."[8] Prominent Mormon leader Marion G. Romney reinforced this principle when he stated, "What they say as a presidency is what the Lord would say if he were here in person."[9]

The LDS church, like most religious denominations in the 1800s, expected absolute obedience to church authority and doctrinal precepts. Like the Pilgrims before them, who were governed by strict obedience to authority and frowned upon dissension over numerous religious issues, Mormonism followed a similar trajectory in establishing a community of faith where church members often faced reprisal from local leaders, family members, and friends if they appeared overly critical of the church hierarchy or in disagreement with church leaders.[10] Psychologists have maintained that authoritarianism "happens when the followers submit too much to the leaders, trust them too much, and give them too much leeway to do whatever they want."[11] But to Latter-day Saints, their strict adherence to church leadership is viewed much differently; it shows a commitment to a life of Christ by following the will of a living prophet of God on earth, the divinely appointed representative of Christ, as seen in their undying devotion and abiding faith. They believe what church leaders say *is* the word of God.

While religiosity has been a source of support, guidance and strength for many believers, those same concepts—when infused with a history of white racial knowledge production—become the basis for institutionalized group disenfranchisement and existential marginalization beyond the confines of individual prejudice and bias. In other words, religion becomes a weapon of exclusion, allegedly authorized by the Most High. It is in the Book of Genesis of the Bible that the story and framing of race begins in Western theism.

A BRIEF HISTORY OF RACE WITHIN JUDEO-CHRISTIAN TRADITIONS: DEMONIZING AND FRAMING BLACKNESS IN AMERICA

Early European American immigrants came to the eastern shores of modern-day America racially primed with Judeo-Christian tales about the continent of Africa as the land of Ham's descendants. As described in the Book of Genesis, Canaan, the son of Ham, was placed under a "divine curse" after his father saw the prophet Noah (his grandfather) drunk and naked in the wilderness and did not cover his shame.[12] Enraged by his son's voyeurism, Noah pronounced a curse on Ham, declaring that he and his posterity be servants to his siblings and their descendants. Until recently, many believed the representation of the curse pronounced on Ham was that of black skin.[13]

These Christian beliefs date back to the fourth century, at the time when the Roman emperor, Constantine the Great, converted to Christianity and introduced sacred Jewish texts (what is now the Old Testament) and translated Greek text (the New Testament) into Roman society after the ancient First Council of Nicea in 325 A.D.[14] The early Eurocentric ideas that God placed the divine curse of the skin of darkness upon blacks were beliefs firmly established in budding Christian liturgy. Religious studies professor Stephen R. Haynes notes,

> In Western Europe prior to the modern period, the curse was invoked to explain the origins of slavery, the provenance of black skin, and the exile of Hamites to the less wholesome regions of the earth. But these aspects of malediction were not integrated in an explicit justification for racial slavery until the fifteenth century, when dark-skinned peoples were enslaved by the Spanish and Portuguese, and the European slave stereotype was stabilized.[15]

These white racial frames were embedded within Christian religious traditions and were subsequently transported across the Atlantic Ocean to the Americas in the 1600s in the form of folk theology.[16,17]

By the nineteenth century, the link between black Africans and Ham's progeny was a widely accepted racist frame in America that deeply affected the religious sensibilities and beliefs of all who came in contact with it. Samuel Dunwody, a southern Methodist minister, preached, "It is by no means improbable that the very name Ham, which signifies burnt or black, was given to [Ham] prophetically, on account of the countries that his posterity were destined to inhabit."[18] Even some prominent blacks were influenced by the divine Curse of Ham theory as expressed by Edward Blyden, a black clergyman. In 1869, Blyden wrote, "It is not to be doubted that from the earliest ages the black complexion of some of the descendants of Noah was known. Ham, it would seem, was a complexion darker than that of his brothers."[19]

Because blacks had allegedly been "cursed" by God, they were doomed to perpetual servitude at the hands of Japeth, the father of white people.[20] This religious position was then taken up and used by white slave owners to justify the subordination of black people under a system of chattel slavery. Echoing the curse in a proslavery pamphlet written in 1838, the author of the pamphlet declared, "The blacks were originally designed to vassalage by the Patriarch Noah."[21,22]

Along with the institution of chattel slavery, Christian interpretations of the Curse of Ham thesis also provided rational fodder for wealth and wealth-generating opportunities for whites in a rapidly expanding agrarian economy in the South and the emerging industrialization of the North. These interpretations of Ham as cursed developed over centuries through the two evolving economies.[23] Both methods of commerce were equally abusive, but in different ways, as white entrepreneurs profited off the backs of blacks by rationalizing that their severe treatment was deserved because of the sins of their fathers.

The Curse of Ham frame was well entrenched in the North, and it was repeatedly used in the South as a defense for slavery and an excuse to commit brutal acts of violence against enslaved black Africans.[24] The renowned abolitionist Frederick Douglass experienced these atrocities in his own life as a slave and witnessed them in the lives of other enslaved Africans and African Americans around him. In his famous narrative, Douglass remarked, "For of all slaveholders with whom I have ever met, religious slaveholders are the worst,"[25] as they found justification in their ruthlessness through the Bible. As Douglass explained, religious slaveholders often called on God while beating, raping, and dehumanizing black people with all the amplified force of righteous indignation against blackness.[26]

The white founding fathers of the nation and framers of the Constitution, fearing that a national religion would give rise to the religious persecution that was fresh on their minds, refused to establish a single state church.[27,28,29] Yet, although Christianity was unable to solidly unite the country as a whole through the establishment of one state religion, American Protestantism nevertheless did succeed in introducing an authoritarian race-based religious standard that all believers could agree upon—that chattel slavery and Native American land theft were divinely sanctioned enterprises.[30] Indeed, both were seen as part of a Manifest Destiny[31] authorized by [the white Christian] God.[32]

EARLY MORMONISM AND THE CURSE OF BLACKNESS

Mormonism's use of the Holy Bible as a spiritual source of authority on the question of a cursed black lineage was very much intertwined with its own rapidly expanding body of canonized works on blacks developed by the LDS Church founder, Joseph Smith. A prophet to the Mormon membership, Smith believed and taught that blacks were the literal descendants of Ham.[33] Not surprisingly, then, his nineteenth-century Mormon followers believed much the same thing as did other white Christian sects—that blacks were perfectly suited to function as the white man's perpetual servant. Interestingly, there were black Saints during that time, and at least two black men, Elijah Abel[34,35] and Walker Lewis[36], were ordained into the Mormon Priesthood during Smith's time as Church President (before his untimely death at the hands of a lynch mob[37]). It is additionally known that the Smith family had a close personal relationship with Jane Manning James, a free black woman, a servant who lived with them for a period of time.[38] Joseph Smith seemed to have had less personal prejudice toward black Americans than his predecessor, Brigham Young. As the second president of the LDS Church, Young spoke for all Mormons when he declared, "We knew that the children of Ham were to be the '*servant of servants*,' and no power under heaven could hinder it, so long as the Lord should permit them to welter under the curse, and those were known to be our religious views concerning them."[39]

Mormonism, however, extended the established interpretation of the Hamitic Curse on black people by expanding the notion that the curse actually originated with the biblical counter-figure, Cain (a predecessor of Ham), for having committed the world's first murder against his brother, Abel. In 1835, Joseph Smith claimed to have translated an ancient papyrus scroll that contained the writings of Abraham and Joseph during their sojourn in Egypt.[40,41] Inscribed on this ancient scroll were curious passages that many Mormon leaders and LDS religious scholars believed established the divine principle needed for black priesthood denial, an ecclesiastical position held by all worthy male members. According to the Mormon interpretation, God's displeasure with Cain caused a sore cursing to fall upon him made visible with dark skin. Moreover, Cain's progenitors, the so-called black race, were to be forever racially marked as a reminder of his transgression, enslaved to serve their white brethren and denied the opportunities of freedom and liberty.

Mormon elder and leader George A. Smith further explained the subordinate position of blacks in the LDS church who "in consequence of their corruptions, their murders, their wickedness, or the wickedness of their fathers, had the priesthood taken from them, and the curse that was upon them was decreed should descend upon their posterity after them, it was decreed that they should not bear rule."[42,43] Other church leaders throughout LDS history echoed these sentiments regarding the accursed standing of blacks. According to Joseph Fielding Smith, the tenth president of the LDS church, "It was well understood by the early elders of the Church that the mark which was placed on Cain and which his posterity inherited was the black skin. The Book of Moses informs us that Cain and his descendants were black."[44]

The Mormon hierarchy gave further insight into the Cain and Ham frame by arguing that in a pre-earth state, a population of spirits could not decide who to serve, God or Satan, in the Great War in heaven. According to Mormon beliefs, because of their indecisiveness, these spirits were deemed less valiant in support of God and His plan in the pre-existence. As a consequence of their presumed failure, these same less-than-worthy spirits were then born into the mortal world in sable bodies that were part of the "accursed lineage of Canaan," the son of Ham.[45,46] Left unspoken but understood in this message was that whites, as compared to blacks, had been more righteous in the pre-existence, manifested by having been born into white bodies rather than into bodies damnable with black skin. Reinforcing the idea of pre-mortal culpability among blacks, Mormon Church leader Bruce R. McConkie opined that "those who were less valiant in the pre-existence and who thereby had certain spiritual restrictions imposed upon them during mortality are those known as Negroes. Such spirits are sent to earth through the lineage of Cain, the mark put upon him for his rebellion against God and his murder of Abel being a black skin. . . . The present status of the Negro rests purely and simply on the foundation of pre-existence."[47] Thus, LDS leaders associated dark skin with saintly unworthiness and white skin with holy virtue for well over a century.[48,49]

During the mid-1960s, knowledge of Mormon teachings about blacks began seeping outside the isolated confines of the Salt Lake Valley headquarters of the LDS Church. In response, Mormon authorities sought to rationalize their negative beliefs about blacks as less deserving by drawing on larger white society's racist past. These notions of race often solidified white group cohesiveness through the deployment of religious conviction. And the "Curse of Cain" frame provided the basis to view blacks through a deficit lens, making it much easier for the white membership to accept and participate in patronizing, yet seemingly benevolent forms of racist practices.

White Mormons, in all their pretentiousness, also took extraordinary measures to ensure that people of African lineage could not marry in the temple, perform proxy work for their loved ones, or receive their endowment, all of which are profoundly defining experiences in Mormon theology. They were emphatic that the priesthood ban placed on black men would remain until God, through His ordained prophet (one of their own), chose to lift the ban.[50] Only then would blacks be allowed full access to the Jesus Christ of the Mormon faith.

For Mormons, the "mark" of black skin was a literal curse, an irreducible sign of difference. Mormon authorities perpetuated enduring racist frames about blacks as deficient and cursed among white members of the faith. This, in turn, necessitated that any persons with black skin, whether through interracial marriage or direct African lineage, be singled out and set apart for deferential treatment from God's emissaries on earth (LDS church leaders). This Mormon version of the "one drop rule" resulted in rejection from church rites both for black men and black women for differing reasons.

THE ONE DROP RULE: RACE MIXING AND A CURSED LINEAGE

It is remarkable how quintessentially American Mormon thinking is regarding black people in that it closely mirrors larger configurations of systemic racist patterns and other forms of oppression found in white America. Mormonism, like most white-dominated Christian religions in the United States, created policies, practices, and rules that excluded black people from full participation.[51] And like other white Christians, Mormons also believed that segregation of the races was good for society, which included a strong aversion to miscegenation—black-white unions.[52] Laws originating in the 1600s prohibited or limited the practice of interracial marriage.[53] These anti-miscegenation laws dominated the Southern states, but most places in the country had some form of restriction against marriage across racial lines.[54]

Mormonism was no different in its stand against interracial marriage. Early Mormon leaders, like the rest of mainstream white America, made it clear that race mixing with the impure, cursed blood of Cain was prohibited and deemed unnatural in the eyes of God and, therefore, in the eyes of the faithful believers.[55,56] They wrote about those fears and expressed them often to the general membership. In a statement to the young women of the LDS church, church president Harold B. Lee extolled the virtues of white womanhood when he enlightened them as to their "favored lineage." He strongly discouraged interracial relationships "with a race that would condemn your posterity to penalties that have been placed upon the seed of Cain by the judgments of God."[57] He taught that any offspring with a drop of "black" blood would be cursed as well.[58,59]

Other LDS leaders were equally vocal in their condemnation of interracial relationships. J. Reuben Clark (1946), a prominent church authority member, warned the youth of the church to "treat them [blacks] as brothers and sisters, but do not ever let that wicked virus get into your systems that brotherhood either permits or entitles you to mix races which are inconsistent."[60] This sort of racist rhetoric and teaching was not uncommon—in fact, many presumed these teachings to be doctrine.

Among the concerns of many Mormon leaders was the notion that the civil rights movement was a scheme designed to reveal blacks' true intention of race mixing their blood with the "pure" white race. Mark E. Petersen, a member of the Quorum of the Twelve Apostles, addressed this very issue in a speech that he gave to educators during the Convention of Teachers of Religion on the College Level. Citing an interview with African American congressman Adam Clayton Powell Jr., Petersen revealed the mania circulating through church leadership. In the interview, Congressman Powell discussed the way in which America was lagging behind in social progress. To Powell, Europe seemed less concerned over loving across the color line. Petersen, however, took that to mean that the black man was obsessed with this idea of marrying and copulating with whites. "He isn't just trying to ride on the same street car—or the same Pullman car with white people. It isn't that he just desires to go to the same theatre as the white people . . . it appears that the negro seeks absorption [*sic*] with the white race. He will not be satisfied until he achieves it by intermarriage. That is his objective and we must face it."[61]

This unfounded distress over "race mixing" was further highlighted in a written exchange between sociology professor Lowry Nelson and President George Albert Smith, discussing the state of racial affairs in Cuba and the Church's potential mission work. During this communication, these letters revealed Smith's hysteria over the very real possibility of interracial marriage.[62] Though this was completely out of context of Nelson's remarks and clearly not the intent of Nelson's conversation, it revealed much of what guided the thinking of early Mormon authorities and officials. Ultimately, the Church had to make a decision as to their preference—to advance the Church and its teachings worldwide, which included exposure to and interaction with blacks, or maintain their position on racial segregation. The ban on blacks from the priesthood assuaged this fear of race-mixing for the time being. But in the end, the opportunity to reach and extend its global membership and influence was too much, and it could not be done with such an antiquated and troubling philosophy on blacks.

THE PRIESTHOOD AND CORE TEXTS IN MORMONISM

Today, thousands of missionaries are dispatched throughout the world to share the Book of Mormon with potential believers and converts to the LDS faith. Based on the Book of Mormon and its teachings, scores of students likewise descend on BYU each year to experience firsthand what is, in the words of former BYU president Ernest L. Wilkinson, "a comprehensive indoctrination of Mormon theology."[63] Mormonism, like other white Christian traditions, anchors its theology in the teachings of Christ Jesus as contained in the Bible. But for Mormons, their beliefs extend beyond the confines of biblical writings as the sole definitive word of God. In addition to the Holy Bible, the principal teachings found in LDS theology center around the Book of Mormon, Pearl of Great Price, and the Doctrine of Covenants as all a part of the official cannon (i.e., Holy Works) of the LDS church. These additional sacred texts are intended to encourage church members to lead a more sanctified life, while buttressing the belief in Jesus Christ in a world beleaguered by sin.

Further distinguishing itself from mainline Christianity is its emphasis on continuing revelation, as the heavens remain open for God to communicate with humankind through His chosen prophet. Just as the Book of Mormon is the cornerstone of LDS beliefs, the lay priesthood, then, is the glue that holds the faith together by allowing men to officiate in church affairs, ordinances, and rituals at the local, regional, and national level. The priesthood is intended as a spiritual office and functions as a stair-step process with a lesser grooming priesthood leading to a more responsible higher priesthood.[64,65]

Within Mormonism, the Aaronic priesthood, or the priesthood of Aaron, is the lesser priesthood given to adolescent boys from twelve to eighteen years old. In the Aaronic priesthood, there are different roles or offices that carry responsibilities for young men as they prepare to be ordained for the higher office of the Melchizedek priesthood. This instruction begins early, as Mormon boys aspire to higher responsibilities, dutifully working toward building and sustaining the Mormon kingdom worldwide. Importantly, the worthiness and eligibility of young men for priesthood ordination is initially determined by age and maturity level guidelines set by LDS church headquarters and enacted by the local ward (or congregation) bishop who oversees all aspects of spiritual life (and to some extent secular life) among members in the Mormon faith within that community.[66]

The Melchizedek priesthood, in turn, is the higher office of priesthood that Mormon boys progress toward as members of the Church.

The higher priesthood enables worthy males (which, initially, was limited to only white men) to serve in various church assignments, offices, positions, or callings while acting on behalf of the Lord and guided by God's power through prayer.[67] One such office that each of these men hold is that of an "elder" of the Church. Additionally, among those priesthood blessings that men in the Mormon faith aspire to obtain is the right and privilege to solemnize all things necessary on earth for personal salvation. This includes the ordinances of baptism (for both the living and dead), the gift of the Holy Ghost as a constant companion, and most important, eternal marriage, which is performed on only the worthiest of saints in the holiest of sanctuaries, the LDS Temple.

The priesthood is the pinnacle of aspirations for Mormon men. It is a gift that must be earned through good works, culminating most commonly in serving a proselytizing church mission typically when men come of age at eighteen years old. But it is also a right of passage for all males of the LDS faith. That is, those who are capable and do not attain the level of worthiness to be ordained and to hold the priesthood are essentially branded with the letter "A" (or, if you will, "P" for "priesthood") on their chests for all within the Mormon community to see in their failure to be righteous. By not attaining and holding the office of priesthood, it is, for many practicing Latter-day Saints, a mark of shame for a Mormon man and his family as he is unable to fulfill his priesthood responsibilities in ways that reinforce the hyper-masculine world of gender politics in Mormonism.

To deny black males the priesthood, then, is to mark them as not fully worthy, not fully men. The priesthood ban against blacks may not seem like much of an issue to the outside observer. But to members of the Mormon faith, particularly to Mormon men, the priesthood is a significant and defining moment in their spiritual development and advancement as well as that of their families.

Practicing black Mormons, not surprisingly then, wanted the priesthood in part as a way to dis-identify with the everyday realities of being black in an often hostile, color-conscious society dominated by whites. They wanted to be seen as "ordinary" Mormons, which meant race neutrality or a colorblind Church. Black Mormons felt the mantle of the priesthood should trump race. In other words, having the priesthood would mean *some* level of status and equal standing between black and white Mormons in a purportedly universal church. In actuality, as Mormon history demonstrates, that did not happen.

DIVINE AUTHORITY AND THE EMERGENCE OF THE MORMON CHURCH: LINKING OLD WORLD AND NEW WORLD CHRISTIANITY

Prior to the official enactment of the priesthood ban by Brigham Young circa 1852, the Mormon church was a fledgling New England-style religion created by its young founder, Joseph Smith Jr. (1805–1844), who was spiritually troubled by the religious passions of his day. The region in which Smith grew up in rural Western New York was a source of intense Protestant activity, with preaching over the particulars of the millennial reign of Christ and religious rivalry in the early part of the nineteenth century.[68,69,70] The contentious eschatological debates between the Presbyterians, Baptists, and Methodists touched the Smith home personally, fragmenting family members, pushing them to investigate and explore different faith traditions. Meanwhile, Smith searched for spiritual guidance from on high through prayer.[71]

Joseph Smith was about twelve years old when he began questioning the shortcomings of the various organized religions and the hypocrisy of Christians as it pertained to the things of God in his vicinity.[72] According to Smith, "[M]y intimate acquaintance with those of different denominations led me to marvel exceedingly for I discovered that they did not adorn their profession by a holy walk and Godly conversation agreeable to what I found contained in that sacred depository this was a grief to my Soul."[73]

Not knowing which church to join, the young Smith came across a passage in Scripture, "If any of you lack wisdom, let him ask of God, that giveth to all men liberally, and upbraideth not; and it shall be given him."[74] The compelling nature of the Scripture inspired Smith to seek specific answers from God as to which Christian sect he should join. He retreated to a grove of trees where God the Father and his son Jesus Christ reportedly visited him in a miraculous and supernatural encounter known in Mormondom as the "First Vision." Visions, such as the ones Smith alleged, were not uncommon during this time period, as many claimed similar heavenly encounters.[75] Joseph Smith had many more visitations by heavenly messengers, particularly Peter, James, and John, New Testament disciples of Christ in glorified form, who revealed to Joseph that God intended to restore the primitive church and its teachings. This restoration would soon usher in the second advent of Jesus Christ, and thus reestablish order to the universe. Joseph Smith taught what he learned through his divinely inspired visions to the Saints—the Mormon membership and body of believers.

According to Mormon history, in 1829, these same heavenly messengers embarked on the banks of the Susquehanna River to confer the Melchizedek priesthood, or higher priesthood, upon Smith and fellow acolyte, Oliver Cowdery.[76] Joseph Smith then had the authority he needed from God to organize and bring forth the restoration of the ancient church made anew in nineteenth-century America. And in 1830, under the leadership of newly ordained Mormon prophet Joseph Smith, the Church of Jesus Christ of Latter-day Saints was officially organized; a church that would one day come to boast members and congregations in the millions throughout the world.

According to LDS beliefs, Jesus Christ established his true Church (calling its members Saints) on earth during antiquity, and shortly after the death and ascension of Christ into heaven, He visited His "other sheep" in the Americas. For Mormons, the other sheep, whom Christ referred to in the Bible,[77] denotes two groups of people who migrated from the Old World Jerusalem to the New World in the Western Hemisphere. The Book of Mormon is the story of these two groups of people and their journey to, and history in, the Americas.

Coming from the Old World, the second group of these peoples are believed by Mormons to be the descendants of Lehi, an ancient Israelite prophet,[78] and his posterity, who were commanded by God around 600 B.C. (before the fall of Jerusalem to the Babylonians) to leave the area and settle somewhere in Mesoamerica. The history of these Pre-Colombian Christian peoples and their various wars, conflicts, prophecies, and experiences with Christ were said to be compiled on gold plates buried in an earthen mound known as the famed Hill Cumorah site near Joseph Smith's Western New York home.[79,80]

In the fall of 1823, approximately three years after the "First Vision," the angel Moroni (who presumably lived during 385 A.D.) appeared to Smith and unveiled the location of these long-buried ancient texts. The translation of these gold plates by the prophet Joseph Smith is what became the source material for the Book of Mormon, which is the core of LDS beliefs.[81] The subsequent publication of the Book of Mormon in 1830, along with the restoration of the "true church," set in motion a particular universal call to action to share with non-Mormons, or gentiles, important teachings for personal salvation that can only be found, according to Mormon traditions, in the LDS faith. These truths are saturated with images and understanding of whiteness as symbolized in their interpretations of Christ as a preferential being.[82] Mormons have been traditionally socialized, under the auspices of Jesus, to call on Him through the white male leadership on matters of faith, often venerating and deifying church authorities in ways that leave little room for doubt or questioning.

One aspect of the white racial frame in Mormonism is the privileging of white racial knowledge over other forms of epistemologies, as high-ranking church officials "created and reinforced racial hierarchies by spiritualizing social concerns."[83] Such was the case with the exclusion of blacks. By linking Christ with Mormon racial folklore, church authorities could circumscribe the criticism of dissenting voices both inside and outside the faith while the Mormon membership blindly followed. Issues like interracial marriage and the black priesthood ban were matters of faith attributable to the biblical ages and religious freedom as opposed to a broader and more accurate history of white supremacy. The confidence and unwavering faith that church members have for their leaders made the negative framing of blacks more sustainable. According to Richard Wright, the "apex of white racial ideology was reached when white domination was a God-given right."[84]

IS IT DOCTRINE OR POLICY? MORMON CONTRADICTIONS ON THE PRIESTHOOD BAN

If there were ever any doubt as to the dogmatic convictions around the status of people of African lineage in Mormonism, it would be put to rest by the encounter between the First Presidency[85] and fellow Mormon and sociology professor Lowry Nelson, who taught at Utah State Agricultural College (what is now Utah State University). Nelson studied in Cuba right after World War II and was familiar with the sociocultural and religious practices of the people. Following Nelson's work in

Cuba in 1944 where he researched rural life in the Caribbean, his old childhood friend, Heber Meeks, reached out to him. Meeks was mission president over the Southern states, and he had been asked by members of the First Presidency (then-President and Prophet George Albert Smith and his two counselors, J. Reuben Clark and David O. McKay) to engage Nelson in an inquiry as to the feasibility of missionary work in the island nation of Cuba.[86]

The first of the letters Nelson received in 1947 informing him of the Church's interest in missionary work in the region was frank regarding Mormon racial attitudes toward blacks. Due to his sociological work in the region, Nelson was well prepared to render them an expert assessment of the situation. Unfortunately, the answer that Nelson provided to Meeks and the First Presidency was not well received nor was it one they were looking for. In Nelson's response, he raised serious concerns regarding the Church's position of "white supremacy," something that he could not condone.[87] In subsequent letters to the First Presidency, Nelson responded that he found justice in neither the Curse of Ham folklore nor the doctrine of inequality as interpreted in the teachings of Jesus by high-ranking LDS authorities in Utah. Acknowledging the long history of teachings regarding blacks as inferior, he respectfully questioned the credibility of such a racist church "doctrine."

President G. Albert Smith, however, in his correspondence with Nelson, declared that all God's children were, in fact, *not* equal, and the Church's teachings on blacks was, in actuality, LDS doctrine since its inception.[88] The First Presidency's retort discounted Nelson's objections to Mormon bigotry. They attempted to stifle his argument by indicating that he was straying from the Gospel and the sacred teachings of the Lord for allowing himself to be led astray by the "worldly learning" and contemptible philosophies of man.[89] This tactic of silencing dissenting voices has long been used by white Americans on anyone (especially people of color) considered a threat to the established order of white power and authority. For the Brethren,[90] this included Mormon intellectuals who have been portrayed as falling victim to the whims of Satan, as no man should question the Church. Elder Dallin Oaks accented this feeling of the Brethren when he stated in a 2007 PBS interview, "It's wrong to criticize leaders of the Church, even if the criticism is true."[91]

But Professor Nelson was not alone in his confusion on the doctrine. Church leaders have long been illusive and contradictory on the topic of black priesthood denial. Until this point, there had been no official writings affirming these teachings as doctrine. But two years later, in 1949, the first of three official LDS statements regarding black male priesthood ordination was delivered. At that time, The First Presidency of the LDS church declared, "The attitude of the Church with reference to Negroes remains as it has always stood. It is not a matter of the declaration of a policy but of direct commandment from the Lord, on which is founded the doctrine of the Church from the days of its organization, to the effect that Negroes may become members of the Church but that they are not entitled to the priesthood at the present time."[92]

This statement delivered by the Mormon high leadership continued by citing Brigham Young's racist assertion that blackness comes as a result of the "consequence of their fathers rejecting the power of the holy priesthood, and the law of God. They will go down to death. And when all the rest of the children have received their blessings in the holy priesthood, then that curse will be removed from the seed of Cain."[93] Hence, this quasi-doctrine carried within Young's statement was enough to grant the Mormon hierarchy the rationalization to continue the prohibition against black people.

The contradictions became even more evident with the writings and teachings of David O. McKay from his apostleship through his presidency. Ironically, less than a decade after then-Apostle McKay lent his signature to the letters penned to Lowry Nelson and just five years after the LDS hierarchy released the first official statement on black folk in which it was declared that the priesthood ban was indeed doctrine (elevated to the level of the sacred), he released a statement confuting his earlier support. Once sustained as president of the Church of Latter-day Saints in 1954, David O. McKay stated privately to his son, "There is not now, and there never has been a doctrine in this Church that the Negroes are under a divine curse. There is no doctrine in the Church of any kind pertaining to the Negro. We believe that we have scriptural precedent for withholding the priesthood from the Negro. It is a practice, not a doctrine, and the practice someday will be changed. And that's all there is to it."[94,95] Despite McKay's ambivalence in proclaiming the priesthood ban as doctrine, the racist practice of reducing blacks to second-class citizen status continued until 1978.

Considering the fact that these white racial frames of inequality were conveyed as an essential part of Mormondom, Nelson responded with a disconcerted comparison between Mormon racial folk theology and the beliefs of segregationists Theodore G. Bilbo[96] and John Elliot Rankin, both prominent and unabashedly racist politicians from Mississippi. While both of these self-proclaimed white supremacists had equal disdain for the intermingling of races, Bilbo went further by composing a racist manifesto in the culmination of his life, often invoking biblical prose in warning his people of the ensuing "mongrelization" of the white race. In his book *Take Your Choice—Separation or Mongrelization*, he referred to himself (as he often did, in the third person) when he said, "Personally, the writer of this book would rather see his race and his civilization blotted out with the atomic bomb than to see it slowly but surely destroyed in the maelstrom of miscegenation, interbreeding, intermarriage and mongrelization."[97] This passage summarized the entire message of his racist literature.

Mormonism's patronizing form of racism is similarly aligned in many ways to the racist practices of Bilbo and Rankin, each man invoking the name and image of Christ to inflame racial tensions. In essence, Christ did the work of injustice for white people in destructive ways.[98] This form of theological violence attacks the soul though the implementation of whiteness and religious imperialism.[99] African Americans responded by establishing their own sanctuaries and later changing their conceptions of Christ as a symbol of liberation.[100]

THE CONTINUED SIGNIFICANCE OF HAM'S CURSE

Enacted and implemented as policy, black men were named as ineligible for priesthood ordination due to their (presumably) divinely relegated status, though most members were unaware of a "doctrinal" pronouncement, just as was Lowry Nelson. In fact, it is not uncommon to hear present-day Mormons bemoan that the past teachings of the Church were mere folklore and a reflection of the times. But extensive research has demonstrated that leaders, at one point, claimed this as doctrine, among official canonized works. In the end, the Church generated more questions than answers, leaving the members unclear as to the depths of systemic racist practices.

Yet, regardless of the incongruity of the Church, the ban against black male priesthood ordination was, in the very least, considered LDS church policy from 1852 through 1978. Thus, the seeds of hate were planted and given theological nourishment to flourish. These racist views among Mormons reflect a widespread deficit orientation that existed about blacks. They further informed the decision making, actions, and interactions of LDS church leaders who drew on whiteness as institutional authority supposedly coming directly from God Himself. The ban became an unquestionable, commonplace practice over time within the faith. But to deny black men access to priesthood ordination in the Mormon faith was to also deny the families of these men full rights and privileges of the faith. Priesthood restriction against black men was, therefore, no insignificant matter within the LDS community as it carried considerable authority and power.

These LDS discernments of the spiritual genesis and subsequent demise of black people due to their presumed lack of valiance formed a corpus of racial knowledge about blacks held and acted on by whites. This white racial knowledge was passed down through seven generations of Mormonism as it was taught and supported by elite white men considered by the rank-and-file membership to be prophets, seers, and revelators who led the Mormon church by divine inspiration. Deemed God's literal power on earth, the priesthood decides which whole groups of people are included and excluded from participation. In the case of African Americans and their families, the Mormon priesthood was used as an exclusionary tool of metaphysical manipulation and control.

As is the case with all white racial frames and ideologies of indifference, the racist mythology of black inferiority found within Mormonism specifically served a function among the white membership. By legitimizing whiteness through the marking of blackness as the racial and spiritual "Other," church leaders maintained the oppression of blacks through the coercive weight of white male patriarchy cloaked in the white robes of priesthood authority, none of which could be maintained without an unswerving and colluding body of believers.[101] The spiritualized process of the priesthood demonstrates its essential nature within Mormonism as it has been since the formation of the Church.

STAYING THE COURSE: WHITE AMERICAN MORMONISM AND THE UPHEAVALS OF THE CIVIL RIGHTS ERA

Racist philosophies of the Hamitic Curse and black inferiority were inherited from Western European thought and applied to American contexts and conditions. These theological beliefs about blacks as cursed were put forward by elite white men in the founding of the nation and slowly infused into popular culture through the influx of race-based ideology through the generations. In a dynamic and shifting racial order, racist views applied to reasoning around black bodies created acceptable systemic advantages and the continued domination by white people of African Americans and other "expendable" Americans.[102]

Within Mormon theology, the divine curse frame provided the basis for a myriad of interpretations on the causes of black suffering. Tropes of blackness were created, produced, and passed off as official doctrine. And for much of the Church's history, blacks were subsequently considered anathema in LDS doctrine, much the same way as they were in other mainline white Protestant faiths, as subordinate beings unworthy of God's grace and destined to be "servant of servants."

Mormon memes of black-skinned people as cursed in society fit well within the prevailing viewpoint held by most whites that blacks only had themselves to blame for their own circumstances. This perspective enabled white Americans to refuse to see the humanity in black people and further emboldened conservative analysts like sociologist Bill Wilson. Wilson contends that "poor black Americans, like poor white Americans, are poor because they are located in the low-waged sector of society and that race has little to do with."[103] White racist frames have made it easier for white Americans to sleep well at night while black Americans remain structurally in the margin and unjustly disadvantaged.

Early framers of Mormon theology, following in the footsteps of the nation's leaders, drew on general deficit-based discourse about people of African descent. But during the 1960s, a seismic change began to force the country to examine its racist practices and discriminatory laws against black Americans. Much of U.S. society was waging war against racial injustices long committed by white America during 85 percent of its history, from slavery to Jim Crow racism. And while society was generating optimism toward the enactment of civil rights legislation, Mormons remained resolute in their convictions about the debased status of blacks. After all, it was God Himself who told the conservative leadership this was the correct path toward redemption. While other churches and religious sects were quickly conforming (at least publically) to the laws of the land, Mormons, by contrast, stayed the course and continued to teach contempt and practice discrimination without apology. But despite the overall isolation, closed ranks, and unified actions of white Mormons in Utah, the race-based exclusionary practices of the LDS church could not forever escape the scrutiny and challenges faced by white America during the civil rights era of the 1960s.

The strict framing of blacks and their descendants by the Mormon faith generated a new wave of activism in the West. While black activists during this period desired to draw attention to institutionalized forms of racism that they encountered, black college athletes within the Western Athletic Conference (WAC) found a way to protest against the racist doctrines of the Mormon church, which was otherwise protected by the Constitution's Freedom of Religion clause. As the LDS church–owned Brigham Young University was a founding member of the WAC charter, black athletes at that time were able to use college sports as a vehicle to expose the hypocrisy of the Church's racism. Meanwhile, students were ever more critical of the WAC for ostensibly tolerating the practices and teachings of the Mormon flagship school and not denouncing, sanctioning, or otherwise disciplining its teams and leadership. Though many of the black protestors heard some unsettling rumors about Mormon beliefs, which led to the protests, they truly had no idea of the scope and magnitude of racist framing of black people that existed in the LDS church since its earliest days.

4

POLITICAL UPRISING IN THE LATE SIXTIES AND EARLY SEVENTIES

Fanning the Flame of Black Student-Athlete Revolts

> It is time for American Negro athletes to join in the civil rights fight—a fight that is far from won.—Mal Whitfield, Olympic veteran[1]

For much of our racial history in North America and what later became the United States, we have lived in a nation where oligarchy—the rule of a few over the many—continues to exacerbate social inequalities that divide us in a number of significant ways. Much social science research affirms that these systems of inequality were created and maintained by a small group of English blue bloods who held considerable power and influence over the U.S. economic and political systems.[2,3] Such power, obtained partly through land theft, led to the near destruction of native peoples in North America.[4,5] And since the beginning of this nation's history, these same white elites—the early landowners and slave-holding colonists—produced various forms of despotic institutions aimed at capitalizing on stolen labor through unspeakable forms of terror enacted on the body and soul of black people.[6] This system of chattel slavery had long-lasting effects as the descendants of early slaveholders continued the violence on the progeny of men and women in forced bondage. These unjust, foundational and oppressive hierarchies and structures continue presently into the twenty-first century, and they are still widely felt in contemporary times as reflected in pervasive mistrust of whites held by African Americans and other Americans of color.[7,8,9]

This history of white racial dominance through countless manifestations of savagery forms the contextual backdrop of the sociopolitical, economic, and racial lattice from which the events of the civil rights era occurred. This chapter traces the development of historical iterations of white supremacy in the United States as it played out during the turbulent years of the 1960s and 1970s wherein black athletes were thrust into the social upheaval of U.S. society. The intent of this chapter is to track ways that black male student-athletes contributed to the toppling of one hundred years of Jim Crow racial segregation. It was during this era that the racial ideologies of white bureaucracy in America began to formally transition from race or color consciousness to race neutrality or colorblindness.

Pointedly, organized religion—Christianity in particular—had long been used to subjugate blacks through white aggression. This chapter explores how religion of the New World, Mormonism specifically, continues to serve as a stronghold of protection for the historical privileging of whiteness and preservation of racial ideologies of black inferiority. Black athletes took on and challenged the "divinely" sanctioned notions of black inadequacy within Mormonism and the church-owned educational institution, Brigham Young University.

COUNTER-FRAMING TO CONTEST JIM CROW RACIAL IDEOLOGIES

Ninety percent of American households had at least one television between 1950 and 1960; thus, images of the struggle for civil rights were transmitted into the living rooms of homes all across the country[10], as U.S. racial brutality was unveiled to the world for the first time on the nightly news. Unable to escape these gripping broadcasts, the Civil Rights Movement began to evoke white sympathy from those who typically turned a blind eye to black suffering. Americans watched in shock and horror as what began in the 1950s as an otherwise peaceful and nonviolent movement "quickly"—in the minds of many white Americans—escalated into a more combustible and less containable movement. They witnessed, firsthand via the technology of television, the graphic and bloody display of pure white racial hatred against blacks enacted in a most vivid manner.

This further generated an embarrassing, worldwide story for human rights that, consequently, proved of great importance to American interest abroad.[11] According to Professor Derrick Bell's theory of interest-convergence, the United States was not motivated by a desire to improve and atone for its shameful human rights record and treatment of black Americans as much as it was to hide their dirty laundry in order to advance its image and standing in the world, which was of vital importance to the nation's Cold War allies.[12] If the United States could have maintained its world image as a superpower while retaining its racial oligarchy, there likely would have been another hundred years of "separate but equal." Instead, images of lynched and mutilated bodies stunned the globe.

Pictures of mostly black men hanging from southern trees, seared into the consciousness of ordinary people, inspired jazz great Billie Holiday's haunting ballad "strange fruit," which exposed the hypocrisy of American racism in a deeply unequal and divided society.[13] As the United States attempted to save face, the country began to distance itself from more overt forms of white racist violence, like the scourge of lynching that was no longer tolerated outside the South. It was not until Russian propaganda drew attention to the treatment of American blacks that the country's hand was forced, and the legal walls of oppression began to crumple.[14] Thus, the sympathy generated by television exposure of white-on-black brutality created a watershed moment that facilitated the push for long-overdue legal changes.

Black Americans, though, had been fighting this fight for centuries, as whites used domestic terrorism to preserve and maintain the racial order. This harsh mistreatment was not just physical in nature, but also psychic against the soul, thus ensuring black self-doubt, the enemy of self-esteem.[15,16] African Americans have historically employed countermeasures to resist slavery and other white-imposed racism(s) in attempts to redefine themselves by what Feagin and his associates dubbed "counter-framing."[17,18,19,20] Black resistance to white rule occurred in a multitude of ways throughout history. Early examples of counter-framing included slave narratives, music, and religious expression. The civil rights movement marked an explosion of counter-framing approaches from exasperated blacks. These ranged from nonviolent marches to the cherished victories of the black athlete over a white opponent to the more extreme threat of armed racial conflict.

REWARDS AND LOSSES FOR RACIAL RESISTANCE AND CIVIL RIGHTS ACTIVISM

At this point in history, the nation was engrossed in a struggle for the soul and conscience of America. This racial battle would bring to a head and expose the gross contradictions contained in Francis Bellamy's emblematic Pledge of Allegiance, which, in theory at least, epitomized the notions of freedom, justice, and equality brought to fruition with the formation of the United States.[21] Mired instead with generations of extreme white racism, the country had, in truth, been resting on a shaky foundation of systemic injustice rather than the ideals of the pledge.

During the 1950s and 1960s, the civil unrest in the American South spawned profuse acts of white-on-black violence all across the country, some more bloody and brutal than others. Blacks resisted where they could. Some quietly, others loudly, whether with large protests or individual acts of defiance. Dr. Martin Luther King Jr., who emerged as the young leader of the Montgomery bus boycotts, is generally envisioned as the face of the civil rights campaign. But countless unknown individuals also participated in the freedom struggle, often supported by organizations such as the Southern Christian Leadership Conference (SCLC), the Congress of Racial Equality (CORE), and student-led organizations such as Student Nonviolent Coordinating Committee (SNCC). Though the philosophy of the civil rights resistance led by King's faction combined Christian moral principles with the Gandhian notion of pacifism to undergird the movement, mayhem and bloodshed were often unleashed on protesters, particularly in the South where white-framed racist traditions ran deep.[22,23]

This was never more vividly illustrated than when four black students sat down at a Woolworth's lunch counter in Greensboro, North Carolina, and politely asked for service. When asked to leave, the students remained in their seats until the store closed that evening. This youth-led tactic of peaceful resistance ignited one of the largest sit-in movements across the South, throughout multiple stores in multiple cities. Importantly, it would take six months of daily mass sit-ins, occasionally resulting in force and injury by whites on the peaceful black protesters, for Woolworth's to desegregate the lunch counter. Though these racial protests started long before the 1960s, this time period was a crucial turning point in the civil rights movement. The following year, in 1961, the most famous of these nonviolent protest groups emerged, the Freedom Riders.

James Farmer, the cofounder and first national director of CORE, led the original Freedom Riders. Farmer enlisted the help of thirteen young people (seven black and six white) from different areas of the country to participate in a movement that had more foresight than anyone other than Farmer himself could have imagined.[24,25] Many of the participants were from other nonviolent protest groups like the Nashville Student Group, an organization that had successfully staged student sit-ins to desegregate lunch counters and movie theaters.[26] Similar nonviolent strategies would be employed during the Freedom Rides into the Deep South to test federal law intended to end legal segregation in interstate transportation[27] and to demonstrate against the South's wonton disregard for the law.

The CORE strategy was simple enough—put black and white bodies in close proximity on buses bound for the Deep South in an effort to deliberately violate segregationist laws. The bus riders challenged this "American apartheid" most notably by eating side by side at segregated lunch counters in bus terminals and by disregarding the rules of racially designated public washrooms. These undertakings were designed to contest the resolve of whites hell-bent on upholding their customs and traditions rooted in a system of white racial domination and supremacy—a power structure that was successively built up over twenty generations to keep blacks and whites separate and *unequal* before the law and to preserve white privilege and the Southern way of life.

The riders were anticipating a two-week trip that would end in New Orleans in time for the anniversary of the *Brown v. Board of Education* decision. They encountered little resistance initially during their trip but would soon face racially instigated beatings, arrests, and other forms of harassment and violence at the hands of angry white mobs. The threat of dismantling the whiteness of Southern hegemony invoked negative white racial frames about black progress, which included the image of blacks acting too "uppity" and forgetting their place in society, a standpoint that incited racial mistreatment directed at the riders and other organizers committed to bringing about an end to Jim Crow.

As time elapsed, the civil rights counter-framing strategy of theological passivity—the gospel of "turn the other cheek"—that called for assimilation and integration had come to a standstill. By the late 1960s, younger generations of African Americans—students, athletes, black faculty, staff, and others—impatient with King's long-suffering, less overt approach to white injustice, began to demand deeper democratic changes in laws, customs, habitude, and practices. These new civil rights activists had abandoned their suits and ties for dashikis, braids, and naturals. Proud of their blackness and seeking self-determination free from white intrusion, this new generation of black Americans was no longer afraid to speak treason to the white establishment.

These latest tactics sparked a new generation of civil rights activists who relied on provocative language and images, boycotts, and walkouts, even resorting to some form of violence (including hostile takeovers of university buildings) if need be, to get their point across. This willingness to use force terrified white America.[28] The old paradigm of nonviolence had given way to a groundswell of an explicitly more confrontational form of activism directed at ending institutionalized racism and oppression, including racial exclusion found within institutions of higher learning.

Sweeping legal and political changes resulting from years of protest defined the 1960s with seminal legislation that made it possible for African Americans, especially the black middle class, to have some semblance of parity with whites. Most notably, the Civil Rights Act of 1964 outlawed discrimination on the basis of race, color, religion, sex, or national origin.[29] Still, more victories began to accumulate, and laws were passed that further defined the civil rights era. The Voting Rights Act of 1965, for example, prohibited states from imposing any prequalifying condition for voting that denied the right of any citizen of the United States to vote on the basis of race or ethnicity.[30] Additionally, *Loving v. Virginia* ended the ban on interracial marriage that had long criminalized interracial couples who chose to violate state antimiscegenation laws.[31,32,33] And the Civil Rights Act of 1968 (fair housing) afforded stigmatized Americans some governmental protection regarding racial discrimination in the housing industry.[34]

Yet these "victories" were earned at a high price. Medgar Evers, an NAACP field worker, was murdered; the Sixteenth Street Baptist Church was bombed and four young, innocent girls were senselessly killed in the fray; President Kennedy was assassinated while campaigning in Dallas; three civil rights workers were found dead and buried in a dam in Mississippi; Malcolm X was gunned down before a public address; the Selma March turned into Bloody Sunday; the Watts Riots erupted;[35] Martin Luther King Jr. was assassinated on a Memphis balcony;[36,37] and many more "anonymous" names in history gave their independence, their humanity, and, more than occasionally, their lives to the sacrifice for the advancement of a more civil and humane society. As the ultimate price of civil rights activism, the black community as a whole suffered the profound loss of life and talent. These experiences of death and pain for human and civil rights were seared into the minds and hearts of many African American children whose parents had been involved in the movement in some particular way, whether directly or indirectly. These same black children would grow up with a fighting spirit, the will to push the status quo by any means necessary. Their anti-racist resistance to the enduring supremacy of whites served as a catalyst that fostered the creation of the black radical tradition of activism. The racial protests that ensued in response to pervading debauchery were widely captured in the national and global media. This tradition of counter-framing against widespread racial inequities set the stage for a new form of freedom fighter—the black athlete activist.[38]

A NEW KIND OF FREEDOM FIGHTER

One of the most well-recognized activists and athletes of the time was Muhammad Ali. But when he first entered the boxing ring, he was known as Cassius Clay. Clay grew up in the segregated world of Jim Crow racism, which likewise influenced his involvement in the civil rights movement. Accordingly, he knew all too well the race hatred that whites individually and collectively held. He was well aware of the consequences, for blacks in particular, of living in a society dedicated to upholding racial frames of black marginality. Indeed, it may be that Clay's experiences with white racism likely drove him to boxing in the first place. As an athlete, he was expected to remain aloof to the harsh realities of white-on-black oppression all around him. The expectations of white America were that black folks would act in deference to whites' shared interests at the expense of their own group insights. But Cassius Clay would later transform himself into the "Great American Boxer" and social activist, Muhammad Ali, who was, in turn, indifferent to white sensibilities, as a promoter of black group uplift.

Likewise, one of the most compelling and enduring images in sports history took place during the 1968 Summer Olympic Games in Mexico City. The late 1960s was a time when the United States proudly exploited the skill and prowess of the black athlete as a means to show dominance and power to the world while abusing and discriminating against those very same citizens back in their own neighborhoods. Virtually everyone can recall the image of the two black U.S. track and field stars standing on the winner's podium with a black-gloved fist raised to the sky—in the black power salute— with heads bowed during the national anthem.

This rebellious image of black resistance, unity, and power against U.S. white supremacy left an indelible stain upon America in the eyes of all of humanity. For the first time in U.S. history, the reigning superpower had its own human rights drama unfold on a world stage. If the nation did not want global attention drawn to the persistence of racial unrest among African Americans back in the States, then they had a problem on their hands with the 1968 Olympic Games. Gold medalist Tommie Smith and bronze medalist John Carlos, quietly, yet forcefully and unforgettably, informed the world of white-on-black injustices back at home, a place that purported a rich tradition of democracy and freedom. And there are countless other remarkable black athletes who have pushed toward social justice and robust democracy. Jim Brown. Arthur Ashe. Kareem Abdul Jabbar.[39] These athletes, using their national prominence in the sporting world to make a statement regarding social justice, paved the way for black student-athlete defiance.[40,41,42,43]

CHALLENGING SYSTEMIC WHITENESS IN HIGHER EDUCATION

In 1962, the Western Athletic Conference (WAC) was newly formed to unify the then-fragmented Border, Skyline, and Pacific Coast conferences into one powerhouse division with the intent to showcase the top college athletes from across the Western United States. BYU led the effort in the formation of the new conference, which, in its heyday, was fairly competitive. The inaugural WAC charter touted some of the best teams in western college athletics including the likes of Arizona, Arizona State, BYU, New Mexico State, Utah, and Wyoming.[44]

Shortly after its formation, to maintain its powerhouse status in the highly competitive arena of intercollegiate athletics, the WAC began increasing the recruitment of black student-athletes through the 1960s. Yet, what the conference did not bargain for was that these black students had been racially socialized, which is to say they were prepared as children by their black parents to effectively contend and cope with race-based mistreatment long before they arrived at these white universities and colleges.[45,46] For much of their lives, the black athletes who came of age during the late 1960s grew up seeing and hearing acts of civil disobedience against white supremacy enacted by blacks all around them. Whether on television or by word of mouth, the black student-athletes recruited to white universities in the Western Athletic Conference from 1968 to 1972 were racially socialized in terms of having received wisdom on how to challenge racism from their parents, grandparents, and other elders from the black community immediately around them. They also received wisdom on resisting whiteness by watching key figures in the African American community including Rosa Parks, Fannie Lou Hamer, Septima Clark, Malcolm X, Stokely Carmichael, and countless others having the courage to stand up for freedom's dream and, if need be, engage in more confrontational and less passive acts of defiance and civil disobedience.[47]

The black radical tradition of counter-framing white supremacy was in full swing by the late 1960s and early 1970s and was newly marked by the emergence of the Black Power movement, which as far as J. Edgar Hoover was concerned was part of a "communist" plot.[48,49] The Black Power movement's avant-garde ideas of economic self-determination and racial group uplift through black self-love—race pride for African Americans—were expressed differently and often more assertively than Dr. King's eloquent, yet passive, pleas for social integration and political inclusion for blacks. The children of the civil rights era had quickly morphed into a more politically cynical group of young dissidents—branded "militant"—aimed at speaking black truth to white power.[50]

The Black Power/Black Nationalism perspective influenced scores of revolts within predominately white academies and their athletic departments all across the country.

By the time competing black athletes of the late 1960s reached the world of college sports, they had grown tired of a lifetime of undisguised and unabashed racial mistreatment at the hands of white America. This black weariness spawned a generation of activism. Black athletes expressed deep concern over racist bureaucratic structures contained within the university system and athletic departments of predominately white institutions (PWIs), taking full advantage of the white sports establishment as an effective platform to bring attention to the shameful conditions they faced on campuses.[51] In hopes of bringing about radical change in American life, these black athletes used their bodies against the establishment by withholding their highly regarded athleticism from competition. According to Bullock, "They protested against unsympathetic coaches, rules against 'Afro' haircuts, lack of housing for blacks, lack of jobs for athletes' wives, policies against interracial dating, lack of black coaches and cheerleaders, and indignities suffered on and off the field at the hands of bigoted fans, opposing players, and game officials."[52]

Tommie Smith and John Carlos, the two former San Jose State athletes and U.S. medalists on the Olympic podium that October day in Mexico City, became an inspiration for many black activist students and professional athletes. The courage and conviction of these two competitors started with a call to action by sociologist Harry Edwards. In 1967, Edwards's disdain for white American exploitation of black athletes drew national attention when he organized a successful campaign against the athletic department at San Jose State College. Through his advocacy on behalf of black athletes, Edwards had gained considerable popularity and understanding as to how organized sport could be used to challenge and counter-frame the whiteness of athletics.

By 1968, prior to the Olympic Games, Edwards and his organization, the Olympic Project for Human Rights (OPHR), successfully picketed the prestigious, all-white New York Athletic Club (NYAC). Edwards would bring to light the troubling history of NYAC's race-based restriction to only white and Christian members.[53,54] The NYAC track meet was the premier indoor track and field event for aspiring Olympic hopefuls.[55] And yet, despite their personal ambitions for Olympic glory, the black athletes originally scheduled to participate in NYAC's 1968 competition heeded OPHR's call to dissent and thus put their own careers and futures in serious peril.[56]

There was a reported 50 percent decline in attendance that year. The few fans who did arrive witnessed only nine black trackmen, six of them from the University of Texas at El Paso (UTEP), cross the picket line and compete. At the behest of UTEP's track and field coach Wayne Vandernburg, his athletes were reportedly threatened with expulsion and revocation of their scholarships if they chose to involve themselves in the demonstrations. The UTEP runners conceded to their coach, competed, and returned to El Paso as heroes, thus maintaining the status quo. Just two months later, however, Edwards would meet with those same black UTEP track club members. The encounter invariably gave them the resolve and fortitude to resist, oppose, and stand up against the racial injustices they consistently faced on and off campus and in and out of competitive arenas by refusing to compete against BYU in an upcoming track event in Utah.[57] Significantly, each of these happenings served to set the stage for and further fan the flames of outrage experienced by the 1968 black student-athlete protests that were launched against BYU and the Mormon church's racist policy regarding the rights of blacks within the faith.

A CALL TO ACTION: BLACK STUDENT-ATHLETES AND THE STRUGGLES AGAINST FAITH-BASED DISCRIMINATION

When it came to BYU—the school that represented and reflected the negative racial views of the mainline LDS church—the Mormon school had been able to hide behind the cloak of the First Amendment in their ability to invoke religious folklore as a basis to discriminate with impunity and free of legal recourse. Even as the rest of white America was being challenged on their overtly racist practices of discrimination, Mormon leadership used the constitutional right to freedom of religious exercise to resist changes to their faith-based assumptions of black inferiority. White supremacy, in this case, had the law on its side, granting institutions of religious worship carte blanche immunity under the First Amendment.

Historically, blacks grappled to find ways to protest effectively against the race-based bigotry within religious institutions such as the LDS Church. But faced with the daunting prospect of competing against the racist institution, incensed and exploited student-athletes saw a loophole to fight religious intolerance. Since BYU was the academic extension of the Church's educational system, collegiate sports provided a prime opportunity to engage the LDS Church in the court of public opinion on their racist religious doctrines and practices. Realizing the only way to counter and "dismantle" the racist practices of a church was to battle on a so-called neutral ground, these young radicals took to demonstrating by using their bodies and athletic talents, this time by their standards in a variety of strategies and tactics.

The early demonstrations of racial resistance leading up to the infamous Black Power salute at the Mexico City Games turned out to be the initial spark that galvanized the athletes in the WAC to openly challenge American racism at white universities.[58] Emboldened by the counterculture revolution of the 1960s, culminating with the assassinations of Robert F. Kennedy and MLK in 1968, the six student track athletes at the University of Texas-El Paso led the first of many university-wide protests across the West against BYU and the race-based discriminatory religious practices of Mormonism and the LDS Church. In response, many white-controlled institutions were unprepared to contend with the barrage of demands put forth by black student-athletes.[59]

The six black UTEP runners, comforted by their meeting with Edwards, gained the necessary courage and foresight after the February NYAC meet to eventually defy the duplicity of their white coaches and the white administration. They organized to boycott the upcoming meet against both BYU and Utah State, two institutions known for their official and unofficial Mormon affiliations respectively. The UTEP athletes, along with many other black student organizations, targeted BYU specifically because of the LDS church's persistent racist teachings, attitudes, and discriminatory views toward black people and civil rights. Blacks at UTEP were not just protesting against religious intolerance but also against the burdens of Jim Crow racism that they felt Mormon theology affirmed. When media officials asked UTEP runner Dave Morgan why he protested, he responded by saying, "There were about a dozen reasons. The Mormons teach that Negroes are descended from the devil. As a reason for the track team's boycott it may sound like a small thing to a white person, but who the hell wants to go up there and run your tail off in front of a bunch of spectators who think you've got horns."[60] These black collegians were dissatisfied with the degree of isolation and relegation on every level within university life and in the collegiate sports world.

This challenge to Mormonism through sports caused contention in many forms. Aside from the negative public attention to the LDS church received by these racial protests, it is conceivable that this turmoil also caused the BYU athletic department some damage both financially and image-wise to its morally upright, clean-cut reputation. Such disruption to the athletic program included the cancellation of games, low spectator attendance due to poor team performance and the ever-present threat to fan safety, and even the likely relinquishment of future athletic commitments. When it came to confronting boycotts, the Church could no longer put up the First Amendment as a defense for its racist practices and doctrines without suffering severe reprisal as an educational entity.

Unfortunately, the UTEP track athletes, like many other athlete activists, found little sympathy or support from the white administration and coaching staff at their school. The black students nevertheless held firm to their demands by not attending the track meet in Provo, which subsequently led to their dismissal from the UTEP track team. The greater cause was to push forward direct challenges to the race-based exclusionary practices of an otherwise shielded institution, but this was not without great personal loss to educational and potential athletic careers.

RACIAL PROTESTS AND MOUNTING PRESSURE: BLACK AND WHITE AGAINST MORMONISM

Though it took some time to garner steam, this single act of defiance had important corollary effects. The UTEP track athletes' boycott of the BYU-sponsored track meet initiated a wave of more student-led protests against BYU that spanned across the Western United States over the next four years. Black Student Unions, black student-athletes, and other independent student-based groups on various campuses organized demonstrations targeting BYU. Sit-ins during halftime of basketball games and the wearing of black armbands by student-athletes were common forms of protest. Some student-athletes actually succeeded in convincing their respective schools to stand against religiously protected racial discrimination by withdrawing their programs from competition against BYU. But these demonstrations occasionally turned violent.[61] In some instances, the protestors threw eggs at opposing Mormon players and even resorted to throwing flammable material onto the basketball court.[62]

When the BYU basketball team played against the University of Arizona, for instance, a small group of protestors tried to force their way into the building before they were met by security. This racial demonstration led to damage of property and a modest game delay. At Colorado State University, a Molotov cocktail was thrown during a basketball game against BYU.[63] Similarly, the University of New Mexico–BYU basketball game was delayed for an hour after protestors threw eggs and kerosene-filled balloons onto the court.[64,65] Prior to this same game, it was reported that bricks were thrown at the homes of university officials.[66] But the most widely known racial protest against BYU and its athletic teams was the infraction that took place at the University of Wyoming.

In 1969, the University of Wyoming experienced its own campus-wide unrest when fourteen black players were kicked off the team for attempting to organize a protest by wearing armbands against BYU.[67,68] The mere mention of a protest against BYU by the black Wyoming football players, later to be known as the "Black 14," drew the ire of their coach and attracted the national media to the mostly white and conservative town of Laramie. Further, this brought widespread outside attention to the West regarding the previously little-known priesthood ban in the LDS faith.[69,70] Lloyd Eaton, the football coach of the Wyoming Cowboys who was known to be a tough disciplinarian of his players, had little tolerance for black demands. Coach Eaton, like so many of his white contemporaries, operated from the prevalent white antebellum frame that intimates that black athletes need white control. And the conservative athletic department at Wyoming, like other schools in the WAC, gave its coaches absolute authority over their respective teams and athletes.[71] The Black 14 had little time to respond to Eaton's tirade when he revoked their scholarships and promptly dismissed them from the team, but not before berating them with racially insensitive remarks.[72,73]

These racial protests by black student-athletes were pervasive through the 1960s and 1970s. The intensity and frequency of these events of unrest revealed the recalcitrant nature of white supremacy in America. They likewise confirmed the degree to which black folk were determined to directly confront and bring to an end all forms of white racial exploitation and control, particularly as they manifested on white college campuses. Many other black students and black student-athletes experienced a variety of race-based indignities on their campuses, and the BYU protests gave them a reason to fight to better their circumstances. Though many of these racial dissents ended poorly for some black athletes in terms of their personal education and professional career aspirations, it is important to note that these black-student-led and black-athlete-led rebellions signaled a shift in white America's enduring racial authority, a unitary counter-framing of white power and privilege. This rebellion against systemic racism spread across U.S. society, using the nation's obsession with sports, collegiate sport in particular.

The more difficult part of the struggle for human rights, however, lay ahead in changing white institutional priorities, which informed the racial attitudes and beliefs of whites inherited from previous generations. This included a persistently robust inclination to discriminate in their decision making and practices. The successful counter-framing of white supremacist ideas, beliefs, and practices, religious or otherwise, did not end the African American struggle for full inclusion and representation in college sport and academic life. But it did garner the support of a few select white institutions, mostly in the self-professed liberal states of the West, that appeared to find the cause of the black student-athletes as a just one and had their own protests and boycotts.

In the wake of the University of Wyoming's national image crisis, Stanford University president Kenneth Pitzer boldly and unreservedly severed all athletic relationships with BYU, naming the athlete's "Right of Conscience" as justification for his support to locate Stanford University behind the cause of the black athletes. As defined by Pitzer, "Right of Conscience" refers to the right of all students to empower themselves by boycotting any event that they deemed "personally repugnant." Defying his colleagues, Pitzer allowed the black athletes from

Stanford University a way to resist the white power structure from which he himself benefited. Further, his special assistant, acting as an official mouthpiece for the University's president, stated that if BYU wished Stanford to change its policy, the Mormon church would have to "reinterpret God's word and establish doctrines compatible with Stanford's policy."[74]

Following the pattern set forth by Stanford University, other white educational institutions began to support their students and athletes in their socially conscious protests against white racism. The coaches and administration of San Jose State College, California State University at Haywood, and the University of Washington all instituted some form of compromise for the aggrieved athletes, in the form of armbands, abstaining from competition, or other ways of exercising their First Amendment right to free speech.[75] Meanwhile, the LDS church and BYU continued to stand behind their own First Amendment right to freedom of religion. With differences over which faction of the First Amendment took precedence, freedom of speech or freedom of religion, both opposing views represented sides that were equally right in their interpretation of the law, but with contravening effects.

TURNING A BLIND EYE TO PROTESTS OF INJUSTICE: CLINGING TO THE IRON ROD OF RACISM

The real debate lies at the core of the First Amendment's rights dilemma. Each individual—athletes, students, and educators alike—were all declared equal (regardless of race or creed) in the eyes of the nation. But did freedom of religion give a religious institution the right to discriminate on the basis of race? Ignoring the obvious pretense that Jesus taught to love everyone free from judgment, the LDS Church and BYU asserted that God's law was the highest in the land and their interpretation of it would stand. But how long would Mormonism be able to withstand the mounting national pressure to change its fundamentally anti-black doctrines and practices?

Just like its Southern counterparts were slow to partake in this process of "integrating" their campuses, Brigham Young University only began to admit its first few African Americans to the university on sports scholarships in the early 1970s. BYU, like other predominately white institutions (PWIs), needed black muscle to win games and fill stadiums and arenas, and despite church leaders' personal feelings toward black people, they yielded (though reluctantly) when it came to college athletics. Student-athlete Bennie Smith (1971–1972) was a transfer from Western Arizona Junior College and the first African American student who was recruited strictly for his football strength.[76]

Pointedly, the notion of controlling the bodies of blacks was in no way new. Instead, these age-old white racial frames have been firmly entrenched in our nation's past, as established Eurocentric beliefs historically informed by science and ritualized in practice. The idea has persisted throughout U.S. society that races of mankind are distinct biological entities with differences thought to be related to mental capacity, physical prowess, and sexual behaviors despite DNA evidence to suggest otherwise.[77]

These standards along with other dehumanizing treatment in the classroom and campus life brought forth a need for black players to demand greater systemic changes consisting of a sense of fairness and decency. The efforts of many black student-athletes began to bear fruit at PWIs, with the exception of church-owned institutions such as BYU whose administrators saw no contradiction within their beliefs of black inferiority. Despite considerable protests against its educational institution and the new introduction of blacks on the BYU campus, the LDS Church was unshakable in its convictions to teach racist folklore—that BYU was obliged to uphold—regarding black people as the sons and daughters of Cain. The Church was determined to maintain its position despite public scrutiny and a societal shift in white racial attitudes.

To this day, black athletes are often genetically viewed as the embodiment of white racial understandings about human difference. The white sport establishment continually reinforces these beliefs (sometimes consciously or unconsciously) about the need to control black bodies by imposing white norms or expectations on them in the form of defining acceptable and appropriate types of hairstyles, music, clothing, tattoos, and more. These restrictions served to reinforce the status of blacks as reluctant houseguests at BYU.

5

MORMON ATTITUDES TOWARD CIVIL RIGHTS

It's God's Law, We're Not Racist!

> Our living prophet, President David O. McKay, has said, "The seeming discrimination by the Church toward the Negro is not something which originated with man; but goes back into the beginning with God."—1969 First Presidency Statement[1]

While efforts were being made at the federal level to dismantle Jim Crow practices of racial segregation, the LDS church was determined to stay their course of framing people of African ancestry as being under a divine curse and, therefore, unworthy and ineligible to hold the Mormon priesthood. Over a century had passed since the early 1800s when the founders of Mormon theology had first formulated and then expanded racial knowledge about black people as the sons and daughters of Cain marked as cursed with skin of blackness. By the time the civil rights era had commenced in the late 1950s and into the 1960s, the LDS church had a sophisticated media network in place to disseminate its official writings, doctrinal pronouncements, and conference talks to the general body of the church membership.[2] Contained within those writings were the positions and beliefs regarding race (among other issues).

This chapter will examine some of the ways the LDS church, with its racially exclusionary practices and doctrines, attempted to navigate through the volatile racial, political, and social landscapes of the civil rights era. In particular, this chapter will explore how the authority of religion was regularly invoked to protect, perpetuate, and justify white racism within the Mormon church. Meanwhile, throughout the nation, other institutions began to make amends on matters of race in response to the force of the civil rights movement. BYU, as the academic mouthpiece of the Mormon faith, represented the racial perspectives of the LDS church and its privileging of white interests. Thus, the school became the target of attacks for its manifestations of Jim Crow–type, legally sanctioned racial segregation.

MORMON UNIVERSALISM AND ITS EXCLUSIONARY BIND

Many of the writings by LDS church authorities from the time period of the civil rights era demonstrate the degree of Mormon ambiguity and hypocrisy toward civil rights and blacks, despite Mormonism's claims to universalism. The 1969 First Presidency Statement, the second of three official statements on race by the Church, epitomized this dichotomy of rhetorical acceptance and global alienation of blacks. The statement reads:

> It follows, therefore, that we believe the Negro, as well as those of other races, should have his full Constitutional privileges as a member of society, and we hope that members of the Church everywhere will do their part as citizens to see that these Rights are held inviolate. Each citizen must have equal opportunities and protection under the law with reference to Civil Rights.
>
> However, matters of faith, conscience, and theology are not within the purview of the Civil law. . . .
>
> From the beginning of this dispensation, Joseph Smith and all succeeding presidents of the Church have taught that Negroes, while spirit children of a common Father, and the progeny of our earthly parents Adam and Eve, were not yet to receive the priesthood, for reasons which we believe are known to God, but which He has not made fully known to man.[3]

Pointedly, BYU student reporter Judy Geisler summarized the Church's values and tenets in her intentionally ironic statement in the school paper, the *Daily Universe* (or *DU*), when she declared that she was "thankful for being of the white race in a land where the white is supreme," but also "thankful for having the sense of social responsibility to know it is my job to do everything I can to end the hypocrisy of the racial double standard in America."[4]

The ultraconservative ideology of the governing Mormon hierarchy, coupled with racist thought and commentary, reflected the larger white nation and its general antipathy for black Americans. The vast majority of them shared a conservative vision of blackness as culturally, spiritually, and morally inferior. Other Mormon leaders believed that the civil rights movement was a "Communist program for revolution in America."[5] Rarely did church leaders publically denounce racism or theorize around the idea that social and material conditions of U.S. race and class inequalities were attendant to black suffering.[6]

Indeed, for Mormon leaders, black suffering and the exclusions faced by blacks had been divinely imposed by God and, therefore, were not to be disturbed, challenged, or changed by mere mortals, especially not by scholars with their fallibility and dependence on the limited knowledge generated by man. LDS prophet and church president David O. McKay put it this way: "there is an explanation for . . . racial discrimination, dating back to the pre-existent state, but modern sociologists will not accept it . . . they are writing appealing to us to lift the ban upon the Negro race, and adopt racial equality in the Church."[7] But McKay could not fathom the sociologists' appeal because in his mind, black suffering was God's will. Throughout much of the twentieth century, Mormons were fairly dismissive of sociological explanations of black oppression and, instead, relied on the LDS canon, which members of the Mormon church considered holy writ.

As articulated in earlier pages, the notion that some spirits were more virtuous than others in the eternities was commonsense knowledge in Mormonism throughout its history. Not surprisingly, the white spirits were the more righteous ones and blacks, by contrast, were the less righteous ones, according to Mormon teachings. Official church publications produced and circulated a sizable body of literature on the question of whether or not blacks even had a place in the LDS faith. Under the guidance of the First Presidency, church authorities continued to not only produce racist discourse on pre-earthly black inferiority but also to teach negative and unfavorable views about blacks as unqualified and therefore undeserving of society's rewards and opportunities throughout the late 1940s and 1950s. Mormon racial concepts provided church members an easy and readymade racial framework to make sense of and justify the world around them, alleging that God sanctioned black priesthood denial and other race-based exclusionary practices to which blacks were subjected within Mormonism. It was taught that "[n]egroes are not equal with other races where the receipt of certain spiritual blessings are concerned."[8]

At a time when de jure racist practices in larger U.S. society were under assault from black American victories such as the 1954 landmark decision in *Brown v. Board of Education,* high-ranking church leaders were hard at work, instructing the Saints that segregation was an inspired enterprise by the Lord to separate the races by blood and habitation. The Church's form of race-based discrimination was sanitized in nature by comparison to more overt and violent forms of discrimination that was occurring in other parts of country. Thus, church leaders truly felt absolved in their beliefs and practices, scapegoating God as the source of black priesthood denial.

By the time the African American student revolts began in the 1960s, the divine curse framework was well established in the heads and hearts of many Latter-day Saints, and Mormon deficit-oriented frames of blackness were becoming increasingly more public knowledge. The negative media attention that surrounded church headquarters was extensive, capturing the public's reactions to Mormon racial ideologies and practices. Well-respected news journalist Wallace Turner penned several compelling columns in the *New York Times* trying to make sense of the Mormon position on blacks. He wrote, "For the African and his children's children the doctrine of eternal progression has little meaning. The doctrine of marriage for time and eternity is for others, not for them. The mortal existence offers lesser opportunity for the improvement of their souls than for other races."[9] He saw this sanctimonious view on the status of black people in the LDS faith to be a significant barrier to the advancement of the cause of the Church.

The Mormon hierarchy did not help matters when it came to defending their racist behavior against a rising tide of opposition. When asked about the Church's position on blacks, Joseph Fielding Smith, the

10th President of the LDS church, enthusiastically replied, "I would not want you to believe that we bear any animosity toward the Negro. 'Darkies' are wonderful people, and they have their place in our church."[10] This attempt to show acceptance through blatantly racist remarks from an educated, prominent leader turned out to be an embarrassing quandary, which did not help the Church's reputation in changing times.

IRON FIST DIPLOMACY: WILKINSON'S UNYIELDING CONTROL OVER UNIVERSITY AFFAIRS

The leadership at BYU, unapologetic for their racism, only further enraged the Church's detractors. Ernest L. Wilkinson, an attorney by trade, served as the seventh president of BYU (1951–1971) during the African American student uprisings against LDS racial bigotry as well as against the university for its complicity in the discrimination of blacks. He was a politically conservative[11] man who questioned the motives of the U.S. government's expansion of federal spending embodied within the New Deal era and, later, Kennedy's perceived "socialist" agenda. When President McKay appointed Wilkinson as president of BYU, he charged him to "have [the] vision to understand more than anyone else in education circles the dangers of communism and . . . be a leader in our schools in protecting our people against this ungodlike philosophy."[12] Many of the members of the board of trustees, which comprised fifteen "general authorities" (high-ranking Mormon leaders) who were appointed by the First Presidency as a church calling, likewise, were thrilled with Wilkinson as the new BYU president. Known to be a vocal critic of Washington and the federal government, he was a self-professed anticommunist during his twenty-year reign as head of the university.

For Wilkinson, however, the world must have seemed to be decaying right before his eyes. Much to his dismay, he witnessed the continuation of factionalism within the Republican Party, which then gave way to the Democratic administrations of the Kennedy and Johnson era. Given his extreme views, he found himself disillusioned at having to contend with not only unpopular racist commentary of the Church and what this negative view of Mormonism meant for BYU but also with some of the nation's most pressing contemporary issues. Those issues ranged from growing resistance to the Vietnam War and the draft to the perceptual proliferation of communism and support for the civil rights movement, all of which Wilkinson was determined to prevent from entering the campus of BYU.

The counterculture movements of the late 1960s and early 1970s, which included environmentalism, the rise of feminism, drug experimentation, rock music, and a culture of "free love," all accented the philosophical and political happenings of the times that spread across many of the nation's colleges and universities. The dynamics of the counterculture movements both influenced and were reflected by the protests against BYU and its intercollegiate athletic program. This was a clear sign that America, from Wilkinson's viewpoint, was in serious moral peril because his generation failed the (white) youth by ineffectively teaching young people the proper love of country as enshrined within the Mormon interpretation of the U.S. Constitution, a document considered by the Church to be divinely inspired.[13] This view of Wilkinson's was his version of Allen Bloom's popular 1987 book, *The Closing of the American Mind*, a book that blames the so-called decline of American universities on antisocial, anti-authoritarian liberals.

Across the country, the perceived impending doom loomed large in the minds of dissatisfied conservatives, particularly the right-wing faction of the party, as they felt the nation was crumbling at their feet into an immoral, Godless morass. This perception of coming destruction provided fodder for Wilkinson to shape BYU in a way that aligned with his "traditionalist" values, as he sought to promote and preserve his conservative agenda by hiring faculty and staff closely aligned with his perspectives. Toward his goal of keeping "worldly" influences out of BYU, Wilkinson reconceptualized the University Honor Code System to better constrain the wilds of an emerging rebellious youth culture.[14]

In his attempts to find "trusted" and "suitable" faculty members, Wilkinson created a campus of fear and paranoia at BYU, believing that a certain radical element of the faculty secretly sympathized with communism. He labored to initiate a covert "spy ring" typical of many tactics that anticommunist, conservative Cold Warriors engaged in during the "red scare" to monitor faculty members' activity, particularly those believed to have politically left leanings.[15,16] In the president's journal, he stated, "We are clearly in the midst of a great campaign to create a socialistic state." He further condemned "liberals [who] want to make the BYU a pulpit for all of the left-wing groups in the country."[17]

This red scare–type thinking pervaded BYU in nearly every facet of life and served as a beacon to keep the world's sinful influences out and the institution "pure" and unmolested from the increasingly more strident voices of discontent throughout the protest years of the 1960s. This drive to keep carnality out of BYU even included a strict filtering and selection of the invitations extended to guest speakers who visited the campus and who were asked to share differing opinions and viewpoints about world and national events. Wilkinson opined, "I am looking for the very best speakers in the nation, but they must have honest-to-God American thinking, who inspire us to greater heights rather than sow the seeds of disillusionment."[18]

The campus racial climate at BYU reflected, in many ways, the whiteness of the nation as a whole and the struggle to desegregate not only the material and political conditions of life but also the deficit-oriented racial thinking about blackness that has long permeated the social fabric of America. The Mormon church itself was no different from other institutions in rationalizing its racial mistreatment of black people. However, instead of using overt physical violence to control access to and distribution of society's valued resources in ways that continued to privilege whites as a group, the Mormon church and its leaders and membership utilized "God," ironically, as a means of exclusion in their meeting houses, conference halls, and academic institutions. Consequently, He was exploited as a weapon to protect continued white racial dominance.

THE MORMON CHURCH, THE MEDIA, AND THE FLOW OF INFORMATION AT BYU

Civil rights were antithetical to the revealed word of God from the LDS point of view, at least as it was put forward by church leaders, who are the definitive authority on dispensing and interpreting Mormon theology. Oftentimes, what the Mormon leadership personally believed about black people was passed off as theology or matters of faith.

> Were we the leaders of an enterprise created by ourselves and operated only according to our own earthly wisdom, it would be a simple thing to act according to popular will. But we believe that this work is directed by God and that the conferring of the priesthood must await His revelation. To do otherwise would be to deny the very premise on which the Church is established.[19]

In reality, these understandings were instantiations of inherited dominate frames of the larger white world around them. According to Feagin, "Human beings gain most of our racial frame's understandings, images, and emotions from imbibing and testing those of parents and peers, the media, and written accounts handed down over generations."[20] Thus, after more than 120 years of Mormon institutionalized racial framing (that began with their new leader, Brigham Young, in 1847[21]), the transmission of such discourse informed discriminatory thinking and behavior of generations of progeny from the original LDS framers. Two specific ways that Mormon racial knowledge is transmissible to succeeding generations is through personal experiences (formal education, socialization, and conversations) and through mediated communication.[22]

Negative representations of blacks, particularly with regard to black men, have historically been readily visible and conveyed to the public through the news, film, and other forms of media.[23] Images of docile dancing "darkies" and other forms of (mis)representation were, by design, intended by whites to control black bodies, thus rendering them less human while fully validating their restriction to society's valued resources. If these images do anything for the psyche, they reinforce essentialist understandings of blackness as an inherently dangerous space—a geography of fear. Likewise, Mormonism impressed upon its members, through official church-sponsored media, these deep chasms that supposedly existed between blacks and whites. The majority of the students who attended BYU during the protest years were from mostly white and conservative Western states and had very little, if any, contact with black Americans. As a result, these young white Mormons relied on the power of the media (whether print or audiovisual) to make sense of the idea of blackness in a number of productive and unproductive ways, indisputably shaping their destiny.

Furthermore, the view that students at BYU needed controlling, and if left to their own devices, they would revert to the dangers of liberalism is one of the particular motivations that informed the president's thinking on handling student unrest. President Wilkinson continued to believe that "communist revolutionaries" were responsible for undermining the sanctity of white American values by inciting political and racial dissent. He was determined to protect the university from this worldly wickedness as McKay had entrusted him to do.[24] One way Wilkinson could keep the students in line and away from what he saw as the destructive influences on them was to control (to the extent possible) their learning environment, from aspects of the students' behavior (including the attire of young women) and organizing activities to the flow of information that penetrated BYU's campus. By limiting student access to world events, Wilkinson created a community sheltered from sinful influences and especially from the reality of the contemptuous civil rights movement underway outside the university walls.

The *Daily Universe* provided an excellent medium to curtail outside hot-button issues deemed unacceptable for students and faculty, which included matters of "war, morals, economics, social problems, law, crime and punishment, [and] housing," otherwise known as "news."[25] A more exhaustive list of banned topics included:

> advocacy of communism, socialism, fascism, and other extremist doctrines or systems of government;
> advocacy of apostate religious doctrines or sects;
> advocacy of ideas, programs, or actions contrary to the declared purposes of the university;
> advocacy of birth control, illicit sex, drug abuse, illegal procedures, invasion of privacy, and other antisocial practices;
> debate on the validity of the LDS church doctrine; and
> ridicule of university and church leaders.[26]

Merwin Fairbanks, the *DU*'s faculty advisor, landed in hot water with the university president on numerous occasions when he neglected to properly screen and censor articles, thus allowing some prohibited ones to be disseminated to the masses.[27] For example, the *DU* published an article regarding student reaction to the *Brown* decision. Some BYU students took sides, as noted in the article, arguing in favor of or against segregation as expressed by one student who felt the voting for segregation was skewed because "thousands of negroes were kept from the polls by fear and unfair practices."[28] The student certainly calls into question the very idea of a "free society" that denies its citizens the most basic form of democratic expression, the right to vote. This was exactly the type of discussion and critical thinking among students that Wilkinson was determined to circumscribe.

PROTECTING WHITE MORMON YOUTH FROM MISCEGENATION WITH "NEGROES"

One of the more pressing issues on hand for President Wilkinson was the need to safeguard the youth from amalgamation. Rather than seeing the movement as a means to improve equality of opportunity for African Americans, Wilkinson and other church leaders who espoused similar conservative philosophies saw it as government infringement upon the privileges of whites. What is more, they deemed the civil rights movement to be a front for black people's real purpose—interracial marriage between blacks and whites. Mormon leaders, in other words, feared that young white Mormon women might be seduced into a loving relationship with a black man, a forbidden practice given blacks' debased status within Mormonism.

The Mormon hierarchy expressed great reservation and unease over "race mixing" that the civil rights movement was perceived to embody, particularly on the campus that housed the future of their faith. The concern most pressing on the minds of church leadership was the coming fulfillment of Brigham Young's doctrine of "blood atonement," which meant that for any white Saint from the "chosen" seed of Japeth found mixing with the seed of Cain, the punishment was "death on the spot."[29] Mark E. Petersen proclaimed in his August 27, 1954, speech to LDS church educators, "The negro seeks absorption with the white race. He will not be satisfied until he achieves it by intermarriage. That is his objective and we must face it. We must not allow our feelings to carry us away, nor must we feel so sorry for the negroes that we will open our arms and embrace them with everything we have."[30,31]

Harold B. Lee, who served with McKay as one of his closest advisers and sat on BYU's board of trustees, also expressed his paranoia of black-white miscegenation. Lee, who later became the eleventh president of the Mormon church, warned President Wilkinson directly: "If a granddaughter of mine should ever go to BYU and become engaged to a colored boy there, I will hold you responsible."[32] BYU football coach Tommy Hudspeth explained the real reason why blacks were not recruited to campus concerned the fear of intimate race mixing between blacks and whites. He confessed that the school "discourage[d] the Negroes because [it was felt] they would not be happy in the social situation here. . . . We will not allow inter-racial dating."[33]

Additionally, Wilkinson's opinion was reflected in his views regarding Utah State University president Daryl Chase and his seemingly favorable attitude toward blacks. Wilkinson told Chase that the environment on his campus at USU must be a concern for the white mothers and fathers worried about their daughters. In contrast, the campus climate at BYU reflected the pulse of a growing faction of dispirited ideologues, holding apocalyptic perspectives expressed as warnings of the coming damnation and downfall of an increasingly evil U.S. society. For Wilkinson and many on the BYU faculty, America was a scary and dangerous place, particularly for the rising generation, in jeopardy from hostile takeover by left-leaning plutocrats.[34]

At the heart of Mormon racial attitudes were embedded fears of blacks put forward by Mormon church leadership, which were closely aligned with the racist ideologies found in the American eugenics movement of the mid-twentieth century. The white racist framing of the eugenics movement—said to be grounded in the science of racial purity—used policies and procedures to restrict marriage and immigration with regard to populations of people of color. They, likewise, encouraged sterilization and segregation as an effective means of reducing the chances of interracial procreation with people deemed "unfit" in society.[35,36] In essence, the LDS hierarchy sought to maintain its whiteness by policing the boundaries of the one-drop rule. The Church drew on this racial folklore for the purposes of maintaining a predominantly white church membership completely antithetical to its universalist claims.

MORMON STUDENT RESPONSES TO LDS CHURCH POSITION AGAINST CIVIL RIGHTS

While BYU was steadfast in its convictions regarding black racial inferiority, African Americans were battling for their human rights against a backdrop of Mormon depictions of blackness as a site of theological reprobation.[37,38] As young black students were charged with making their own contribution to the black freedom struggle through the slow and painful integration of predominately white and racist universities throughout the country, black students and student-athletes in the WAC spearheaded change directed at BYU, a school they saw as a significant violator of their civil rights. The Church-sponsored school, however, attempted to distance itself from these claims of white racism by insisting that its governing body was separate from the Church itself and therefore the accusation of racism did not apply. Yet, the general populace viewed BYU and the Church as one and the same. In fact, the Board of Trustees at BYU is comprised of LDS Church General Authorities as a type of ecclesiastical calling from the prophet of the Lord and His Quorum of the Twelve Apostles.[39] Hence, BYU's implication that the lack of racial equality in Church doctrine in no way spilled over into the LDS church-run school (and its sports) was unfounded.

Students at BYU responded to the widely circulated claims of Mormon racism in their own ways. Not all students were passive in their affirmation for or against civil rights. Mitt Romney, for example, the former 2012 GOP presidential nominee, was just a young man at the time. Returning home from his LDS mission from France in 1969, he decided to forgo his return to Stanford and, instead, attend his faith-based school, BYU.[40] Almost immediately, Romney found himself embroiled in the race controversy surrounding the Black 14 at Wyoming and the LDS church's longstanding position on blacks. When Stanford University suspended competition against BYU in October 1969, Romney was not especially enthused, recalled Kim Cameron, a personal friend of Romney's at the time. Cameron stated that he "felt like it was, A, naïve and, B, sort of a bigoted, narrow-minded perspective."[41] Romney did not hesitate to make his thoughts known about the issue of race. As the one-time leader of the Cougar Club—BYU's sports booster organization—he began to organize counter-protests.

During this same riotous period, most students at BYU were not entirely privy to critical information about current events of the times. As "opposing teams would throw tomatoes and worse at BYU players and their fans…there was a pervasive sense in the club that BYU was 'under siege' from the protests."[42] The reaction by Romney and other members of the club was to respond with efforts "to raise more money for the school" recalls Dane McBride, a club member and close Romney friend.[43] Some students took to protesting the protestors. In response to the black armbands worn by the entire San Jose State football team, the BYU counter-protestors chose to wear red armbands because their opponents did not "actively recruit Indians."[44] This showed their ignorance of the gravity of the situation, as SJSU and other Universities were concerned not with BYU's lack of "active recruitment" of black student-athletes but with the school's overt discrimination toward them. San Jose State did not have any unwritten policy to actively deny Native Americans as BYU did with blacks. Brian Walton, then-student body president of BYU, asserted that the Mormon school was not racist, as it had "no admission policies which preclude people from entering the University because they are black."[45] What Walton did not address, however, were the unwritten rules regarding people of African lineage and the ban on priesthood ordination, based on persistent Mormon racist folklore, that placed limitations on blacks' full participation in Church affairs as well as on university admissions.

Not having been educated like most white students on other American college campuses, the BYU students responded to the Civil Rights racial protests by declaring them to be "bigoted." The majority of them, either unaware or unconcerned with the state of racial discrimination and intolerance within the nation and in their own faith, felt that *they*, as opposed to African Americans or other people of color, were the actual targets of racial discrimination as members of the Church. The responses of these students often displayed their naiveté and lack of critical understanding regarding the nation's enduring and shameful past as well as the present state of racial inequality around the country and in their own house of worship. There was a group of students and faculty that actually did understand the changing racial tides of the country and sometimes expressed their discontent openly.[46] BYU's Dean of Students, J. Elliott Cameron, was dismayed at the student responses; he expressed, "I think these BYU kids are real naïve. They don't realize what this means elsewhere."[47,48]

As for the priesthood ban on blacks, the BYU students loyal to the Mormon canon in its current state of privileging whites felt that "the very notion of questioning [it] was considered 'unseemly as well as useless,'" noted McBride.[49] Accordingly, Church members are not free to deviate from the approved and circumscribed dictums of the First

Presidency who have the exclusive right to authorize and interpret any and all things related to doctrinal matters, and the members of the Mormon Church are expected to support and obey the leaders. "You have to understand we are taught unquestioning obedience," said Jim Brield, a BYU junior.[50]

How could Church authorities be so out of step with the rest of the country in moving along the path toward social justice and human rights? Civil rights, as a social movement sweeping through U.S. society, had become an ideological battlefield and source of conflict in the LDS faith. As the rest of the nation was contending with how to address the matter of human freedom, the LDS church not only remained entrenched in its historical position against blacks, it fought hard against any changes to its racial framework. These beliefs were particularly astounding given Mormonism's message of Christian universalism and its robust, proselytizing missionary program. Yet, there has always been a strong history in which religious devotion and implementation of faith has led to the justification of nefarious deeds contributing to the destruction and exploitation of masses of darker-skinned people. A critical examination of the Crusades as well as the ongoing conflict in the Middle East and faith-based politics here at home (e.g., abortion and same-sex marriage) provides ample evidence for the role of religion in tyranny and oppression.

It is likely that the traditional position of the Mormon church on blacks may explain the apparently harsher treatment that black Utahns historically experienced in the Mormon-dominated state. Racial discrimination was severe enough in the Beehive state that in 1963, the local NAACP official Charles Nabors went on record stating that Utah had "potentially the worst race problem in the United States."[51,52] As in most white towns and cities in both the Northern and Southern regions of the country during this era, black folk in Utah faced daily race-based microaggressions and indignities, including debarment from nightclubs, bars, restaurants, hotels, theme parks, and movie theaters.[53] In response, Mormon church leaders felt themselves bound to uphold racial practices and doctrines until God saw fit to remove His curse from blacks, regardless of how much mounting pressure the public exerted on the Church. The divine curse was the reason for black suffering, many Latter-day Saints reasoned, not the effects of continuing racial discrimination and gross inequality. But a movement was now in motion as blacks mounted a gallant campaign to hold America, and institutions such as BYU, responsible for a history of white racism, dishonesty, and brutality.

IRS SEEKS TO TAKE ACTION ON DISCRIMINATORY PRACTICES

Despite criticism from around the world, the LDS church stood staunchly behind its right to freedom of religious practice wherein the law sanctioned and upheld institutional discrimination. This strategy of invoking God as authorization for their actions enabled the Mormon church to defiantly practice its politics of exclusion under the guise of Divinity. The use of religion and God as a source of justification for racial discrimination proved a more difficult fallacy to expose, where the rationale for racial discrimination of other institutions was simply their distaste and prejudice. The Constitution was finding it problematic to argue with God, as He was protected in the First Amendment.

As many students in the Western United States were protesting the discriminatory traditions of BYU and the LDS church, the position on blacks, from the Church's standpoint, was a matter of theology, not a matter of civil rights. The Mormon hierarchy persistently clung to the historical privileging of whiteness in both the public and private realm. Sermons were delivered at the annual LDS General Conference that testified to the hard work of the Mormon elites to amass a large repository of racist rhetoric. Though the U.S. Constitution protected the Church in its contentious racial beliefs under the freedom of religion, the Church-sponsored school *did* have to answer to the U.S. government as an educational institution receiving federal student aid.

A fact-finding commission was dispatched from the Department of Health, Education and Welfare's Office for Civil Rights (now called the U.S. Department of Health and Human Services) in 1968 to investigate rumors of Mormon racial bigotry and discrimination. It was later determined that BYU was in compliance with federal law as it was outlined in Title VI of the Civil Rights Act of 1964.[54] There was no evidence of a written policy that BYU overtly discriminated against blacks. The school would use this finding to proclaim its racial innocence while vehemently condemning attacks as unfair branding on their tarnished image.

In contrast to BYU, Bob Jones University and Greensboro Christian School both codified their racist positions on black people by either placing racially specific conditions on their admissions or outright barring them from matriculation on campus. These overtly racial policies were in violation of Title VI and, before too long, caught the attention of the Internal Revenue Service (IRS), causing it to issue two statements on the matter in 1970. According to the IRS, the agency could "no longer legally justify allowing tax-exempt status to private schools and universities which continued to practice racial discrimination," nor could the IRS continue to "treat gifts to such [overtly discriminatory] schools as charitable deductions."[55,56]

Although BYU never created a frontstage[57] written policy barring black entrance, they certainly never fully encouraged black admission, either. And, in truth, there has been overwhelming evidence of backstage rejection in the form of verbal and written discouragement from attending "The Lord's University." In the 1960s, a letter was sent to potential black applicants from the administration, dissuading them from attending the institution by citing that Utah was, in essence, a cultural desert where few black people lived, especially in Provo, the home of BYU. Hence, in would be in their best interest if blacks attended a more suitable institution elsewhere.[58,59] Although there were some outspoken student and faculty freedom fighters on campus, the actual intentions that blacks were not wanted in the institution were substantiated in backstage conversations and meetings, such as Ernest L. Wilkinson's Board of Trustee minutes.[60] The white administrators relied on the racist framing of church leaders to discourage prospective blacks from attending the university.

The Civil Rights Movement was becoming a source of contention, embarrassment, and debate for many church authorities. Though BYU averted discipline based upon the Title VI findings, church leaders felt the clock was ticking. As the Internal Revenue Service bore down on Bob Jones University, it would seem that the Church was on the radar of the IRS as well. It is conceivable, then, the Mormon Church only began to rethink its religious stance on blackness when the IRS maintained its withdrawal of federal support and denial of tax-exempt status for any private entity that practiced institutional discrimination, intimating BYU's imminent future.[61]

A SHIFT IN MORMON DOCTRINE AND POLICY ON BLACKS

June 2015 marked the thirty-seventh anniversary of the end of the now defunct Mormon priesthood ban on people of African descent, which gave black Latter-day Saint males equal standing in the LDS church with their white counterparts. It was on Friday, June 9, 1978, dubbed "the long promised day," that Spencer W. Kimball, the twelfth president of the Church of Jesus Christ of Latter-day Saints, and the First Presidency and Council of the elite Quorum of the Twelve Apostles received a revelation through prayer and mighty supplication before the Lord almighty.[62,63] In the revelation, God announced to His Prophet that the time had come for the priesthood ban against blacks to be lifted.

With the stroke of a pen, President Kimball, acting under the direction of the Lord, ended a racist policy framed in the language of LDS religious thought that relied on centuries-old, Anglo-themed, socially derived constructions about African Americans as a divinely cursed people. By allowing black men (and through them black families) an equal seat at the table, the Church attempted to absolve the state of Utah and the Mormon people of their institutionalized racism and create an image of the LDS church as a less racist organization.[64]

The news of the revelation circulated quickly around the world, which triggered hope and optimism for many rank-and-file members of the Church. In an interview with the late Tim Russert on *Meet the Press*, for example, Mitt Romney recounted hearing this news. A young businessman at the time the priesthood ban was lifted, he remembered hearing the broadcast from church headquarters while driving through the Massachusetts countryside. Romney recalled pulling his car over and weeping with joy at the announcement.[65,66] President Jimmy Carter likewise weighed in on the announcement, acknowledging the LDS church's efforts at ending the race-based restrictive policy.[67] The *Salt Lake Tribune*, in turn, opined that a "burden has been lifted from all Utahans, whether members of the LDS faith or of other faiths."[68]

The change in policy lifted the Church out of austerity, which could not happen fast enough for more liberal-minded church members who, for years, were expected to act on blind faith with regard to the discriminatory custom of banning black men from the priesthood and denying both black men and women entrance into the LDS Temple. Never questioning church authorities (at least openly) on their positions on matters such as race, members of the faith were instead expected to accept the will and instruction of their leaders prima facie. The lifting of the priesthood ban signified a shift in Mormon theology and practice. The Church gloriously, though ambivalently, entered into the so-called post–civil rights era of new race relations, which consists of the bombast of colorblindness.[69]

In subsequent weeks after the priesthood ban was removed, the LDS church appeared to be practicing what it preached by promising greater resolve among the Mormon leaders to teach its members through example about racial tolerance and integration. The Church worked to provide members with a different lens that emphasized the Christian principle of the atonement of Jesus Christ, often taught in Mormonism and put forward from the pulpit by members of the faith. The notion of Christ's Atonement provided a way for the Church to rectify its racist past by putting forth the position that all mankind has access to the process of repentance made possible through Christ's suffering on Calvary's cross. Since blacks had been less valiant in the preexistence, before coming through birth into mortality, the Atonement of Christ also applied to them and "paid" for their lack of worthiness. According to Mormon leaders at the time, the payment of the Atonement allowed blacks to enter into racial equality with whites within the Mormon faith.

For nearly two centuries, the LDS faith failed to offer a reasonable explanation, point of clarification, or acceptable apology to people of African descent for the spread of LDS racist folklore. Instead what was often uttered within Mormon communities was:

> When our leaders speak, the thinking has been done. When they propose a plan—it is God's plan. When they point the way, there is no other which is safe. When they give direction, it should mark the end of controversy. God works in no other way. To think otherwise, without immediate repentance, may cost one his faith, may destroy his testimony, and leave him a stranger to the kingdom of God.[70]

It has not been uncommon to hear both local and general church authorities speak publicly about the black priesthood ban, saying that "the time was not right for them to hold the priesthood." In response, Mormon people were left to interpret that God has His own time frame when it pertains to racial equality. In Mormonism, this was the standard mantra used by many practicing members to explain the now defunct ban and why the Mormon church would suddenly end its long-standing prohibition against blacks but offer no hint of an apology or cogent explanation for why the policy existed in the first place. For Mormon church leaders, the controversy was settled and did not warrant further review or discussion. After all, according to the LDS church's official logic, the Mormon faith had been acting under the direction of God. Though blacks have been permitted full participation since 1978, the justification for the prior restrictions has allowed continued racist rhetoric by lay members to circulate from generation to generation.

On December 6, 2013, the Mormon church released a surreptitious update to its website entitled "Race and the Priesthood," disavowing the racist theories that LDS officials used to justify prohibiting blacks from full participation in the faith. In referencing past/prior explanations of valiancy and God's will, the LDS church has declared, "None of these explanations is accepted today as the official doctrine of the Church."[71] Confirming what we already knew, the long-awaited explanation provides a historical accounting of the circumstances and conditions, which led to the priesthood ban on black men, and it places the origins of black priesthood denial blame squarely on the shoulders of Brigham Young and others who relied on his wisdom to exclude blacks. In release of the latest declaration, the Church finally addressed the reality of racism that it long denied throughout seven generations of Latter-day Saints. Interestingly, this posting was made anonymously by the Church without fanfare, announcement or groundbreaking "revelation" to clarify it, and certainly, without author credit for the statement.

Also missing from the most recent proclamation is an actual apology for the many decades of racist propaganda and discriminatory action taught by the Church and for its part in the persistence of systemic white racism. Black Latter-day-Saints received essentially a surreptitious "note" obscurely tucked away in a series of keystrokes on the Church's official website for their troubles. Only once an acknowledgment and apology is made can all members seek to do better and right by those the Church offended and psychologically wounded. Otherwise for black Americans, this gesture rings hollow as simply rhetoric. Moreover, it demonstrates that racial discrimination comes in many shapes and sizes, including one bearing gifts of religious salvation, redemption, brotherhood, and divine truth.

6

NO HONOR IN THE HONOR CODE

The Suspension of Brandon Davies and the Incompatibility Nexus between Blackness and Mormonism

> God has always been discriminatory.—Professor Randy Bott, BYU religion professor, in discussing Mormon priesthood ordinations of blacks in an interview with the *Washington Post*[1]

The dismissal of Brandon Davies, a six-foot-nine African American basketball player on BYU's starting lineup, made national headlines in 2011 for all the wrong reasons. Davies confessed to BYU officials and church authorities that he had run afoul of the university honor code system by having premarital sex, a violation of church beliefs and of the school's honor code policy.[2] Davies is a practicing Mormon and local kid from the city of Provo who clearly understood the consequences of his indiscretion, which likely led to an admission of guilt in the first place as well as the subsequent counseling with church leadership. As this chapter will analyze, a Mormon athlete has more options for recourse to include the benefit of the Church and its structured pathways of ecclesiastical counseling for its members. For Davies and many other LDS students and student-athletes alike, the honor code is not just another college entrance form to be signed. Instead, it represents the Mormon canon, a promise to live a particular lifestyle that has an em-

EL CAMINO COLLEGE LIBRARY

phasis on maintaining high moral standards to include living the "law of chastity."[3]

In this case, non-Mormons are at a disadvantage in relating the theological significance of the code to their own values, beliefs, and morals. Moreover, there is a disjuncture in how discipline is meted out and in the opportunity for remedy between Mormons and non-Mormons when a transgression of the rules occurs. In addition to and in spite of religious orientation, the material presented in this chapter also demonstrates a black-white binary[4] in which a discrepancy in punishment between racial groups exists.[5,6] The Davies incident serves as a venue for exploring the complicated intersection of racial dynamics within a race-based exclusionary religion. As both an African American and a Latter-day Saint, Brandon Davies and his experiences epitomize a compelling narrative of how race and religion collide in the world of BYU sports.

This chapter more closely examines the honor code at BYU, what it means to Mormons, and what it ultimately means for non-Mormons and blacks. The BYU honor code system is not like those in other institutions of higher education, where the code centers solely around policies on academic integrity and appropriate ethical behavior; the honor code office exists for the purpose of dutifully reminding young Latter-day Saints to live by the precepts of their faith.[7,8] BYU's honor code contains an amalgamation of church doctrine-based standards, values, and beliefs about how individuals and groups should act and interact. It was designed to keep the integrity of the student body and faculty intact by policing scholarship, information exchange, dress and grooming standards, and especially activity.[9,10] Ernest L. Wilkinson stated in his biography that the honor code, "had to set a proper example of dress, dance, and behavior in keeping with the Mormon philosophy that men and women should shun the world and all its unseemliness."[11]

For Mormons, the rules contained in the honor code are in alignment with the laws that govern their faith. And a breach of these statutes can result in a trip to the honor code office. The actual consequences handed out by the honor code office, however, are dependent upon race and religious persuasion.

THE INNER WORKINGS OF THE HONOR CODE

The LDS gospel message is replete with lessons that encourage church members to tame and discipline their most basic human desires in ways that will allow them to walk uprightly before God. Those desires of the natural man, to include consumption of alcohol and hot caffeinated drinks, tobacco use, and sex before marriage, are known in the faith to be an enemy of all righteousness. Church members believe that such behaviors are signs of moral imperfection that will lead the faithful down the perilous road to carnality and sin and, ultimately, spiritual death. Accordingly, the honor code represents Mormonism's most unyielding beliefs—from its principle of sexual purity and traditional Western views of marriage between a man and woman (memorialized in "The Family: A Proclamation to the World") to the law of health that governs physical and spiritual well-being as reflected in the eighty-ninth section of the Doctrine and Covenants "Word of Wisdom."[12]

In similitude of the commitments that young LDS adults have made as part of abiding by Mormon practices among the faithful, BYU students meet with local church authorities each year, pledging anew in writing to reaffirm and uphold the principles of the Mormon gospel. These principles, exemplified in the BYU honor code, are outlined and prescribed by church elites, who are considered by most members to be men of God in tune with the mind and will of the Lord.[13,14] It is because of these codes of conduct that many LDS families encourage their children to attend BYU, in hopes that they will obtain a strong, quality education while deepening their understanding of the principles of Mormon theology, which include abstaining from activities considered contrary to the revealed word of God.

Discipline for trespassing the honor code is not simply a university infraction. For LDS students, the violation spills over into the general LDS church where membership and standing is often at greater risk for those endowed members,[15] especially for the "elders" or men of the Church who have made solemn covenants in the temple to uphold their priesthood. For more serious transgressions from adultery to criminal offenses, the punishment is often referred over to the church court of his or her home or university congregation where final decisions are made at the local level on matters of personal worthiness. Sanctions vary and depend partly on the disposition of church leaders who meet and discuss the best possible course of action for a young transgressor through prayer and, occasionally, fasting. Hence, the discipline of a Mormon athlete is quite often handed over to their ward bishop for reprimand and repentance. Mormon athletes, like Davies, who attend BYU and run afoul of the honor code, have a multitude of options available to redress the situation, from the church leadership to the student's coach regarding his or her involvement with the team. All of this makes it much more likely to avoid academic discipline, suspensions, and even expulsion. For non-Mormon athletes who attend BYU, however, the story is much different. They are in a predicament with fewer options for recourse. Former athlete Hassan McCullough asserts, "[S]ay it's a white person that gets in trouble, a person that's Mormon gets in trouble, they get to go talk to the Bishop, and they still stay in school. But if you're not Mormon, they don't give you the same treatment."[16]

Likewise, a comparable dilemma is evident if one is nonwhite at BYU. And the intersection between the two constructs, race and religion, creates an intractable double bind, an existential paradox rooted in history that amounts to an even greater burden that is viciously synergistic. This is of particular importance for the black male athletes, many of whom are not LDS, as they begin their collegiate and athletic careers on unequal footing with their white and Mormon peers. Outnumbered en masse in race and religious affiliation, the young men are at a significant disadvantage from the moment they arrive on campus where the administration, faculty, and staff have provided little or no additional services or guidance for these student-athletes to help them succeed in an austere environment.

Approaching race from the standpoint of epistemology of whiteness, most whites are oblivious to the needs of black students. Research confirms the difficult challenges for black students on predominately white campuses, where they suffer from adjustment issues and lag behind their white peers in their academic endeavors.[17,18] BYU created a university nondenominational chaplaincy at the administrative level as an advocate for non-Mormon students who find themselves in need of counsel.[19] Although this change is a positive and welcomed move on the part of the BYU administration and the athletic department, it is a fairly weak indicator of the overall institutional commitment and efforts in place to help all students succeed. Because there is no other support system in place, black students recruited from areas in which the social structure is very dissimilar from that of Provo and the surrounding areas in Utah struggle to find their place. Though it may be argued that a religious institution need not provide alternative faith counseling, the reality is that BYU coaches are making a point to seek out, identify, and recruit top athletes regardless of religious persuasion. Therefore, it is their responsibility to provide student support for those outside of the faith that they bring in with the promises of academic success in exchange for athletic glory.

Not only are these students unfamiliar with the Mormon cultural paradigms and the penalties of stepping outside such a strict religious context, they have no ecclesiastical or academic maneuvers in place to help them navigate the rough intersections of LDS religious thought, white racist inclinations, and the stigma (frame) associated with black male student-athletes at PWIs.[20] Should they violate the honor code, many rules of which are incongruent with their own structural upbringing and/or beliefs, the recourse is often swift and extreme, particularly when the honor code has fewer options of remedy for these individuals without a home LDS church community from which to draw. In other words, their punishment will come entirely from the whims of the institution's honor code office, and such measures will focus primarily on their athletic and/or academic involvement.

READ THE FINE PRINT BEFORE YOU SIGN: UNDERSTANDING THE IMPLICATIONS OF THE CODE

So why would a non-Mormon, black athlete decide to attend BYU, given the setting? Certainly, the chance to play on a competitive level within a Division I college athletic program and the subsequent exposure to the prospect of glory, respect, and a doorway out of deprivation is quite enticing to a seventeen- or eighteen-year-old athlete, particularly one from a marginalized racial group. Adding to that is the opportunity to earn a quality education, another avenue out of the uncertainty of being black in America. Black parents, many of whom are unaware of the LDS church's racist past and its link to BYU, often encourage their sons to attend the wholesome faith-based school that proclaims its mission is developing young minds and characters through divinity.

Knowing all too well the dangers that lurk beyond the relative safety of home, it is not hard to imagine many of the parents of these young men feeling reassured by the school's clean-cut image and relative isolation. But what is most significant among those who accepted scholarships to attend BYU is the almost unanimous report that the honor code is not once discussed beyond a brief sidebar on recruiting trips—an interesting declaration considering the gravity of these core values in the Church and, hence, the university. As Ronney Jenkins, a former BYU football player from the late 1990s, stated, "It wasn't something that we sat down and really spoke about, got into detail about."[21]

In fact, most non-Mormon athletes also report that they were not properly counseled by the coaching staff and given a thorough review of the honor code system, particularly with respect to its ramifications for them as students and athletes. This is not a problem, of course, for students and athletes who grew up LDS, with the knowledge of these rules through church doctrine and their socialization. But what the non-Mormon athletes do not fully grasp are the implications of their trespasses against a religious code to which they do not subscribe, an impact that can be career ending and life altering. Lamenting his dealings with the honor code office and subsequent repercussions, Jenkins further observed, "When the Honor Code stuff got brought up . . . they didn't say 'look, if you drink, this is the Honor Code, this is how they work. . . . This is what's going to happen, possibly. If you have sex, this is what's gonna [*sic*] happen. This is how serious we take it. . . . So if you think you're not gonna [*sic*] be able to abide by these types of rules, as far as sex and drinking or whatever, this is what's gonna [*sic*] happen. And I wouldn't advise you to come into our institution.'"[22]

Many former black BYU athletes have restated similar accounts of how the coaching staff "velvet gloved" the honor code policy by downplaying, intentionally or otherwise, its importance—presumably in the interest of winning games—leaving many unsuspecting and naïve young men vulnerable to punitive measures. Having not been fully detailed on the repercussions of their actions and the disciplinary consequences involved, many non-Mormon athletes conveyed the belief that the rules were a part of the Mormon faith and carried more of a religious significance than an academic one. And seeing as how they are not LDS themselves, the common fallacy is that a "violation" of the rules pertaining to moral cleanliness would not necessarily apply to them, particularly with regard to academic sanctions. That being said, though there are numerous instances of blacks targeted for crimes or violations that they in fact did not commit, those black student-athletes who defiled the honor code did admit to their misconduct. McCullough, for example, was discharged from BYU after pleading guilty to shoplifting. He recounts, "I think everything is totally my fault about what happened. [So] I don't really have bad blood with BYU."[23] What most concerned many of these former players, however, was the apparent discrepancy in how they were disciplined in comparison to their white and Mormon counterparts.

MADNESS IN MARCH: UNEQUALLY APPLIED DISCIPLINE

Before the honor code controversy erupted, the 2011 basketball season was BYU's finest in years, led by National Player of the Year Jimmer Fredette.[24] This was shaping up to be one of the greatest teams in BYU's history, and arguably, the best team since perhaps when the great Danny Ainge suited up more than thirty years earlier. The Cougars were riding high as the nation's third-ranked NCAA basketball team heading into March Madness. The Davies incident and the school's reaction stunned many in the college sports community, coming at the worst possible time for BYU as they embarked on a storied run through the NCAA basketball tournament.

In addition to its academic rigors, college life is often known for its frat parties, excessive alcohol consumption, and sexual escapades, as students transition from young adulthood to mature, societal adults. Though these unhealthy activities are frowned upon by the school administration, it is fair to say most universities would not compromise their chances for national recognition and the potential for millions of dollars in revenue by benching one of its stand-out basketball players for a legal, yet religiously based moral lapse in judgment. To many casual observers, this heavy-handedness on the part of the administration seemed like much to do about nothing. Even the very public Christian athlete Tim Tebow, once the toast of Denver and the religiously conservative nearby town of Colorado Springs, later weighed in stating, "people definitely deserve second chances" and seemingly questioned whether BYU's "punishment" was in fact appropriate.[25]

But many other commentators saw it differently. In *Bloomberg Businessweek*, Scott Soshnick said BYU's action "is reason for celebration" for placing the opportunity to teach moral character to young men above the need to win.[26] Jim Rome, once host of a national and highly popular sports-themed show *Jim Rome Is Burning* on ESPN, declared, "Credit to [BYU] for not compromising its integrity and selling out for the millions they could've made for a deep run in the NCAA tournament."[27] And Pat Forde of ESPN opined, "BYU isn't willing to subordinate its principles for victories."[28] In the end, this "bad press" turned out better for the Mormon school than it could have imagined—recognized, upheld, and praised for its sanctity. But what Soshnick, Rome, and other sports analysts were not cognizant of is the difference in how discipline is partially rendered at BYU for honor code offenses based on at least two significant factors, race and religious group affiliation.

More notably of the two, racial biases are evident in the discrepancy of the reprimands between blacks and whites. In fact, black males are more frequently, harshly, and publicly targeted for honor code–related dismissals than their white teammates—as reported in public records (media accounts and police records) and by interviews with former BYU athletes, some of whom were on the receiving end of BYU's unequally applied discipline.[29] Black male athletes constituted nearly 60 percent of all disciplined athletes over a twenty-five-year period (from 1991 to 2015) whereas only 20 percent where white males. And yet, blacks only made up 9 percent of student-athletes at Brigham Young University.[30] Even more alarming was the rate of black male dismissals/expulsions from the football and men's basketball teams since 1991. Comprising no more than one-third of the football team at any given time, black males were removed at a rate of nearly 80 percent while white male dismissals made up less than 10 percent. The numbers are staggering. A pattern emerges showing black male student-athletes suspended from BYU at a disproportionate rate from whites.

This process of targeting and dismissing black men for honor code violations turns out to be less of a "principle stand" (backed by the honor code), as portrayed in the media, than a reflection of a longstanding tradition of deeply entrenched racist ideology compiled within the expansive body of church liturgical writings, sermons, talks, and other literature. These dominant white racial frames employ early, broad, European-American ideas that criminalize blacks as sexual deviants, ignorant brutes, unruly, and dangerous.[31] The national headlines during the 2011 March Madness conjured up a not too distant past for Mormonism's struggle over basic human rights for people of African descent. Once again, the scandal involving the image-conscious LDS church and its continuing problems with blacks was brought to the public eye.

The other factor, religious group affiliation, also plays a role in how discipline is dealt. When BYU student-athletes who are LDS are chastened, it is typically done in a private manner, as these matters are undoubtedly considered confidential between the individual student, faculty, and the Church. Either the course of action is dealt discreetly, or the athlete silently (with respect to the media) fades into the background, as they are potential distractions to the team and athletic department. Despite being Mormon himself, this was oddly not the case with Davies, who would shamefully endure his punishment in front of a national viewing audience. And it certainly was not the case with the spate of high-profile black student-athlete dismissals at the school over the last twenty years.

THE RACIALIZED PARADOX OF BRANDON DAVIES

Be that as it may, Davies himself is different from most of his African American, non-Mormon predecessors driven out of the institution in past years. He is black, and yet he is also Mormon. A son of Provo, his reality does not mirror that of most African Americans. Brandon is a transracial adoptee raised by a single white mother and reared in a predominately white community and faith he shared with two adopted siblings.[32] Like most black or biracial transracial adoptees reared by white parents in predominately white contexts, he was likely socialized to see the world through the prism of colorblindness.[33,34] It is quite plausible that Brandon was taught to identify less with blackness and more with the attitudes and dictates of whiteness as it intersected with the Church's universal theme of brotherhood and sisterhood. Most transracial adoptees who grow up in similar circumstances are generally taught by their well-intentioned white parents that the best course of action regarding racial identity development is to politely ignore race rather than engage it.[35] Conceivably, from Brandon's point of view, the handling of this contravention had little to do with race and more to do with his disobedience to the principles of the LDS gospel.[36]

Davies was not the stereotypical black student to attend BYU on an athletic scholarship, divested from the community. He was the community, an insider with black skin. Because of this, he knew the secret code. He was given the scriptural "rulebook" by both his mother and the community to navigate the religious topography, which allowed him to be successful at BYU. And relating with his peers, he failed to see his "difference" as different, which usually comes with a cost to racial identity development.

In reality, Brandon was a walking paradox, a social construction.[37] He stood out at Provo High School not just for his above-average height and athletic skill, but because he was exotic, a novelty—one of a handful of students of color. This was only magnified once he embarked on the larger public stage of BYU sports. Whether he realized it or not, he was likely reminded of being black in his daily interactions with friends. Transracial adoptees reared in his environment of Provo, Utah, have spoken agonizingly about the race-based mistreatment they endured at the hands of their white peers.[38] This varied from slights, jeers, and insults to curious fascination, with hair touching, skin touching and the use of popular black, urban slang (including the "ever-cool" Nigger-word).

Just by his physical appearance alone, Brandon embodied dominant white frame(s) associated with black people; these ideas with which whites are most familiar include the presumption of athleticism and a "cool pose" masculinity expressed in unique patterns of speech, walk, and style to include the notion of a smooth-talking ladies man.[39,40] Though he was likely exceptionalized against additional white stereotypes of black intellectual incompetence with a penchant for criminal tendencies (as the good black Mormon, both spiritual and obedient to the teachings of the faith), Brandon was still a departure from what is normal there. And this was evident in how he was treated disparately upon committing an infraction of the honor code. Though he was given an opportunity to redress his sin through his LDS bishop, he was still publicly branded a miscreant in the popular press—a paradigm seen among black expelled athletes.[41,42,43]

THE REVOLVING DOOR OF BLACK ATHLETES

BYU is not like most schools. Since the early 1970s when black players and students began trickling into the institution, the numbers have remained exceedingly small. As of the fall semester of 2013, BYU reported 4,139 students of color on campus. Underrepresented minority students *as a whole* made up just 14 percent of the student body; most of them were Asian-Pacific Islanders. And, specifically, black student enrollment was a paltry 265, less than 1 percent of the student body.[44] Public PWIs typically maintain an average African American enrollment of 13 percent, whereas private PWIs enroll upward of 17.6 percent of blacks on average.[45] By comparison, the numbers at BYU are simply inane.

During his reign, Coach LaVell Edwards (1972–2000) laid a solid foundation in altering the recruitment efforts to include and increase the number of black players.[46] When head coach Gary Crowton took over the program, he looked to build upon those efforts, as he was itching to restore the program to its former glory. Entering into his fourth (and what would be his final) season, Coach Crowton had plans to keep his job by increasing the competitiveness and visibility of Cougar football. One way he sought to accomplish this endeavor was by falling in line with the tradition of most Division I top-ranked football programs and attracting more black muscle to the program. The 2004 football season turned out to be a banner year for the BYU athletic department. That year alone, Crowton brought in a sizable number of African American players—it turned out to be the largest group of both black college students and black student-athletes at one time on the university's campus to that date.[47] And yet, one year later, nearly all of those black recruits were discharged with a multitude of university violations that varied from their mundane presence at a party where alcohol was consumed and/or sexual activity took place to the serious allegations of robbery and rape.

Affectionately named the "Baker's Dozen" after Honor Code Office director Steven Baker and his dismissal of twelve black athletes, Chad Nielsen discussed the vast disparity in his article entitled "BYU Confidential" in the *Salt Lake Magazine*.[48] Within one year's time, twelve African American members of the football team had been discharged from the team and, in some cases, from the university. During that same year, only two other nonblack players were dismissed, one white and one Polynesian. (A second white football player was penalized with probation, totaling two whites disciplined. Meanwhile, a total of fourteen blacks were sanctioned that year.) As it happens, prior to 2004, it had been three years since the last white football player had been dismissed.[49,50] Does this imply that blacks are more likely to commit moral violations?

What it most certainly does is uncover the unfortunate truth that blacks and whites are "handled" differently with respect to the honor code, which was put in place as a method of control over the school's student body (and faculty), and it was found to be particularly useful when it came to the containment of non-Mormon blacks.[51,52] According to former BYU athlete Ibrahim Rashada, a black student (athlete) is presumed guilty by the honor code, and one can only hope to be "exonerated."[53] Ibrahim believed he would have no trouble at BYU, considering that as a member of the Islamic faith, he subscribed to much of the same clean lifestyle as do Mormons, but he encountered his first brush with the honor code by his second day on campus. He was accused of sexual harassment by a store employee but was found to be innocent when store cameras proved no such crime occurred. This did not stop honor code officials from pestering Rashada since his earliest times on campus, beginning with the concern over his facial hair. BYU frowns upon facial hair and requires its students to keep a clean-cut hairstyle and a clean-shaven face. But as a Muslim, he was assured that he could keep his beard, as it's a sacred sign in his Islamic faith. He was informed that he would be issued a "beard card" to present when called upon by any BYU authority.[54] That card never came, and Rashada felt the brunt of it daily.[55]

His greatest struggle, however, came after a seventeen-year-old female accused him and three other African American BYU football players of rape. When the case finally went to trail a year later, Ibrahim was acquitted of all charges.[56] But by that point, the damage had been done, and Ibrahim Rashada likely wished he had gone to another school, given the string of troubles he encountered in Provo. Rashada, like most black players recruited to BYU, did not appreciate how serious honor code violations were until controversy erupted. Reflecting on his experience at BYU, he stated, "That's the last thing that came to my mind—to ask them about rules. I thought it was just another college."[57]

Former Cougar quarterback Steve Young once declared in a *Sports Illustrated* story about the honor code, "There's no bait and switch. It's very out in the open, very clear. It's compassionately administered."[58] But in Ray Hudson's case, there are no other words to describe it.[59] He had a baby on the way when he signed the BYU honor code, and he assuredly made the school administrators and coaches aware of his situation before signing the document. It was not until an "orgy scandal" broke involving other athletes of color that Ray was pulled into the honor code office. Though he had no involvement with the group-sex case, he was subsequently charged with an honor code violation by having a baby out of wedlock. Despite their prior knowledge of his circumstances, he was suspended from school for an entire semester.

This is not to say that all of the twelve athletes of color removed from campus that year were falsely accused. In fact, as stated before, most of them admitted to their improprieties. But for every one black football player involved in breaking the honor code, there is an additional white athlete breaking similar rules with weak and uneven enforcement, including those who were not LDS. The black athletes in the high-revenue sports of football and men's basketball are disciplined at a ten to one ratio compared to the white athletes. The numbers imply that blacks are under constant surveillance. Tico Pringle states, "The black athletes get called on it. Returned missionaries don't get turned in. It's all hush-hush. It's political. You go to the honor code office and then you go and talk to your coach and your coach pulls strings if he needs to. A lot of the guys I know did things and they got away with it because strings were pulled. There are guys who got their girlfriends pregnant and didn't get in trouble. They pick and choose who they want to punish."[60]

A TALE OF TWO STORIES: ILLUSTRATING DISCIPLINE IN BLACK AND WHITE

A classic case in the annals of BYU sports history is the story of Jim McMahon, the legendary BYU quarterback and eventual quarterback of the 1985 Chicago Bears Super Bowl championship team. A white, but non-Mormon student-athlete from Roy, Utah, McMahon survived five years of less than stellar honor code adherence during his college tenure. It was widely known (and McMahon has alluded to this himself) that the quarterback great often engaged in sexual escapades, drinking, and even smoking on campus while coaches turned a blind eye. As he describes it, it was not until his eligibility expired that he was actually punished for his indiscretions and formally suspended from school, a mere four classes shy of graduation.[61]

Years later, however, McMahon was granted the opportunity to complete his bachelor's degree in pursuit of the elusive BYU Hall of Fame, a courtesy not extended to many black players who have suffered similar circumstances.[62,63] Even in recent years, stories have emerged chronicling disproportionate punishments between black and white players. Just by comparing and contrasting a handful of BYU athletes on the basis of race in the sport of football, it becomes apparent that subtle and not-so-subtle differences exist in terms of treatment and student outcome.

The practice of sanctioning for honor code improprieties is, in actuality, a messy business. Honor code infractions cover a large spectrum of "do's and don'ts" with varying degrees of interpretations on how the penalty should be delivered. Hence, justice is applied inconsistently with very little structure. It is rendered on an individual basis, and the outcome depends as much on the temperament and internal workings and values of the disciplinarian as it does on the athletes and their misconduct. This is true across the board. Where one player receives a single game suspension for alcohol consumption, another receives five games, and still other players are completely removed from the team. But there is a trend at large, and it is generally unfavorable for black male athletes.

As discussed, the numbers show black athletes suspended at a significantly higher frequency than white players. But in addition to this, the pattern reveals that black players (particularly non-LDS athletes) typically received stiffer treatment for a similar type of misbehavior. Some noted cases in the differences in treatment between former black and white BYU athletes for fighting, alcohol consumption, and sexual indiscretions, to name a few, are revealing.

For example, in 2001, former footballer and white Mormon Teag Whiting was involved in a fight in which the police were summoned to the scene. Upon their arrival, he ran from the police and was later arrested. Not only was there minimal attention paid to the brawl, as it was essentially downplayed in the public sphere, but also he was only suspended for one game.[64,65] His fate and that of many other white athletes like him were very different from the black and non-Mormon athletes who were even suspected of mischief. Whiting's one-game suspension for fighting and arrest can be compared to a recent violation against the honor code committed by BYU wide receiver Devon Blackmon, a black junior college transfer who was suspended for one game for wearing a pair of earrings during the 2014 summer session.[66] Fighting, evading police, and arrest resulted in the same punishment as a minor (one-time) dress code violation. Blackmon owned up to his mistake and fully accepted his consequences.[67] But he did not have to say anything for the rest of the world to see the hypocrisy. Even Carrie Jenkins conceded in a 2004 interview, "It's extremely rare for a player to be suspended for dress and grooming violations."[68] Though there is an occasional instance when a black athlete receives greater leniency than his white peers (and no doubt there are times when white athletes receive onerous punishment), the trend is to the contrary, and it is disconcerting to say the least.

Dependent upon the gravity of the offense, racial scripts are automatically affixed to the wrongdoing. This is largely determined by dominate white racial frames that dictate and inform conscious and unconscious thought and action about the character and disposition of the contravener. These cognitions further influence the limits of what is the correct and appropriate course of action between black, white, and Polynesians players. Hence, these dismissals stem from generations of deleterious white racial frames that negatively cast doubt on black potential, systemically derailing their chances at college success before it has a chance to get off the ground. That is to say, whites have been racially primed to draw on prescribed notions regarding black behavior as predictable and, therefore, more deserving of stiffer sanctions. For example, former athletic director Val Hale made a self-fullfilling prophecy upon the 2004 recruitment of a large cohort of young black men. Summing up the thinking of many white BYU leaders, he said in his racially coded statement, "I was worried when [Crowton] brought in that many [blacks] from outside this culture at once. It made me nervous, it made my wife nervous. I expressed concern to the coaches about it."[69]

BYU has never had more than 1 percent black students on campus, be they Mormon or non-Mormon. Given the racialized history of the LDS church in regard to people of African lineage and the racist commentary that underscored the practice of exclusion, it should be no surprise that very few, if any, North American blacks find the Church of Latter-day Saints and its flagship school the least bit appealing.[70] But is it any wonder why, when the numbers are so skewed in disciplining black athletes?[71,72] We may never know the full details and rationale behind these disciplinary actions; the story offered here paints an alarming track record and wanton disregard for the needs of black male student-athletes and their unique circumstances.

Because the honor code office has been such a lightning rod of controversy for black student-athletes, BYU has taken a new approach on their communication with the media. They have chosen to no longer report any disciplinary issues to media outlets unless they are a matter of public record. This is an attempt to safeguard student privacy.[73] This action spares the beleaguered athlete public embarrassment and shame. It further allows for the accused to surreptitiously retreat from the complexities of Provo with dignity and to resolve to move on with their lives. For some athletes, this means attending another institution to salvage whatever eligibility is left. But for others, this involves moving back to a life of potential uncertainty, which has been the case in particular for non-Mormon black student-athletes.[74] This initiative aims to improve the public perception of BYU in respect to the honor code as a seemingly fair and impartial process. This does not, however, stop the black players from being discharged from BYU or disciplined for lesser offenses at a disproportionate rate. When asked about the Brandon Davies suspension, McMahon offered up his own less-than-helpful advice on how he beat the honor code system at BYU, "You had to find girls who kept their mouths shut."[75]

"ENTER TO LEARN; GO FORTH TO SERVE"

Ironically, honor code dismissals in and of themselves run counter to LDS doctrine and cultural practices that posit the ethic to teach by example, which includes developing boys into men of character and standing within their communities. The Church's mission demands of its leaders to shepherd its men down the path of righteousness. This is evident in how church discipline is rendered to athletes who are members, especially male priesthood holders. As discussed previously, Mormon athletes are typically extended the opportunity to repent by meeting with their church leaders and drawing support from friends and family. But non-Mormons who have been led astray are not given the same courtesy, nor do they have access to the same channels to redemption. Do these student-athletes deserve any less?

Mormonism anchors its theology in the life and ministry of Jesus Christ, who taught his disciples and followers the importance of the principle of forgiveness. On any given Sunday around the world, Latter-day Saints gather in their places of sanctuary and sermonize from the pulpit how forgiveness has influenced their lives for the better. Church authorities have touted its significance and the necessity of second and third chances for its members in the Church's annual general conference, but for most of the black male student-athletes—the vast majority of whom are not Mormon—this has not been the case. Many of these students come from dire circumstances in life with few moderating factors other than sports, and they have often been steered into sport participation as an unrealistic doorway out of poverty and destitution for themselves and their families.[76] These young adults have little, if any, exposure to Mormon culture, its proclivities, and certainly its rules. This is, in essence, a culture shock for many inexperienced black males coming from low-income urban areas. BYU, like many other PWIs, recruits these academically unprepared black male student-athletes from less prestigious high schools solely for their athletic prowess with the "promise" of an education in exchange.[77] But with the acceptance of their offer must come a change in behavior that is often incongruent with their lifestyle, if not their values and beliefs.

Loyal Cougar fans often insist that the players "knew the rules" before they came to BYU. But many of the non-Mormon athletes have insisted time and time again that the extent to which these moral codes applied to them remained vague to say the least. If anyone should be shepherded by the leaders of the faith, it should be these impressionable men. Hassan McCullough agrees: "[A]s a Mormon person, you know that you shouldn't be doing that. The person that's not Mormon, you don't know all the rules and stuff. So [they] should basically be lenient with you, because you don't know."[78]

As Christ said, "It is easier for a camel to go through the eye of the needle than it is for a rich man to enter into the kingdom of God."[79] Following His example, BYU has an obligation to teach, lead, and mentor these stripling warriors in ways that will embolden and inspire success beyond the gridiron and hoops arena, particularly through their difficult times. Even legendary coach LaVell Edwards expressed similar sentiment: "I just think part of our responsibility is to help them. The easiest thing to do is to kick the kid out, or cut him from the team."[80] These players are the ideal candidates to receive the gospel and rules of the faith and be given a second chance. In fact, BYU could be an extremely encouraging environment for these students who have been given an arduous lot in life due to America's persistent and systemic white racism and the high disregard for black males.

But all too often, BYU has been overly heavy-handed and quick to dismiss non-Mormon offenders of its honor code policy—knowing full well the difficult requirements that the faith expects, even for its members. And given Mormonism's long history of contempt for African Americans, these difficulties are exceedingly relevant for non-Mormon blacks. Rashaun Broadus discovered this contempt first hand.

Rashaun was recruited to BYU on a basketball scholarship during the 2005–2006 season from a small junior college in Nebraska. He concedes that during his recruitment trip to Provo, the BYU coaching staff briefed him about the rules prior to his commitment to attend the school. Eager to play the sport he loved and hasty regarding the details, Broadus likely glanced over the honor code policy. But he, like many other non-Mormon black student-athletes throughout the years, severely underestimated the honor code office and the degree to which it would enforce the code on non-Mormons if a mistake was made. Comparing himself to Brandon Davies, he believes that Brandon's offense was far more egregious according to Mormon teachings, and yet his punishment was far less severe than his own.[81]

Broadus found himself in head coach David Rose's office several hours after his early-morning arrest for suspicion of driving under of the influence of alcohol—a charge that was never substantiated. In that meeting with Coach Rose, Broadus learned his fate. He was kicked off the team almost immediately with no investigation and no remediation plan in place for an offense that was ultimately dropped. In turn, he felt alienated and excluded, as though any vestiges of him were completely eradicated. He reports feeling like a pariah while on campus, a state of being hardly suitable for engaged learning.[82]

It is unrealistic and irresponsible to expect these student-athletes to succeed with so little preparation and understanding of a religion set against a backdrop institutionally different from the one in which they grew up. And it is callous to recruit these teens out of their environment into a completely new milieu for which they are exploited and then expect them to immediately comply to the rules of a house of faith to which they do not belong—in a tradition that is considered one of the most strictly observed in this country—only to subsequently discard them at the first sign of trouble. At a time when the young college students need guidance most (particularly if they came from a disorganized home life), universities and colleges reap enormous benefit from the labor power of the black male student-athlete, all in furthering white interests. But there is not much effort placed on helping these students succeed beyond their athletic careers.

When the Brandon Davies story broke in front of a worldwide viewing audience, BYU appeared to be a diamond in the rough seas of college sports, placing morality over winning. In Brandon's case, despite being publicly humiliated for his mistakes, he was given a second chance. But McCullough and Broadus and others like them were not so fortunate. They did not have the cipher. And it was clear they were not worth the effort to mentor in Christ's name.

To initiate reform, the onus should be on the institution, not the eighteen-year-old teenager who grew up in an urban landscape where life was treacherous, and toughness was an attribute of strength for future survival. But far too often, these are the very individuals who fall through the cracks and are cast aside, proving morality to be too much of an undertaking. Hassan McCullough expressed his opinion: "[I]f they're Mormon, they give them second opportunities. But you see the thing is to me, if you're Mormon, I think you should be way more accountable for what you do than somebody's who's not Mormon. . . . That's how it should be. . . . But it's the total opposite, though."[83] McCullough offers a valid point, which certainly calls into question the hypocrisy between the faith and the school's actions. After all, if Mormon students live by the same ethical standards outlined in the honor code and have full understanding of the repercussions, why are they given more leeway when it comes to punishment?

What will BYU choose to do? Will it continue to discharge black male student-athletes at the first sight of transgression—or will BYU and the Church of Jesus Christ of Latter-day Saints continue to uphold the promises of their namesake and walk the path of the Savior? After all, as Jesus said, "He who is without sin among you, let him cast the first stone."[84]

7

COLORBLINDNESS AND THE HEALTH CONSEQUENCES TO BLACK MALE STUDENT-ATHLETES THROUGH THE ILLUSION OF A FREE EDUCATION

> The elevated compensation of some players obscures the reality of exploitation and contemporary colonization. —William Rhoden, *Forty Million Dollar Slaves*[1]

Education was among the first white public spaces to desegregate by reluctantly opening its doors to African American students eager to improve their lives beyond those of their parents. The initial trickle of hopeful black coeds at PWIs was largely unsupported as most whites were dismissive at their mere presence. The students were deemed invisible, irrespective of favorable changes in the juridical process and, with time, many found themselves struggling at these institutions for their rights to decent and equal accommodations and educational parity with their white peers.[2] The entrenched racial knowledge of yesteryear has since been conferred on newer generations of millennial white students and white officials, with similar devastation.

Despite the repeated claims by most white Americans that they are blind to matters of race, black Americans continue to report high levels of negative encounters with members of the white majority.[3] Indicative of these confrontations has been a statistical rise in outward manifestations of hate toward African Americans since the election of America's first black president.[4,5] For example, in early 2015, Twitter erupted over a leaked video of a group of white male fraternity members from the University of Oklahoma (OU) singing a racist chant on the way to a founder's day event. The members of Sigma Alpha Epsilon (SAE) were recorded gleefully belting the limerick, "There will never be a nigger at SAE. There will never be a nigger at SAE. You can hang 'em from a tree, but they'll never sign with me. There will never be a nigger at SAE."[6]

The anonymous video sparked a firestorm of controversy on campus, bringing to light one of many indignities that black collegians face in the shadows at PWIs. As black student-athlete and senior linebacker Eric Striker pointed out in response to the clip, these fraternity brothers at Oklahoma's premier flagship school are the same ones who cheer the loudest at the football games for the black players, so long as they are amusing the white man.[7] But this is not an isolated incident on OU's campus, as many would like to believe.[8] Nor is the denigration of black students exclusively a Southern problem as typically presumed, but instead this is an American one seen at all PWIs across the country from Michigan to Alabama to UCLA.[9,10]

And just as the culture at OU permits a breeding ground for this kind of injurious conduct, BYU's campus climate is no different, as Robert Foster met first hand. The only African American student body president ever elected at Brigham Young University, Foster experienced an onslaught of racial antagonisms that began during his election bid and continued throughout his tenure as president. From the beginning, he faced unfounded allegations of cheating by fellow classmates and university officials that forced Foster to suspend his campaign for a forty-eight-hour penalty. During his time as student body president, he reported pushback from leadership as well as more egregious acts of racial aggression, such as the large amount of hate mail (including one such letter from the White Knights of the Ku Klux Klan) and an incident in which his vehicle tires were mysteriously slashed, forcing him to relocate his family to safer territory. These were ongoing troubles that he experienced over his short one-year term in office.[11]

Over the next decade, the campus culture was not altered significantly on its course as BYU continued to build its legacy through white American antiquity. Just one year after the institution was heralded as "America's University" following the Brandon Davies incident, comedian David Ackerman's 2012 interviews of naïve students on BYU's campus while in blackface caricature highlighted the ignorance and offensiveness that abounds at the Mormon school.[12] In the video, BYU students were asked questions about Black History Month, and their responses fluctuated from the ill-informed—the inability to name any African American historical figure outside Martin Luther King Jr. and Malcolm X—to the outrageous, as they described celebrating Black History Month by eating fried chicken, drinking grape juice, and listening to "lots of Jay-Z."[13] These racist frames are deep-seated and stereotypically castigate black people and the places they occupy. The "humor" in the video perhaps is the astonishing obliviousness of the undergraduates to how actually racist they appeared and how vulgar and embarrassing their remarks are to themselves, BYU, and the LDS faith. But as he aimed to show just how little interaction whites on this campus have with blacks by failing to recognize that even he, himself, is not actually black, but simply wearing darkly applied makeup, Ackerman did so by bringing in the repugnant history of blackface. This was an insensitive attempt at satire. Left uncovered by the video is the reality that the contributions of black Americans are not known on most white college campuses. In such an atmosphere, how can we expect black men and women to feel safe, comfortable, and secure, much less thrive?

Claims of colorblindness persist as a moral defense against personal bigotry toward African Americans. In reality, many white Americans hold unexamined antiblack views, which are evident given that African Americans continue to lag behind on every major social indicator, signaling an ongoing subtle instantiation of race-based discrimination. The degree of inequities that plague the black community in housing, policing, education, health care, and other basic necessities of life are ever present.[14,15] These privations have real life-changing consequences for people of color, such as difficulty in obtaining and maintaining employment, poor academic performance, increased incidents of unwarranted police confrontations, and shortened life spans.[16,17] Contemporary racial oppression has been every bit as relentless and difficult on black people, and it remains a constant threat.[18]

These events further highlight how PWIs systemically fail students of color (and, in turn, all students) by having very little on campus to whom and to which they can relate. By maintaining the Eurocentric curriculum to which students are accustomed, there is no place for critical inquiry and transformative teaching for deliberate purposes.

Halfhearted policies and measures expected to alter the campus climate at many PWIs have uniformly been ineffective and, at some institutions, virtually nonexistent. Most white administrators (i.e., deans, chairs, program directors), faculty, or other gatekeepers do not see the need to cater to black student and faculty requests to solidify equity and achievement. Therefore, PWIs continue to serve the interest of white students through the guise of "integration" while using students of color as little more than window dressing for inclusion. This recursive thinking and unwillingness to examine individual racial attitudes, biases, and beliefs has done very little to reconfigure the footprint of our nation's past; systemic racial oppression has proven much harder to uproot in a society fixated on the myth of race neutrality or "colorblindness."[19]

THE ERA OF CONTEMPORARY RACIAL OPPRESSION AND THE RHETORIC OF COLORBLINDNESS

The civil rights movement brought about a significant shift in white consciousness that seemingly moved the nation toward a commitment to the principles of equality, at least on paper and in rhetoric.[20] Since the civil rights era, current research findings suggest that white adults no longer support scientific and biological racism claims.[21] These more favorable attitudes toward nonwhites have resulted in a change in the societal outlook on interracial marriage, integrated neighborhoods and schools, and seating arrangements on public transportation, for example. These improvements in white racial attitudes, however, have been short-lived and have not translated into less discrimination for African Americans. Conversely, the twenty-first century has continued to reproduce and retool newer forms of the white racial frame daily. Recall from chapter 2 that frames operate in part through direct and indirect messages—the stories we receive from family, friends, and the broader society—about black Americans and other Americans of color, and these philosophies shape the white penchant to discriminate.

Racism has changed in American life from pastimes when "old-fashioned" expressions of bigotry were more the norm during slavery, Jim Crow, and "separate but equal" to a more subtle yet incredibly destructive modus of present-day racial bias.[22,23,24] The ongoing disenfranchisement of black Americans by whites is generally more inconspicuous, focusing less on biological arguments. Instead of relying on racist nineteenth-century pseudoscience as a basis for black marginality, today's racism is automatic—an antiblack affect engrained in the subconscious minds of nearly all Americans, most notably whites.[25] Research in the social and behavioral sciences has generated a sizable body of empirical evidence that confirms the presence and extensiveness of unconscious (or implicit) racial bias in contemporary society.

Implicit racial bias refers to attitudes, beliefs, and values tied to human cognition. They involve the use of mental short cuts—in essence, stereotypes—that influence our understanding of racial difference as well as actions and decision making outside of conscious awareness. Everyone possesses racial bias to some degree. When participants were asked in the Implicit Association Test (IAT) to couple random black or white faces/names and positive or negative adjectives (e.g., love, peace, and joy versus terrible, criminal, and failure) into appropriate columns, the speed at which subjects completed the task demonstrated a pattern interpreted as a high preference for whites.[26,27] In America's highly racialized and stratified society, the vast majority of whites—even those who espouse a personal philosophy of colorblindness—and, in fact, half of blacks "pair photographs of White faces, or stereotypically White names with positive words, and photographs of Black faces or stereotypically Black names with negative words much faster than they pair White stimuli with negative words and Black stimuli with positive words."[28] Since the initial IAT experiments were conducted in 1998, millions have taken the online test, and the conclusions are highly consistent—the speed at which white and black participants respond to the images reveals a pattern interpreted as showing a high value associated with whiteness. According to Lee, "the social science research demonstrates that one does not have to be a racist with a capital R, or one who intentionally discriminates . . . on the basis of race, to harbor implicit racial biases."[29]

Racial biases encompass negative appraisals about black Americans that are triggered involuntarily without awareness or conscious control. This uncritical habit of the mind is an inheritance from our racist past operationalized in modern times through the use of cognitive frames silently residing in the subconscious and not accessible to introspection.[30] The historical negation of blacks as less than fully human is so fundamentally grounded in the minds of whites that the color black itself elicits a contemptible mental reflex, just as we saw in the introduction with the NBA and NHL studies regarding penalties. This is never more evident than when studying the amygdala. The amygdala is a small structure inside the brain related to fear and anxiety, and it has been shown in experiments to be absent of any racial bias stimulus during childhood. However, as children grow and are exposed to the social environment and world around them they become increasingly more sensitive to African Americans such that biases are produced. In other words, by the time these white youth reach adolescence, blackness triggers discord in the amygdala through a process known as "fear conditioning."[31] This suggests that children are indeed socialized to learn their place in the racial hierarchy, and further, the method of sorting and assigning value to difference has important biological implications.

When racial biases are paired with the ideology of colorblindness, the effects on human behavior have real-world consequences for communities of color. In the aftermath of the civil rights movement, the language of colorblindness emerged as an explicit way for white Americans to pretend that race does not matter. Many whites use this strategy to ignorantly convince themselves that U.S. society is now post-racial. Colorblindness, according to Frankenberg, allows "many white people in the United States . . . not to 'see,' or at any rate not to acknowledge, race differences."[32] This standpoint works conveniently for whites, allowing most to nullify their complicity while sleeping well at night in a racist system that privileges and advances their interests.

This same logic allows white Americans to appropriate King's work, principally his "I Have a Dream" speech, inasmuch as it reaffirms the mainstream colorblind narrative. But in reality, this is akin to the proverbial "ostrich syndrome," which happens when white Americans learn to stick their head in the sand and remain unaware of the fact that race does and should matter. The propensity by most whites to feign ignorance as a virtue while turning a blind eye to the vicious realities of racial injustice only prolongs the agony for blacks. Deep public distrust then festers, raising the stakes for future clashes and divisions along racial lines as we have seen recently. In the wake of Ferguson,[33] public outcries for justice and reform reached an all-time high decibel level heard across the country in response to the rash of killings of unarmed black males by white police officers. These "Black Lives Matter" and "I Can't

Breathe" campaigns deliver a sobering truth that colorblindness with respect to law enforcement has not worked in the interest of nonwhites. Long-term tensions and weariness among the racialized subaltern people are detrimental to social cohesion and, understandably, hasten our deepest xenophobic anxieties.[34,35]

In short, colorblindness is the limited awareness on matters of race in North America, thus enabling systemic racism to flourish in a society defiantly resistant to social transformation. Colorblindness has allowed white people to wash their hands of the past by moving forward toward a "race-neutral" society where people are supposedly judged by the "content of their character." In reality, the existence of subconscious racial frames makes this unlikely. Thus, when African Americans interact with whites, whether at their job, the university, in public education, place of worship, or the criminal justice system, they must contend with the higher-than-average probability of discrimination.[36,37] Rather than cultivate a democratic ideal of justice in both thought and deed, colorblindness represents a major stumbling block for African Americans and their pursuit toward full racial justice, particularly in higher education.[38] For most white folk, the illusion of a colorblind society absolves them of past and present "white guilt" over the persistence of racial discrimination in a nation that lays claim to the principles of fairness and progress in life based on hard work.

THE FALLACY OF A "FREE EDUCATION" AND THE FAILURE OF BLACK MALES AT PWIS

Historically, African American male student-athletes were among the first wave of the dispossessed to be allowed to enter the hallowed spaces of PWIs, not as true students per se, but rather as commodities merely masquerading as students. Barred from entering the classrooms or dormitories at many of these PWIs and forced to sit on the floor in the hallway during lectures, black students were told in a number of explicit ways that they did not matter much in the world other than what they could do to win ball games. Such overt racist practices are no longer explicit and evident to the casual observer; therefore, many whites believe this "advancement" is an indication of a colorblind society. In truth, black athletes continue to endure struggles at PWIs. The doctrine of colorblindness has proven difficult to remove from the consciousness of white people, allowing the pain that blacks carry to be hidden beneath the surface and easily ignored.

In the eyes of most white administrations, blacks have been on campus for one purpose only, to fill the coffers by competing and winning. Earning a college degree is merely an ancillary bonus. As Seattle Seahawks and former Stanford Cardinal cornerback Richard Sherman stated during the Super Bowl XLIX media day event, "You're there to play football . . . those are the things coaches tell them every day: 'You're not on scholarship for school.'"[39] The culture of these major collegiate athletic programs is set on furthering the interests of whites through a coordinated method of black exploitation. Black male student-athletes are recruited and admitted to PWIs at a rate higher than black degree-seeking students who are nonathletes, which is telling about the worth and value that black folk bring to the academy. The majority of African American male students on campus at PWIs are overrepresented in the high-revenue sports of football and men's basketball. One study noted that, between 2007 and 2010, black males comprised 57.1 percent of football teams and 64.3 percent of men's basketball teams, but made up just 2.8 percent of full-time, degree-seeking, undergraduate students. Black males are significantly underrepresented in the scholastic side of the student-athlete experience, and they are the least likely to earn a college degree, even when it's "free."[40]

Many of these athletes struggle to find the time or, in some cases, the desire to achieve academically. As former and current players of Northwestern University demonstrated in their brief to the National Labor Relations Board (NLRB), Northwestern football occupies the majority of a player's time at upwards of fifty to sixty hours a week with a highly regimented daily schedule from mealtime to film study to practice.[41] This is not especially unusual; Sherman also elucidated such in the media day events in referencing his time at Stanford.[42] Players nationwide put in an unreasonable amount of training time dedicated to their respective sport as they prepare to fill the seats in stadiums and arenas across the country. Nonetheless, these young men sign a contract; in exchange for their muscle power used to generate millions of dollars for the athletic program and university, they receive the promises of unrealistic rewards under the pretense of a "free education."[43] But this term is a misnomer.

A report by the National College Players Association found that during the 2009–2010 academic year, full scholarship athletes at football bowl subdivision (FBS) schools actually incurred out-of-pocket expenses (a "shortfall") of greater than three thousand dollars per year for basic living needs. This means that, despite a full athletic scholarship covering tuition, fees, room, and board, the student-athlete still accrued debt just to meet the basic necessities of life.[44] These same athletes, by NCAA rule, are only allowed to earn a maximum of two thousand dollars each term, provided they can find the time in the midst of their schoolwork and fifty-hour practice weeks.[45] These are not the only costs that burden the athlete, as Rakim Cox found out the hard way. After claiming his room and board on his taxes as "income," which he was instructed to do, he was slapped with a liability that forced him to pay taxes on the "free" room and board.[46] The common assumption is that revenue-generating athletes in big-time college sports are well cared for by the institution. But, in fact, more than 85 percent of full-scholarship FBS athletes live below the federal poverty line while in school as full-time students.[47] The distress they endure after college has to do with the fallacy of an education they are promised.

The misconception of a free education has been further unveiled, as a recent report shows that the majority of black athletes neither finish their degree nor earn a degree that is consistent with the rigors of the institution from which they attend. Not to imply that all black student-athletes suffer hardship in meeting the demands and academic workload of college life, but the poor graduation rate for black male student-athletes at some of the nation's finest colleges and universities is symptomatic of the crisis in public schools and its continued practices of white racial domination and exclusion of youth of color.[48,49] Research is clear that U.S. public schools have uniformly failed to educate black youth on their own terms, chiefly those from urban settings. Black and brown students, in particular, are vulnerable to the ruthless inequities that exist in education. For example, students of color are more likely to be tracked into low-status classes and programs than their white peers.[50] Because public education in the United States is unequally funded by a system of local property taxes, the masses of young black students who reside in deprived communities obtain fewer resources, receiving a subpar education through no fault of their own.

Yet, PWIs have found ways to admit unprepared black males to campus, who then find themselves languishing in the athletic departments of most major NCAA Division I schools. These men arrive on campus lacking scholastic preparedness from pre-K to high school that is necessary to earn a valid degree. In essence, they are recruited to the university solely on their athletic prowess by the same establishment that denies them entrance and full inclusion in any other circumstance. It is utterly self-serving on the part of PWIs to recruit these players to campus, with many lacking the basic reading, writing, and arithmetic skills necessary to obtain a quality education.[51]

In 2004, the NCAA instituted an Academic Progress Report, or APR score, in its attempts to improve the overall accountability of Division I schools to matriculate student-athletes toward graduation.[52,53] For some students, this requires a multifaceted approach and individualized system of support to ensure academic achievement. This often involves the academic support of tutors and specialized academic advisors. But recently, the NCAA has begun to unearth duplicitous activities by universities and colleges across the country that have hidden their motives under the pretense of "assistance." The most egregious of these occurred at the University of North Carolina at Chapel Hill, one of America's premier public institutions with a long tradition of academic excellence. The deception spanned a twenty-five-year history, whereby advisors steered hundreds of athletes into phony "paper" classes to keep mostly black players academically eligible to compete while at the same time cheating them out of a decent education.[54] With upwards of thirty-seven other reported cases of alleged academic fraud in the last twenty-five years and another twenty institutions currently under the microscope, it is fair to say that this utterly disgraceful practice is widespread.[55,56]

The argument that student-athletes receive the possibility of a "free education" rings hollow when we find institutions like UNC-Chapel Hill pushing players through the system with little regard for the quality of their education but for the chief purpose of keeping the collegian eligible and the athletic department profitable. At the very least, it is educational negligence and fraud to profit off the backs of the least advantaged and then somehow suggest that the predetermined majors and no-show classes resulting in a mock degree is more than sufficient for these students. But at most, this is a form of slavery, as these athletes are not allowed to accept money, due to NCAA rules. For many, expenses outside of what is covered with tuition/fees, room, and board become dire without additional funding. Yet, procuring any monies poses a risk of losing their hopeful ticket out of poverty and the uncertainty of life. If schools refuse to pay them a wage and likewise refuse to extend them a valid education worth something beyond a roll of parchment, these athletes are then working as the mule in the relationship, with little or nothing to show at the end but a broken body, bruised spirit, and concussed mind.[57]

BROKEN PROMISES AND SHATTERED DREAMS FOR THE BLACK BYU ATHLETE

BYU has broken similar promises as they continue to solicit black talent, knowing that the chances of successfully completing their university degree through the sanitized and unnurturing environment of the Mormon campus are low. The Institute for Diversity and Ethics in Sport (TIDES) recently released a report that highlighted this reality. TIDES serves as a clearinghouse for issues germane to race and gender in collegiate and professional sports. The widely respected organization at the University of Central Florida publishes a variety of data on student graduation rates and racial attitudes and a race- and gender-based report card on hiring practices in athletics. The institute assembled a comprehensive review of the seventy-five bowl-bound teams in 2014–2015 and assessed how well they manage to graduate black and white student-athletes over a six-year period. TIDES reported a dismal 33 percent graduation success rate (GSR) for black BYU student-athletes, the lowest of all the teams that were included in the 2015 football post-season bowl series; no other school earned a rate of less than 40 percent.[58] Just 16 percent of the players on BYU's 2014–2015 roster were black out of 123 on the team. The noted subpar black graduation rate translates into fewer than seven black graduates over a four-year span, or fewer than two players a year. Meanwhile, their in-state rivals, the University of Utah and Utah State University, both boasted a black GSR higher than even the white players' on the team. With a GSR for black student-athletes ranked in the top fifteen of all the 2015 bowl subdivision schools, the Utes and the Aggies scored 75 percent and 93 percent respectively.[59]

Despite claims of universalism, BYU has no investment in these young men apart from their ability to produce wins and boost the reputation of the institution. If they did, it would be evident in more black coaches and students on campus; more black student advisors, administrators, and faculty; and more student services to ensure the athletes' success while on campus as well as after their collegiate athletic career. This neglect is not unique to BYU. In reality, the Mormon concept of universalism functions in a similar way to colorblindness. What is unique, however, is the way in which the Mormon institution uses its religious views and the honor code to disenfranchise predominately black athletes in lieu of fostering an environment to teach and model productive behavior for future accomplishments, as its mission suggests. BYU graduate Christian Parker will attest to this. Christian is the older brother of NBA basketball player Jabari Parker, and as a small guard for the College of Southern Idaho basketball during his playing days, he knows something about being a black student-athlete. And though not a BYU athlete, he witnessed firsthand how the BYU honor code can be unevenly applied to black players when he transferred[60] there to finish up his bachelor's degree. A black man on campus with many student-athlete friends, he reflected on a color-based hierarchy with regard to school dismissals, which gives whites and lighter skinned blacks greater leniency than darker skinned students.[61]

In an interview, Christian expressed some reservations about his younger brother, once crowned the top basketball recruit in the country, contemplating Brigham Young as his springboard to the NBA. According to Christian, "I was a major advocate that Jabari should go elsewhere during his college recruitment. The reasons I've shared with him have been based around social abnormalities in a highly Mormon populated environment. This affects everything from honor code issue and sports together and individually."[62] Christian admits that his younger brother never approached these aspects—he was more interested in the team and the coach. But as Jabari pondered whether or not to attend the church-owned school, his older brother was wary of the suspiciously high rate of removals and career-ending actions against black student-athletes (compared to whites).[63]

Though the Parker brothers occupy a different space from most black Americans, they still carry the stigma of race. They both maintain an insider-outsider status on this topic. They are African American student-athletes who competed at PWIs, gaining an understanding of the crucial role of race in sports, and they also share a unique perspective as members of the LDS church, a faith with a self-identified black population of only 3 percent.[64] Jabari himself is what you would call a "unicorn"; his circumstances of being black and Mormon coupled with his emergence as an NBA basketball player are assuredly rare. This allows many white Mormons, and Cougar fans especially, to politely ignore the fact that Jabari's racial identity as a black man is firmly intact and a potential cultural mismatch at BYU where the faculty, staff, and students have little exposure to black Americans. This is an unthinkable probability when universalism is conflated with the frame of colorblind racial ideology, but indeed, most white Americans derive much of their knowledge about blacks from the media and secondhand encounters gleaned from family, friends, and members of their extended white networks.

The reality is that the Parker brothers grew up steeped in the rich cultural landscape of the Southside of Chicago of which they are keenly familiar. The LDS church that Jabari and Christian attended in a largely (and atypically) black LDS congregation in the community of Hyde Park looks very different when paralleled with the predominantly white and Mormon culture of Utah. Jabari would have left Chicago bound for an experience of racial isolation in the overwhelmingly white and conservative setting of Provo, a setting very dissimilar to his circumstances in the sprawling city of Chicago. This is not to suggest that he would have found himself in any trouble in Utah (any more than any normal eighteen-year-old boy). But his high visibility as an outstanding recruit and black Latter-day Saint of his stature make him both an instant celebrity, tokenized for the stereotypical aspects of his blackness, and a target of racial animus at a PWI where he would be one of only a handful of black students out of more than thirty thousand undergraduates.[65] Such a decision means a tough adjustment for any young man coming from a predominately black or more diverse milieu, irrespective of religiosity. In the end, Jabari eventually settled on Coach K—Mike Krzyzewski—and the esteemed Duke University Blue Devils to hone his skills for his solitary year of collegiate play, but not before he paid an "official visit" to BYU.

The LDS church preaches and encourages universalism, stressing to its members on any given Sunday that "we are all alike unto God." But the actions of the BYU honor code office do not reflect the bombast, as evident in the unequally applied discipline standards among black and brown athletes. Otherwise, these men would have been given the same opportunities and second chances at redemption as their white teammates, certainly for those who committed religiously based infractions unassociated with an NCAA violation. As Christian explained, "We do proclaim in the articles of faith 11 'the privilege of worshiping Almighty God according to the dictates of our OWN conscience, and ALLOW ALL men the same privilege, let them worship how, where, or what they may.'"[66] This does not seem to coincide with BYU's "our way or the highway" policies that are strictly adhered to with respect to blacks, specifically non-Mormons. Whether it is a valid and quality education lacking at UNC-Chapel Hill or the ability to stand on equal footing with rules, standards, and consequences lacking at BYU, these young black men deserve an exceptional education, as all men and women do, that will set them on a path toward a bright future. Instead, they are left with capitalistic interests that place property rights over human rights, a system rigged to leave black men and women exposed to unconscious bias and virulent racial subordination through practices and performances of institutionalized discrimination—a pathogenic stressor implicated in early mortality.[67]

CLOSE PROXIMITY TO WHITE COMES AT A RISK TO BLACK HEALTH

African American student-athletes routinely face race-related stressors—microassaults and microaggressions—in the form of low academic expectation, unfair and differential treatment, and even tokenism. Black student-athletes at PWIs such as BYU further suffer from the "only-ness" factor where they must learn how to cope with being the only black person (or one of a few) in isolation from other same-race peers, mentors, or faculty members.[68] Being the "only one" in white spaces as a collegiate athlete leaves the black student vulnerable to contending with dubious racial stereotypes. Renowned scholar-activist Harry Edwards wrote, "They must contend, of course, with the connotations and social reverberations of the traditional 'dumb jock' caricature; they are burdened also with the insidiously racist implications of the myth of 'innate black athletic superiority,' and the more blatantly racist stereotype of the 'dumb Negro' condemned by racial heritage to intellectual inferiority."[69] Though Edwards was referencing the athletic milieu of the 1960s, 1970s and 1980s, contemporary black student-athletes, likewise, withstand many of these same indignities presently in operation at many PWIs all across the United States.[70,71] Such racist barriers and negotiations leave many black men and boys susceptible to harmful aspects of psychological stress.

Jacquelyn Fleming's work on the qualitative experience of black student life at PWIs is very helpful at uncovering the sources of psychological stress that impede black undergraduates' abilities to thrive in post-secondary education. In her book, *Blacks in College*, she examined experiences of black students at eight PWIs compared to those at seven historically black colleges and universities (HBCUs). Making her study unique, she used a range of variables from serial blood pressure checks and reports of sickness to the student academic records and surveys of racial stress to determine their degree of well-being and coping.[72] Fleming found that black undergraduate students at PWIs suffered from higher levels of self-reported stress and social isolation and poorer academic performance than did their same-race peers at HBCUs. Referring to one PWI in her study, Fleming observed:

> Black students at Georgia Tech suffer from some of the worst intellectual deterioration found in a white college in this study. Their academic energies are apparently frustrated by classroom incidents and then withdraw from the classroom into extracurricular pursuits that afford no intellectual benefit. These trends in no way describe the educational experience for white students.[73]

Fleming's work revealed the difficulties black students face in achieving their dreams and aspirations at PWIs. She contended that black students on PWI campuses combat a hostile environment, which triggers a defensiveness that interferes with their intellectual development, interpersonal well-being, and, ultimately, their racial identity development. In other words, these students experienced what William

Smith coined "racial battle fatigue" (RBF).[74] Developed as a consequence of the cumulative effect of systemic white racism coupled with the sting of interpersonal racial bias and mistreatment, RBF exacts resources from the soul of its victim, siphoning precious energy and dousing creativity. Just as military personnel experience symptoms of mental health collapse after years of multiple deployments in areas such as the Middle East, RBF develops in response to distressing mental and emotional conditions that result from the daily insults of racial harassment and aggression in the schoolhouse, in the boardroom, and on the gridiron.[75]

Social isolation caused by racial conflict suffocates the opportunity to engage in the well-rounded activities of college life. Fleming notes that black males often retreat to extracurricular activities to cope with the campus stressors.[76] In some ways, participation in college athletics shields black male students from the persistent racial encounters that are rampant on most PWIs. But this is only temporary. In the end, the negative aspects of being racialized on a predominately white college or university campus outweighs the positive gains of teamwork and sportsmanship that athletics gives them. Evidence-based research has determined that HBCU campuses are more affirming places for black students, where they are made to feel as though they belong. PWIs, on the other hand, routinely frame black students as second-class citizens undeserving of college admission.[77] The thought of being made to compete at (or against) an institution perceived as racist comes at a high cost for black mental and emotional health and well-being.

Experiencing everyday racism and bearing the brunt of white domination exacerbates individual and group dispossession felt by African Americans, accelerating the biological aging process and hastening the development of certain types of diseases of slow accumulation. Research over the last four decades has mounted strong evidence that race-based mistreatment on the basis of physical characteristics (i.e., hair, bone structure, lips, skin color, eye shape, etc.) takes a heavy toll on black people not only at the social, political, and economic levels of society but also at the physiological level where stress hormones surge at elevated levels in African Americans. Disease does not exist in a vacuum. The process of being racialized combined with chronic daily stressors creates conditions that give rise to a perfect storm for disease deep within the physiology of individuals and groups.[78,79]

The psychoneuroendocrine system in the human body is generally well equipped to adapt to situational variations of daily stress. Under sympathetic control, the initial stress response is acutely activated. This is known as the "fight or flight" response that happens within seconds to minutes, preparing the body to cope with a specific threat, whether real or imagined. Indeed, just thinking about a stressful event inside the brain is enough to stimulate the stress response, which increases the energy demands on the body, from increased heart rate, blood pressure, and respiration to the production, release, and utilization of blood sugar and free fatty acids circulating through the vasculature. The stress response is our biological alarm system that prepares the body for imminent physical danger. Interestingly, this system responds to psychological and sociological mediated stressors in exactly the same manner. In other words, being confronted with racial slurs such as the word "nigger" can, and often will, elicit the exact same physiological arousal as being chased by a knife-wielding attacker.

Once the acute event resolves, the parasympathetic nervous system should activate and return the body to normal function. But this does not always happen efficiently, particularly in the bodies of African Americans where stressors tarry throughout the school day, the workday, and other social environments, keeping the body's stress response in a continued state of heightened awareness. During times of extended duress, a secondary stress response known as the "hypothalamus-pituitary-adrenal" (HPA) axis is triggered. The HPA axis system culminates in the production of cortisol, which can then re-trigger the HPA axis cascade for a continual loop.[80] Though cortisol is necessary for the body in short bouts to decrease inflammation, among other functions, it is well documented in the research literature on stress as having a pernicious effect the longer it remains elevated. As cortisol levels endure throughout the day, physiological damage to the small vessels occurs in the vital organs such as the kidneys, eyes and heart.[81] With long-term exposure, cortisol has a blunting effect on systemic immunity, leaving the body more susceptible to disease. The end result of the impact of stress is a greater risk toward developing diabetes, high cholesterol, cancer, hypertension, depression, anxiety, and other forms of lifestyle related maladies.[82]

There is strong evidence that posits that social factors contribute to the production of disease and earlier death for African Americans.

Black males have been historically singled out and restricted from access to economic resources and opportunities afforded to most white Americans. Whether on the playing field as a pawn of big corporate money or in the classroom where the education is a sham, the pounding mistreatment can have serious consequences for blacks and their mental, emotional, and physical well-being.

Black male student-athletes and other African Americans of the 1960s did not realize that the turbulent racial tensions that ensued during the protest years would lead to a secondary, but silent battle—a physiological wear and tear on the body beneath the surface of their skin. Race-based discrimination (whether real or imagined) affects the human condition in more harmful ways than what was previously understood. Research has uncovered an important link between perceived discrimination and negative mental and physical health outcomes.[83,84,85] The impact of daily microaggressions is mentally taxing, but the psychosocial stress can be deadly.[86]

THE INSIDIOUS DEGREE OF RACISM IN THE AGE OF OBAMA

The post–civil rights presence of African people in white public space has yet to remodel the prefrontal architecture where mental framing emanates. As distorted images arose from the smoldering, but ongoing, embers of the black freedom struggle, a familiar image of black men in the modern age of sport has lingered across time, personifying them as ignorant brutes in genetically constituted superhuman bodies. Though these attitudes and beliefs have changed in some respects with the passage of time, vestiges of old-fashioned or Jim Crow racism can still be heard and easily found in society.[87,88,89] Unequivocally, over the last seven years since the election of the nation's first black president, African Americans have been catching hell, struggling against a barrage of racial animus.[90] Whether in the schoolhouse, in the neighborhood, or innocently tending to their own affairs, black Americans and specifically black men and young boys are under constant assault. It is as if the floodgates of white angst, built up over the past fifty years, have been opened since President Barrack Obama took his first oath of office in 2008.

The breadth and scope of white racism is severely underestimated in the United States and is often mistakenly equated with "cross burning" and "name calling," individual acts of meanness. But this does not explain race-based mistreatment in established settings like public schools, which are routinely charged with casting out scores of young black males as young as four years of age to the streets, expelling them, often for no sensible or compelling reason.[91] Such limited understandings by the white educational establishment add very little toward progressive school restructuring and the promises of equal opportunity guaranteed by the Constitution. When young black males are disproportionately ousted from the scholastic process, they are at considerably more risk to live a life consigned to the whims of the underground economy, merely biding time until they reach the walls of the prison-industrial complex.[92,93]

Many African Americans grind onward and find a way to matter amid the depravations in one form or another. Some blacks have developed coping skills through received wisdom, collective experiences of family members who counter-frame the mainstream white narrative. But many cope through the school of "hard knocks" where they acquire a tough exterior shell that becomes difficult to penetrate.[94] In the final analysis, black male student-athletes have many formidable challenges and obstacles that block the pursuit of social justice. Though the situations for black students vary per campus, the underlying shared theme is that race still matters and continues to define the quality of life of black Americans in the twenty-first century.

8

PIPELINE TO A PIPEDREAM

The Elusiveness of Change in the Era of "Black Lives Matter"

> The first lesson a revolutionary must learn is that he is a doomed man.—Huey P. Newton, *Revolutionary suicide*[1]

Black athletes born in segregation and who came of age during the civil rights era witnessed their parents struggle against second-class citizenship in a nation deeply divided by race. These same athletes stood up for justice and would use their prominence and visibility to draw attention to issues that afflicted the black community. Even though both amateur and professional sports during this period had modest numbers of black athletes, they still galvanized around matters key in the freedom struggle. These competitors would blaze a path for future black athletes to follow, leaving a legacy for the next round of freedom fighters.

Following the robust black pride movement, the contemporary black athletes of the 1980s and 1990s maintained a race-neutral façade, borrowing from the colorblind mantra of whites in an effort to remain nonpartisan, at least in the public domain. During this time, players were increasing their presence in the realm of the burgeoning professional sports industry. And as sports developed into a commercial enterprise, the black athlete found a niche for making millions.

As activist voices like Kareem Abdul-Jabbar fell silent, those of a new era focused more on their brand and the balance sheet. These players were in their infancy in terms of realizing the power they had to negotiate contracts and celebrity endorsement deals. Michael Jordan undeniably changed the game with respect to opening additional revenue streams by pitching and developing products for consumption for corporations like Nike. One's brand and its financial implications became the main priority for the black professional athlete of the 1990s. This was never more evident than when Jordan famously stated, "Republicans buy shoes, too," as he declined to politically endorse the black North Carolina incumbent running for Senate against proud southern racist Jesse Helms.[2]

In *Forty Million Dollar Slaves*, author William Rhoden laments the missed opportunities for big-time professional athletes like Michael Jordan and Tiger Woods.[3] Both men are living examples of the fear of speaking out in a multibillion-dollar industry. But whether it was fear of expendability, or more appropriately, fear of the expendable paycheck when taking a stand (such behavior might be construed as "bad for business" in an industry controlled by white corporate elites), many black athletes took their cues from whites, choosing to remain neutral on matters of social and racial inequality. This is not to suggest that athletes back then did not champion causes, but for the most part, those decades saw less activism and more procurement of wealth and status. Issues that might compromise their bottom line were strongly discouraged by marketing and sports executives. Hence, most black athletes steered clear of the polemics of race and other topics perceived as inflammatory and/or contentious.

As many black athletes publically and strategically deployed a colorblind veneer, they further subverted the collective opportunity to seize power and control of their brawn, style, and talents. Speaking truth to white power had all but faded from the consciousness of the black athlete. Instead, for decades, Jordan inspired legions of captivated black youth to unrealistic aspirations, hoping for their "river Jordan" out of the circumstances of their birth.[4] But eventually a new athlete arose with a different mindset and understanding of his worth to white stakeholders.

REDISCOVERING THE HERITAGE OF BLACK ACTIVISM THROUGH SPORT

This modern black athlete has the ability to reconcile some aspects of capitalism's seductive allure with communitarian impulses reminiscent of the black radical tradition. LeBron James, arguably the most formidable among his peers, is a towering figure who exemplifies both of these ideals. He recognizes the enormous sway that he holds in a sport-frenzied and capital-driven society. Feeling an obligation to use that power in the cause of social justice, James has been deliberate in taking a position to support blacks. Whether it be a protest picture supporting Trayvon Martin, his vocal criticism of former Clippers owner Donald Sterling, or, following Derrick Rose, donning the "I Can't Breathe" t-shirt during warm-ups, his voice is often heard loud and clear. But James certainly has not been the only audible dissident.[5]

The end of 2014 saw a resurgence of black-athlete activism following an epidemic of killings of unarmed black men without subsequent accountability. After the ruling to not indict officer Darren Wilson in the shooting death of Ferguson teen Michael Brown, protests erupted throughout the St. Louis-area neighborhood and soon spread around the country.[6,7] Members of the St. Louis Rams, unable to partake in the citywide protests for various reasons, staged their own demonstration. Five members walked out on the field during pre-game introductions with their hands raised high in solidarity, symbolic of "hands up, don't shoot."[8] The former Olympian John Carlos, known for defiantly raising his black-gloved fist against U.S.-based racism, praised the St. Louis Rams for their insurrection. He stated, "They may be under contract to play, but greater than that, they have a right to care about humanity. . . . Asking them to 'shut up and play' is like asking a human being to be paint on a wall."[9]

That single incident sparked a larger crusade among black athletes who recognized their right to stand with the oppressed. Following the news that Eric Garner's killer would not be indicted as well, a few individual football and basketball players such as Detroit Lions running back Reggie Bush and Chicago Bulls guard Derrick Rose sported shirts embossed with the "I Can't Breathe" protest declaration.[10] This action spread to many more professional athletes like San Diego Chargers linebacker Melvin Ingram, Jacksonville Jaguars wide receivers Marqise

Lee and Ace Sanders, and Cleveland Browns cornerback Johnson Bademosi.[11,12] Soon entire teams, including the Brooklyn Nets, Cleveland Cavaliers, Sacramento Kings, Charlotte Hornets, and Phoenix Suns, were honoring the senseless slayings they witnessed as caught on tape and the persistent tribulations between white American law enforcement and the black community. These concerns, however, were not isolated to the professional athlete.

Collegiate programs like Notre Dame women's basketball and Georgetown men's basketball also involved themselves in the fray. And when students at the University of Maryland staged a "die-in" in protest of the Eric Garner decision, UMD football player Deon Long walked among them holding a sign that would define his generation. He asked, "Are we still *thugs* when you pay to watch us play?"[13] His question, followed by the emblematic hashtag #BlackLivesMatter, signified all that is wrong with U.S. race relations. Blacks are the center of this particular commercial entertainment enterprise, revered for their skill but ridiculed for their opinions and emotions. The black body is nothing more than an object of amusement for white delight that possesses little ability to reason outside of the *X*'s and *O*'s of the game; their presence is strictly for the purpose of entertaining the fan.

WHITE FOLKS PAY WHILE BLACK FOLKS PLAY: BLACK MUSCLE AS A BARGAINING CHIP

Against this backdrop of racial exploitation, black student-athletes are rediscovering their purpose beyond the sport. Black athletes today seek greater self-determination, realizing the value of their muscle as a bargaining tool in the demands for their rights. One such issue that remains essential to power and control is the national debate over whether Division I college athletes should be able to receive compensation for their highly regarded talent.

In a recent sit-down interview with *The Huffington Post*, President Obama indicated the need in the future for the NCAA to do a better job of taking care of the student-athlete, putting the responsibility on the college or university to afford greater protection to the athlete. For starters, he outlined a plan where these competitors receive health-care provisions, should they get injured while playing.[14] This may seem incredulous to most, but the reality is that not all student-athletes participating in the NCAA are medically covered by their school, and this includes scholarship athletes. Though the NCAA requires that each athlete have some form of health insurance before competing, it does not place that responsibility on the university. This means that an injured player is not only at risk for incurring his or her own medical costs, but that student also runs the risk of losing both a scholarship and a place on the team.[15,16] Obama further detailed that what bothers him about college sports is that "coaches getting paid millions of dollars, athletic directors getting paid millions of dollars, the NCAA making huge amounts of money, and then some kid gets a tattoo or gets a free use of a car and suddenly they're banished."[17] The president, however, stopped short of calling the NCAA what it is, a band of thieves driven by white cupidity.

Typifying this point is the six-year legal ordeal involving a suit filed by former UCLA basketball star and lead plaintiff Ed O'Bannon on behalf of FBS football and Division I men's basketball players against the NCAA over the commercialized use of names, images, and likenesses (NILs). O'Bannon and the nineteen other current and former collegiate athletes argued that upon graduation, student-athletes should be eligible for remuneration for the millions, if not billions, of dollars made by the NCAA in the use of athletes' images and names. In this case, funds were acquired when the NCAA contracted with electronic game giant EA Sports for their college basketball videogame.

Judge Claudia Wilken recently ruled in favor of the plaintiffs in federal court. She agreed with O'Bannon et al. that the NCAA's rules, "unreasonably restrain trade in the market for certain educational and athletic opportunities offered by Division I schools."[18] At the time, student-athletes could not receive any monies above a full grant-in-aid[19] scholarship based upon their athletic abilities, but this ruling would allow schools to "fund stipends covering the cost of attendance for those student-athletes"[20] based on a portion of revenue the school earns from athlete promotion. In addition, Judge Wilken's solutions would permit the establishment of a deferred compensation–like plan for student-athletes over a period of their eligible playing time. For example, each year the student-athlete remains academically eligible, they would earn an equivalent of one NIL that is limited to no less than five thousand dollars per year of eligibility, to be acquired following their academic stint.[21] Not only will the student-athlete leave the university with degree in hand, but also a small nest egg to begin the next chapter in their new life, lifting many of them to a fresh start out of poverty. Of course, the NCAA has appealed this ruling, vowing to fight on as they believe that payouts for the student-athletes compromises the mission of the university and cheapens the value of a college education (irrespective of the evidence that the "payout" referred to in this legal battle is only after the athlete fulfills his obligation with the member institution). But as of now, any school within the Big Five conferences has the opportunity to offer an athlete up to two thousand dollars above grant-in-aid to cover cost of living expenses.[22]

On the heels of this ongoing deliberation came an unexpected ruling in 2014 by the National Labor Relations Board (NLRB) allowing the Northwestern University football players to be considered university employees and, hence, eligible to unionize.[23] Kain Colter, former Northwestern quarterback and current spokesman for the team's efforts to unionize, has ensured that monetary compensation is not their main concern (but instead health-care coverage, academic assurances, etc.[24]). This ruling was appealed by the NCAA and has since been overturned.[25] But it still raises the decades-old question—should players receive financial payment for their role in a multibillion-dollar industry?

Those on one side of the debate believe that paying players would ruin the sanctity of college athletics. The NCAA responded to the initial NLRB announcement by stating, "This union-backed attempt to turn student-athletes into employees undermines the purpose of college: an education. Student-athletes are not employees, and their participation in college sports is voluntary."[26] The belief here is that players should compete solely for the love of the game where paying them would bring about an end to the innocence of their youth and change the dynamics between the players, coaches, and other stakeholders.

On the other hand, critics point to the $10.8 billion deal that the NCAA signed with CBS/Turner Broadcasting for the NCAA basketball tournament alone.[27] Billions of dollars are made through lucrative TV contracts, corporate sponsorships, and apparel sales. The high-revenue sports of football and men's basketball deliver the bulk of return on investments that then provide the resources to fund other entire sports programs on college campuses. Perhaps not coincidentally, African American males are overrepresented in both of these sports.

THE REALITIES OF TOPPLING SYSTEMIC WHITE RACISM

The NCAA's rationale has been publicly called into question, as Mary Willingham, former Tar Heel reading tutor and whistleblower to the UNC-Chapel Hill scandal, pointed out the hypocrisy in one of their primary arguments involving the integration of education and athletics. She notes that the student-athletes "did not have equal access to a real education because the academic experience for athletes is separate and unequal. They arrived unprepared and remained unprepared because of institutional priorities."[28]

Many black student-athletes come from neighborhoods where they often receive a less-than-adequate primary school education.[29,30] Kunjufu found that teachers stop caring about the learning and advancement of black boys as early as four years of age, and the boys, therefore, effectively stop caring about school around the end of elementary school.[31] This fact is further evident in the numerous publications that highlight their lack of academic preparedness.[32,33] If the school, then, chooses to accept the athlete despite low academic performance (secondary to a racist and stratified public education system) in favor of their physical talent, the university must bare the responsibility of effectively bridging the gap for students to secure a road to achievement.

Currently across the United States, PWIs are engaged in the act of sabotage by refusing to instruct black male students. Instead, they offer a mock degree as a consolation in exchange for the use of their bodies. The university has an obligation to prepare these men and women for their place in the workforce outside of sports. Moreover, it is their educational mission to help these students achieve the goal of degree attainment and living the "American Dream" of a fading middle-class existence. Short of that—presuming there is not enough time, manpower, or resources to fulfill the agreement to provide these young men with a legitimate prospect to earn a viable education and degree—these corporations (universities) must consider adequate restitution.

Higher education has been entrusted with this public confidence, yet has failed to live up to the promises for black male student-athletes.

The irony has not escaped college sports that these students, a vast majority from urban landscapes, stand the most to gain from the reform. Like so many white institutions and organizations in U.S. society, race prejudice and discriminatory practices of alienation and exclusion abound, constantly rearing their ugly heads, dashing career aspirations and extinguishing hope. The only difference here is that these athletes hold a good/service that PWIs can use for their own commodification and "personal" gain, and thus, the institution of sport has found ways to prostitute these young men and women.

College athletics for many black males is a means to an end with the primary goal of making it to the pros. This process starts at a young age for black boys. Growing up in a cycle of scarcity, abuse, and despair, many young black men long for a shot at the professional ranks where their hopes and dreams of gaining financial independence for them and their families might finally be realized. In reality, less than 2 percent of college athletes are drafted into the NFL and NBA.[34] The alternative reward is the chance at a free education from the ivory tower. This is undoubtedly enticing to the casual observer. But to the seventeen-, eighteen-, and nineteen-year-olds from deprived settings, a college education is impractical and an improbable recompense for a multitude of reasons.

This reality, however, does not detour the athletic departments at PWIs from combing the nation for high school prep stars to recruit for their team. The black student-athlete must exercise wisdom and prudence in deliberations of where to attend college with the best chances to play with an eye toward degree completion. To start, these men should also pay close attention to the history of race relations on a campus, whether public or private. Additionally, the player graduation rate for black athletes is a good indicator of where an institution's priorities lie.

The psychological energy (stress-induced pathology) that black student-athletes expend when they attend a PWI can be extraordinarily burdensome and dissatisfying for their social and intellectual development.[35] When combined with the objectification of their bodies, they leave the ivy tower battered, bruised, and empty-handed. These athletes learn to survive such austere, white-dominated spaces by organizing for change. Their strength lies in their numbers, as a special class of oppressed beings that predominate in the most profitable of college sports. Unionizing would allow student-athletes to negotiate with the university for provisions unique to them and specific to their needs, which is precisely why the NCAA fought this ruling so hard. Such advocacy on the part of the student-athletes can have positive benefits for the health of black males, reversing the effects of mental health decline and potentially delaying the onset of chronic disease later in life. This is what Harry Edwards, John Carlos, and others envisioned for the next generation. As Carlos expressed in his sentiments during the recent protests, "I remember saying in 1968, you think I'm bad, just wait until this new generation comes out. I feel like that new generation is here at last."[36]

STRATEGIES FOR CHANGE AT BYU

How do we reverse the trend whereby black students often feel relegated on predominately white campuses? The entrenched nature of systemic white racism makes improvement difficult to secure, particularly when the lust for capital is intertwined with furthering the cause of humanity. Predominately white colleges and universities actively seek out, recruit, and rely on young men of color to win contests, only to see them depart empty-handed. Such a blight upon collegiate athletics makes it evident that the attendant white racial frame undergirds our racist society and accents the institutionalization of policies, practices, procedures, and methods that are utterly discriminatory despite being cloaked in the language of post-racial tranquility.

Reform is not a guarantee. In truth, the athletes are the catalysts that initiate the movement by using their worth as a collective whole to force the hand of those in power. Though the athletes are the true change agents agitating for a better tomorrow for those that follow, systematic remedies only occur once stakeholders are affected in the pocketbook and, in turn, invest in efforts to restructure the academy in ways that meet the needs of black students and other disenfranchised populations. The NCAA as a governing body as well as college and university presidents, provosts, trustees, and other role players have the capacity to improve collegiate athletics and must do so by calling for greater accountability in the process. This begins with transparency. The NCAA has an obligation to find cogent ways to aid prospective student-athletes and their families to better vet universities and colleges, not just for wild-eyed dreams of televised miracles and the widespread exposure to pro scouts, but for ways they can advance the likelihood of graduation and a new sense of purpose after college.

There are several ways in which BYU can facilitate substantial improvement of black life on its campus. One important tool would be to collect and maintain accurate demographics on its student body and faculty. These numbers are serviceable for prospective black and brown students, who would likely be more sensitive to seeing faces on campus that resemble their own. The university administration can also use this data to track institutional effectiveness in efforts to increase racial and ethnic diversity, improve the graduation rates, and bring about other positive endeavors. As a private university, however, BYU has a voluntary system in place that enables students to self-report if they choose. The result is that only limited information is available on racial diversity and equity throughout the campus. But as the TIDES report concluded, BYU has a less-than-stellar record of degree completion for black student-athletes to tout as a selling point.[37] It is imperative that BYU maintain open and unconcealed records on the graduation trends between black and white players as there is no other way to quantitatively assess change without a plan of action and measurable benchmarks. Dieter F. Uchtdorf, second counselor of the LDS First Presidency, recently told a gathering of church history enthusiasts in the Salt Lake City conference center that as Mormons, "we always need to remember that transparency and openness keep us clear of the negative side effects of secrecy or the cliché of faith-promoting rumors. Jesus taught the Jews, 'Then you will know the truth, and the truth will set you free.'" He further stated, "Truth and transparency complement each other."[38] Without a commitment to accountability through full disclosure—some semblance of transparency in their own right—impartiality can never fully be realized at BYU.

Additionally, BYU must create an inclusive environment for students of color as they strive to prepare these young people to be productive members of society. Non-LDS black students who attend BYU have no additional programming or other interventions that aim to improve their overall experience and atmosphere on campus. Instead, the presumed strategy for success of these black guests is to convert them to the Mormon faith as an acceptable means of adapting. In reality, these young men need caring advocates who can relate to their plight and act as a sounding board. BYU must get more creative and accepting rather than secretive and punitive. Black males need a multifactorial approach to feeling less of an outsider at the community level, the university level (both athletically and academically), and at the interpersonal level with discussions surrounding morality and the application of the honor code.

One way that BYU can create this kind of environment wherein the students of color feel included and validated is by building a coalition with members of the local black community in Provo. In addition, BYU could extend a lifeline to the local black churches in the Salt Lake valley to assist in providing stable mentors for their players while on campus. Whether locals or transplants from other regions of the country for school, work, and/or faith, these extended hands may be able to relate to black players who are outsiders in the community, allowing them to establish relationships of trust beyond the walls of the university.

Moreover, former players acting as mentors can especially offer valid advice as to the inner workings of the honor code and provide clarity and specificity to the rules, especially regarding recourse if the statutes (including religious ones) are violated. Even if the player does not subscribe to the principle behind the infraction, they are still subjected to the same (if not more) punitive measures. At the end of the day, BYU is a private university and has more onerous moral requirements for its students, the vast majority of whom belong to the very faith that established the proscriptions. Prospective non-LDS student-athletes must recognize that, for Mormons, religious conviction trumps what may seem to be unreasonable requirements. But with the aid of alumni, the nonmembers will have the ability to navigate the system and circumvent pitfalls.

BYU and its athletic teams can support and encourage this process by establishing relationships with various graduates in the athlete's home city prior to their arrival on campus. Once players have signed their letters of intent, designated individuals should begin to formalize contact with the player and their family members. This buddy-system approach might help to ease the transition and culture shock for black players who grew up in an urban landscape naïve to the rules of white suburbia and the LDS culture.

Arguably, the singlehandedly most impactful undertaking that the university could have for these young men and women of color would be the institution of a volunteer sponsor-family program. This would benefit not only the student-athlete but also the athletic department and the university/community at-large as the students learn to traverse the potential minefields of the LDS stronghold. BYU would not be the first school to consider such a program. Former football player and graduate of the United States Naval Academy Lieutenant Commander Marlon Terrell discussed the enormous benefits of having a sponsor family in nearby Annapolis to help his adjustment to life away from home in Dallas, Texas. The Naval Academy offers this program to all its midshipmen who live outside of a thirty-mile radius. In a way not dissimilar to the culture shock on BYU's campus, Commander Terrell encountered life in the navy culture as rigorous and stringent, but also positively life changing. "Having a support system in close proximity, yet removed from the daily grind of football and the Academy was highly advantageous and influential on my life. And at the same time, those families benefited from having a black male role model around their young sons."[39]

When African Americans of differing faith traditions arrive at the sanitized Pleasantville-like campus of BYU, they are at a clear disadvantage. A sponsor family within the community that is relatable to their circumstances would serve as mentors for guidance and support.[40] Where LDS student-athletes already have a stand-in family through their locally assigned ward and stake affiliation, non-Mormon student-athletes can undertake the same sense of community and family in a home away from home with a sponsor family. The athletic department can then establish an ad hoc committee where such host families might be able to voice their concerns or simply advocate for the student in an official capacity as a designated spokesperson. When it comes to the business of the honor code, a sponsor who can vouch as a character witness would go a long way for these young students if they were to run afoul of university policy with an ill-advised mistake.

In addition to community inclusion, the university itself must consider the impact that black faculty and coaches have on young men and women of color and their role in reducing racial bias. Research analysts recently studied the effects of racial bias among professors at elite universities. The sample included more than six thousand professors across an array of fields at both public and private institutions. In the experiment, fictitious students sent identical letters to faculty seeking mentors to discuss graduate school opportunities. The investigators first tested racialized and gendered stereotypical names and randomly assigned them to faculty members. European-sounding names like Brad Anderson were used for white males while black-sounding names such as Keisha Thomas were used for black women. Raj Singh was one of the names assigned for an Indian male. Mei Chen was a Chinese female and Juanita Martinez, a Latina female. The researchers found across the board a significant gap in the response rate of faculty members mainly at private institutions (like BYU), who were much more responsive to white male students than other groupings of students.[41]

The BYU athletic department must surely grasp by now that black players need other blacks in key roles all across campus. In an environment where religious identity is overwhelming and stifling, BYU can straightaway hire more coaches, staff, administrators, and faculty of color who reflect the needs of black student-athletes and other black students on campus. Currently at Brigham Young, the hiring process is done quite differently from the democratic process at most liberal arts schools. A candidate is recommended for hire by a search committee, but unlike other schools that recieve the stamp of approval from the dean of the department, the final decision on faculty hiring at BYU is made by the higher authority at church headquarters. So much depends on the applicant's background, church affiliation, research interests, or other potential controversial matters that threathen the image-conscious faith. Hence, given the conditions and hiring practices at BYU joined with the church's racist history, racial diversity in the faculty seems overly ambitious. Without resolving to restructure the organization in ways that make the academic work environement less hostile to divergent opinions and viewpoints, the effort to add more faculty of color as well as coaches, counselors, academic advisors, and even the honor code office personnel is futile.

BYU is an equal opportunity employer with an unspoken rule of hiring, to the extent possible, only active members of the Mormon faith who have not been led astray by the "philosophies of men." Although this is their right, this action serves to undermine the very notion of a "liberal democratic education" as it impacts student learning while at the same time re-centering market policies, values, and practices that privilege white epistemology. BYU students are taught instructional material that does not stray too far from the seam lest they be deemed "out-of-step" with the Lord. Unfortunately, BYU has been under fire before for violations of academic freedom wherein scores of intellectuals were removed from their teaching positions. The anti-intellectualism, policing of faculty scholarship, and the general attitude of surveillance on campus make it difficult to teach courses that demand critical dialogue and exchange about the world students inhabit. But there is no better way to understand and be transformed by the experiences and histories of raced peoples in North America and Western society than to have a classroom full of students who engage one another, deconstructing the white dominant narrative by contextualizing race within the greater society.

The recent paradigm shift among today's college athletes regarding their inherent worth and value in the marketplace of brawn must be harnessed against the interest of a self-serving and white-controlled sports-industrial complex. It cannot not be assumed that greater minority representation at a PWI is, in and of itself, evidence of progress; to the contrary, organizational restructuring is paramount for any PWI to address the legacy of its racial past. The Utah-based school comes with a distinct set of guidelines that deserve to be valued. But the incoming athletes deserve the opportunity to examine the university for what it truly is in all its religiously codified stipulations. As long as BYU and other Division I big-time college sports schools are recruiting black students to campus, the academy has the same responsibility to ensure their success as it would all other students. It is incumbent upon the university to meet black and brown students on their own terms and refrain from imposing a particular unrealistic construct upon them.

THE ELUSIVENESS OF CHANGE AT BYU IN THE ERA OF "BLACK LIVES MATTER"

Thirty-seven years ago marked a significant shift in policy for the LDS church when it lifted its priesthood ban against black males. Church authorities once claimed that black skin was a sign of God's displeasure with them according to various Mormon beliefs and interpretations of the Bible. These differing interpretations of why blacks were denied the priesthood in the Mormon faith would serve as justification for LDS bigotry for decades. The vestiges of this tainted past remain a cornerstone of Mormon religious thought. In truth, black folk have never been elevated as a group on the priority list for the LDS church as referenced throughout its history. Currently, there is no visible African American leadership at the highest levels of church leadership, neither in the elite Quorum of the Twelve nor the First Quorum of the Seventy. And since 1978, only two blacks (both Africans) have ever been called to either of these two quorums, both supremely regarded positions.[42] This glaring omission serves to undermine the proscribed claim that the LDS church has moved beyond the Curse of Cain. The all-white-male Republican leadership (with an average age of eighty) has done very little throughout its racial history to ameliorate the damage done to the black community.[43]

Hence, when the recent slugfest broke out at the conclusion of the 2014 Miami Bowl between the predominately black University of Memphis Tigers football team and the majority white BYU Cougars, it served to mark just how little progress America and its native Mormon faith have made in the name of race relations. The melee seemed more than just post-game angst, but more emblematic of a lifetime of racial animus defined by the relationship that the Mormon faith initiated and maintained with black folk as their spiritual "Other." Cheap shots were thrown and three-on-one duals ensued on live cable TV for sports enthusiasts to glean. But as if driven by a counterforce, the Tigers emerged from the contest that night victorious, beating BYU 55–48 in their first bowl win since 2005—a triumph for the black players symbolic of their battle over the continual oppression they encounter at the hands of whites.[44]

When it comes to BYU football and men's basketball, recruiting any significant number of black male athletes appears to be a thing of the past. Because the honor code has been such a lightning rod of controversy at BYU, the athletic department has resorted to a "grow your own" athlete mentality through natural increase or the practice of transracial adoption. But when the coaching staffs head out on recruiting trips, targeting non-Mormon men from inner-city neighborhoods to boost the playing power of their football and basketball teams, they have a duty to avoid any misrepresentation of themselves for both their own sake and the sake of the student-athlete. The dubious Mormon record on race relations is considerably troubling and should give any

African American student-athlete pause before they consider attending the church-owned school.

Black male student-athletes have long withstood a legacy of overt discrimination at PWIs, having been excluded from them longer than given opportunities to matriculate.[45] BYU is representative of most PWIs nationwide, but when the racism is steeped in religiosity, the patterned behavior is much more difficult to unlearn. What sets the Mormon school apart from other PWIs is its repeated use of God as the source of bigotry to sidestep its role as men and women who profess Christ with their lips. Their actions reveal that their hearts are far from doing what is right in His name and mentoring these young adults who are in most need of guidance, acceptance, and unconditional love. And as it happens, these are also brothers and sisters who have been discriminated against by the Church for almost two centuries. To then speak of God as a means to justify race-based mistreatment constitutes the very definition of blasphemy.

If BYU plans to maintain an active roster of black male student-athletes, it has to reevaluate its current honor code policy to ensure fairness and equanimity across the board and further avoid even the hint of racial bias. In just the last twenty-five years (since 1991), eighty-four players have been suspended or dismissed from the BYU football or basketball team. Approximately 80 percent of the disciplined players were people of color, almost 60 percent of them black. Given the history of the revolving door of black male student-athletes at BYU (since they started in 1972), there has yet to be any implementation of sincere enough reform to effectuate measurable improvements. BYU has the ability to be a positive and supportive environment for these young men, teaching them how to become successful and productive citizens. But in addition to winning in the sporting arena, they must develop a reputation for winning in the classroom much like at Vanderbilt, Duke, Stanford, and other private schools that have an applaudable black-male graduation rate.[46] The halfhearted approach they have in place now cannot sustain itself. And until corrections are made, the recommendation for BYU would be to cease all recruitment of young black men and women for the protection of their fragile and developing mental and emotional well-being.

NOTES

INTRODUCTION

1. Picca, L. H., and Feagin, J. (2007). *Two-faced racism: Whites in the backstage and frontstage.* New York: Routledge.

2. Hawks Insider. (2014, September 7). Hawks owner Bruce Levenson statement regarding team sale. Retrieved from http://www.nba.com/hawks/hawks-owner-bruce-levenson-statement-regarding-team-sale

3. Hawks Insider. (2014, September 7). A copy of Bruce Levenson's e-mail. Retrieved from http://www.nba.com/hawks/copy-bruce-levensons-email

4. He further stated that many blacks do not have disposable income to spend on season tickets or additional amenities such as food and beverages at games. While this is presumptive, particularly with a large professional black population in Atlanta, there is a sobering truth in his claims. Blacks are three times more likely than whites to be in poverty in this country.

5. Fleming, J. (1984). *Blacks in college: A comparative study of students' success in black and in white institutions.* San Francisco: Jossey-Bass.

6. Kareem Nittle, N. (n.d.). How four Christian denominations in the U.S atoned for racism. *About News*. Retrieved from http://racerelations.about.com/od/historyofracerelations/a/How-Four-Christian-Denominations-In-The-U-S-Atoned-For-Racism.htm

7. In December 2013, the Church issued a statement acknowledging its racist past. This is discussed more thoroughly in Chapter 5. But it should be made clear that there was no official declaration that we have seen with other revelations. (The First Presidency usually signs official declarations.) And furthermore, the Church still did not offer up any such apology.

8. Feagin, J. R. (2009). *The white racial frame: Centuries of racial framing and counter-framing*. New York: Routledge.

9. Lakoff, G., and Johnson, M. (1980). *Metaphors we live by*. Chicago and London: University of Chicago Press.

10. Lakoff, G., and Johnson, M. (1999). *Philosophy in the flesh: The embodied mind and its challenges to western thought.* New York: Basic Books.

11. Smith, D. T. (2013). Actual and symbolic prison in black male life in US public schools. Manuscript submitted for publication.

12. Boccato, G., Capozza, D., Falvo, R., and Durante, F. (2008). The missing link: Ingroup, outgroup and the human species. *Social Cognition, 26*, 224–34. doi: 10.1521/soco.2008.26.2.224.

13. Pickler, N. (2015, March 6). On eve of Selma tribute, Obama says Ferguson probe exposed broken, racially biased system. *U.S. News & World Report*. Retrieved from http://www.usnews.com/news/politics/articles/2015/03/06/obama-holding-town-hall-at-historically-black-college

14. Hawks Insider, A copy of Bruce Levenson's e-mail.

15. Goff, P. A., Eberhardt, J. L., Williams, M. J., and Jackson, M. C. (2008). Not yet human: Implicit knowledge, historical dehumanization, and contemporary consequences. *Journal of Personality and Social Psychology, 94*, 292–306. doi: 10.1037/0022-3514.94.2.292.

16. Schwarz, A. (2007, May 2). A study of N.B.A. sees racial bias in calling fouls. *New York Times*. Retrieved from http://www.nytimes.com/2007/05/02/sports/basketball/02refs.html?pagewanted=all&_r=1&

17. Vedantam, S. (2012, April 26). Power (dis)play? Teams in black draw more penalties. NPR. Retrieved from http://www.npr.org/2012/04/26/151383136/power-dis-play-teams-in-black-draw-more-penalties

18. Feagin, J. (2006). *Systemic racism: A theory of oppression*. New York: Routledge, p. 27–28.

19. Psychosis is described by the mental health profession as a "loss of contact with reality."

20. Cheng, Y., Yang, C.-Y., Lin, C.-P., Lee, P.-L., and Decety, J. (2008). The perception of pain in others suppresses somatosensory oscillations: A magnetoencephalography study. *Neuroimage, 40*[4], 1833–1840.

21. Mujcic, R., Frijters, P. (2013, March). Still not allowed on the bus: It matters if you're black or white! Retrieved from http://ftp.iza.org/dp7300.pdf

22. Feagin, *The white racial frame*.

1. THE MEANING OF SPORT IN THE POPULAR IMAGINATION

1. Cohen, W. B. (1980). *The French encounter with Africans: White responses to Blacks, 1530–1880*. Bloomington, IN: Indiana University Press, p. 222.

2. Goldenberg, D. M. (2003). *The curse of Ham: Race and slavery in early Judaism, Christianity, and Islam*. Princeton, NJ: Princeton University Press, p. 2.

3. Cole, C. L., and Andrews, D. L. (1996). Look—it's NBA showtime! Visions of race in the popular imaginary. In N. K. Denzin (Ed.), *Cultural Studies: A Research Annual, 1*(1), 141–81.

4. 53% say pro sports have helped race relations in U.S. (2013, April 19). *Rasmussen Reports*. Retrieved from http://www.rasmussenreports.com/public_content/lifestyle/general_lifestyle/april_2013/53_say_pro_sports_have_helped_race_relations_in_u_s

5. Hartmann, D. (2000). Rethinking the relationship between sport and race in American culture: Golden ghettos and contested terrain. *Sociology of Sport Journal, 17*, 229–53.

6. Ferber, A. (2007). The construction of Black masculinity: White supremacy now and then. *Journal of Sport and Social Issues, 31*(1), 11–24. Quoted on p. 19.

7. Kane, M. J. (1996). Media coverage of the post Title IX female athlete: A feminist analysis of sport, gender, and power. *Duke Journal of Gender Law & Policy*. Quoted on p. 95. Retrieved from http://scholarship.law.duke.edu/cgi/viewcontent.cgi?article=1225&context=djglp

8. Kane, Media coverage of the post Title IX female athlete, 97–98.

9. Douglass, D. D. (2002, November–December). To be young, gifted, Black and female: A meditation on the cultural politics at play in representations of Venus and Serena Williams. *Sociology of Sport Online, 5*. Quoted on p. 9. Retrieved from http://physed.otago.ac.nz/sosol/v5i2/v5i2_3.html

10. Thompson, M., II. (2010, July 20). Golden State Warriors sign ex-Palo Alto High star Jeremy Lin. *San Jose Mercury News*. Retrieved from http://www.mercurynews.com/bay-area-news/ci_15562510?nclick_check=1

11. Associated Press. (2012, February 17). Hornets slow down Jeremy Lin, snap Knicks' winning streak. ESPN. Retrieved from http://sports.espn.go.com/nba/recap?gameId=320217018

12. Brennan, M. (2011, January 12). Jeremy Lin using assignment to his advantage. *NBA Development League: News*. Retrieved from http://www.nba.com/dleague/news/lin_110112.html

13. 63 former NBA D-League players on 2009 opening night rosters. (2009, October 27). *NBA Development League: News*. Retrieved from http://www.nba.com/dleague/news/nba_rosters_2009.html

14. Duncan, A. (2012, April 18). The world's 100 most influential people: 2012. Jeremy Lin: point guard. *Time*. Retrieved from http://www.time.com/time/specials/packages/article/0,28804,2111975_2111976_2111945,00.htm

15. Feagin, J. R. (2009). *The white racial frame: Centuries of racial framing and counter-framing*. New York: Routledge, p.13.

16. Ding, K. (2010, September 3). Lin is the NBA's Asian-American inspiration. *Orange County Register*. Retrieved from http://www.ocregister.com/sports/lin-264953-nba-american.html

17. Asian athletes limited by genes or nurture? (2013, April 12). *GoldSea*. Retrieved from http://goldsea.com/Air/Issues/Physiques/physiques_20514.html

18. Gregory, S. (2012, February 27). Linsanity! *Time*. Retrieved from http://www.time.com/time/magazine/article/0,9171,2106983,00.html

19. Harvard University Athletics. (2010). Harvard men's basketball—Jeremy Lin bio. Retrieved from http://www.gocrimson.com/sports/mbkb/2009-10/bios/Jeremy_Lin_Bio

20. Janowitz, N. (2012, March 9). After backing a dark horse, Lin's agent is riding high. *New York Times*. Retrieved from http://www.nytimes.com/2012/03/10/sports/basketball/jeremy-lins-agent-roger-montgomery-is-riding-high.html?pagewanted=all

21. Bolch, B. (2012, February 13). Jeremy Lin's high school coach says race hindered opportunities. *Los Angeles Times*. Retrieved from http://latimesblogs.latimes.com/sports_blog/2012/02/jeremy-lins-high-school-coach-says-race-hindered-opportunities.html

22. Gregory, S. (2009, December 21). Harvard's hoops star is Asian. Why's that a problem? *Time*. Retrieved from http://www.time.com/time/magazine/article/0,9171,1953708,00.html

23. Hartlep, N. D. (2012). Harvard to the NBA: Deconstructing Jeremy Lin as a "Model Minority." *Korean Quarterly, 15*(3), 18.

24. Petersen, W. (1966, January 6). Success story: Japanese American style. *New York Times Magazine,* 20–21, 33, 36, 38, 40–41, 43.

25. Jeremy Lin goes from Harvard to the NBA. (2011, March 10). *CNN*. Retrieved from http://am.blogs.cnn.com/2011/03/10/jeremy-lin-goes-from-harvard-to-the-nba/

26. Greenberg, C. (2012, February 20). Jeremy Lin ESPN interview: Racism, Kim Kardashian, apartment among topics with Rachel Nichols. *Huffington Post*. Retrieved from http://www.huffingtonpost.com/2012/02/20/jeremy-lin-espn-interview-racism-kardashian-video_n_1288875.html?ref=sports

27. DeJohn, I., and Kennedy, H. (2012, February 20). Jeremy Lin headline slur was "honest mistake," fired ESPN editor Anthony Federico claims. *New York Daily News*. Retrieved from http://www.nydailynews.com/entertainment/tv-movies/jeremy-lin-slur-honest-mistake-fired-espn-editor-anthony-federico-claims-article-1.1025566

28. Ding, Lin is the NBA's.

29. Radovich, P. Jr., and Devine, L. F. (2013, April 7). Linsanity: Jeremy Lin's rise to stardom. *60 Minutes*. Retrieved from http://www.cbsnews.com/video/watch/?id=50144360n

30. Hoberman, J. (1997). *Darwin's athletes: How sport has damaged Black America and preserved the myth of race*. New York: Houghton Mifflin.

31. Demby, G. (2014, April 2). Why aren't Asian-Americans getting their "one shining moment"? NPR. Retrieved from http://www.npr.org/blogs/codeswitch/2014/04/02/297287958/why-arent-asian-americans-getting-their-one-shining-moment

32. Lapchick, R. (2002, May 1). Asian Americans athletes: Past, present and future. ESPN. Retrived from http://espn.go.com/gen/s/2002/0430/1376346.html

33. Edwards, H. (2000). Crisis of Black athletes on the eve of the 21st century. *Society*, *37*, 9–13.

34. Gibbs, J. T. (1984, January). Black adolescent and youth: An endangered species. *American Journal of Orthopsychiatry*, *54*(1), 6–21. doi:10.1111/j.1939-0025.1984.tb01472.x

35. Sailes, G. (1987). A socioeconomic explanation of Black sports participation patterns. *The Western Journal of Black Studies*, *11*(4), 164–67.

36. Meanwhile, the underrepresentation of Asians in these same sports leaves the stereotype that Asians are athletically inferior. Ironically, but not so surprising, when Jeremy Lin was named to the first-team all-state in California, he received no Division I scholarship offers. Thus, the self-fulfilling prophecy perpetuates the stereotype.

37. The poverty level for a family of one is an annual income of $11,490, while the poverty level for a family of four is an income of $23,550 per year. U.S. Department of Health & Human Services. (2013). Office of the Assistant Secretary for Planning and Evaluation: 2013 Poverty Guidelines. Retrieved from http://aspe.hhs.gov/poverty/13poverty.cfm

38. Lapchick, R., Hippert, A., Rivera, S., and Robinson, J. (2013, June 25). *The 2013 racial and gender report card: National Basketball Association*. Retrieved from the Institute for Diversity and Ethics in Sport website: http://www.tidesport.org/RGRC/2013/2013_NBA_RGRC.pdf

39. Lapchick, R., Beahm, D., Nunes, G., and Rivera-Casiano, S. (2013, October 22). *The 2013 racial and gender report card: National Football*

League. Retrieved from the Institute for Diversity and Ethics in Sport website: http://www.tidesport.org/RGRC/2013/2013_NFL_RGRC.pdf

40. O'Reilly, K. B. (2013, February 25). Black men increasingly hard to find in medical schools. *American Medical News*. Retrieved from http://www.amednews.com/article/20130225/profession/130229975/2/

41. Goldsmith, P. A. (2003). Race relations and racial patterns in school sports participation. *Sociology of Sport Journal, 20*, 147–71.

42. Beamon, K., and Messer, C. (2014). Professional sports experiences as contested racial terrain. *Journal of African American Studies, 18*(2), 181–91. doi:10.1007/s12111-013-9261-6.

43. Harrison, C. K. (2000). Black athletes at the millennium. *Society, 37*(3), 35–39.

44. Feagin, J. R. (2001). *Racist America: Roots, current realities, and future reparations*. New York: Routledge.

45. Feagin, J. R. (2006). *Systemic racism: A theory of oppression*. New York: Routledge.

46. Therborn, G. (2013). *The killing fields of inequality*. Cambridge, UK: Polity Press.

47. Foucault, M. (1977). *Discipline and punish: The birth of the prison* (A. Sheridan, Trans.). New York: Vintage Books.

48. Foucault, M. (1980). *Power/knowledge: Selected interviews and other writings: 1972–1977* (C. Gordon, L. Marshall, J. Mepham, K. Soper, Trans.). New York: Pantheon.

49. Mercer, K. (1992). "1968": Periodizing postmodern politics and identity. In L. Grossberg, C. Nelson, and P. A. Treichler (Eds.), *Cultural studies* (pp. 424–38). New York: Routledge.

50. Carrington, B., and McDonald, I. (2002). Sport, racism and inequality. *Sociology, 11*, 8–13.

51. Gallup. (2013). Gallup historical trends—Religion. Retrieved from http://www.gallup.com/poll/1690/religion.aspx#1

52. Maranise, A. M. J. (2013). Superstition and religious ritual: An examination of their effects and utlilization in sport. *The Sport Psychologist, 27*, 83–91.

53. Quoted in Jona, I. N., and Okou, F. T. (2013). Sports and religion. *Asian Journal of Management Science and Education, 2*(1), 46–54, p. 49.

54. Mandel, S. (2009, August 27). With one year left, Tebow well positioned to become all-time best. *Sports Illustrated*. Retreived from http://sportsillustrated.cnn.com/2009/writers/stewart_mandel/08/27/tim-tebow/

55. Richardson, A. (2009, April 27). Kiper: Tebow not an NFL-caliber quarterback. *Tampa Tribune*. Retrieved from http://tbo.com/sports/colleges/kiper-tebow-not-an-nfl-caliber-quarterback-93629

56. Schefter, A. (2010, February 22). Tebow to unveil new delivery at pro day. ESPN. Retrieved from http://sports.espn.go.com/nfl/draft10/news/story?id=4935351

57. Matuszewski, E. (2010, April 23). Tebow, Bradford drafted in NFL first round; fellow QBs Clausen, McCoy wait. *Bloomberg*. Retrieved from http://www.bloomberg.com/news/2010-04-23/tebow-bradford-drafted-in-nfl-first-round-fellow-qbs-clausen-mccoy-wait.html

58. Pompei, D. (2009, January 12). Scouts: NFL doesn't know what to do with Tim Tebow. *Chicago Tribune*. Retrieved from http://articles.chicagotribune.com/2009-01-12/sports/0901110403_1_tebow-nfl-scouts-west-coast-offense

59. Pompei, D. (2010, April 7). Draft: Rating the quarterbacks. *Chicago Tribune*. Retrieved from http://articles.chicagotribune.com/2010-04-07/sports/ct-spt-0408-quarterbacks-nfl-draft--20100407_1_sam-bradford-nfl-draft-tim-tebow

60. Jones, L. (2011, September 30). Tim Tebow billboard urges Denver Broncos coach to change quarterbacks. *Denver Post*. Retrieved from http://www.denverpost.com/broncos/ci_19011687

61. Associated Press. (2010, May 5). Tebow leads April jersey sales. ESPN. Retrieved from http://sports.espn.go.com/nfl/news/story?id=5165547

62. Schuman, D. (2012, January 13). Wes Welker, Victor Cruz and Arian Foster prove there's value in undrafted players. *Athlon Sports*. Retrieved from http://www.athlonsports.com/nfl/wes-welker-victor-cruz-and-arian-foster-prove-theres-value-undrafted-players

63. Schuman, D., Wes Welker, Victor Cruz and Arian Foster prove there's value in undrafted players.

64. Trademark looks, moves in the NFL. (2013, February 27). *Sports Illustrated*. Retrieved from http://www.si.com/nfl/photos/2013/02/27trademark-looks,-moves-in-the-nfl, http://sportsillustrated.cnn.com/multimedia/photo_gallery/1008/nfl.trademark.looks/

65. Ted Haggard and James Dobson are both leaders of the Christian conservative movement. Dobson is the voice of the Christian right and self-proclaimed moral leader.

66. Brady, J. (2005, January 17). Colorado Springs a mecca for evangelical Christians. NPR. Retrieved from http://www.npr.org/templates/story/story.php?storyId=4287106

67. It should be noted though that Tim Tebow still received a standing ovation from the Philadelphia fan base when he came on the field for the Eagles as a fourth stringer in the 2015 NFL pre-season. He had not played NFL football in a year, and he had not been on any regular team roster in 2 years. That alone is evidence that his fame is more than his play.

68. Associated Press. (2011, October 11). Tim Tebow named starting QB, Brady Quinn "best boyfriend." CBS News. Retrieved from http://www.cbsnews.com/8301-31751_162-20118588-10391697.html

69. Shpigel, B. (2012, March 21). After hours of uncertainty, Jets complete deal for Tebow. *New York Times*. Retrieved from http://www.nytimes.com/2012/03/22/sports/football/jets-acquire-tebow-in-trade-with-broncos.html?pagewanted=all&_r=0

70. Krattenmaker, T. (2010). *Onward Christian athletes: Turning ballparks into pulpits and players into preachers*. Lanham, MD: Rowman & Littlefield.

71. Tim Tebow SUPER BOWL AD VIDEO: See Tebow TACKLE Mother Pam. (2010, April 9). *Huff Post Sports*. Retrieved from http://www.huffingtonpost.com/2010/02/07/tim-tebow-super-bowl-ad-v_n_436383.html

72. Blum, E. J., and Harvey, P. (2012). *The color of Christ: The son of God and the saga of race in America*. Chapel Hill, NC: University of North Carolina Press.

73. Goldenberg, *The curse of Ham*.

74. Jordan, W. (1968). *White over Black: American attitudes toward the Negro, 1550–1812.* Chapel Hill, NC: University of North Carolina Press.

75. Haynes, S. R. (2002). *Noah's curse: The biblical justification of American slavery*. New York: Oxford University Press.

76. Disparities between LDS men and women abound and appear to be growing while the rest of the nations' gender gap is narrowing. The reasons are multifactorial and have much to do with the level of education between the genders and traditional gender roles strongly encouraged and reinforced in the LDS faith. According to Heaton and Jacobson (2013), Mormon women in Utah have less education than their non-LDS counterparts in Utah. Heaton, T. B., and Jacobson, C. K. (2015). The social life of Mormons. Forthcoming in T. Givens and P. Barlow (Eds.), *Oxford Handbook on Mormonism.* Oxford University Press.

77. See Paul Reeve's seminal book, *Religion of a Different Color*, to understand how Mormons were initially racialized, as the media understood them to be in cahoots with abolitionists whether real or imagined. And like other peculiar ethnic or religious groups in U.S. society that looked to conform to mainstream practices, Mormons eventually metamorphosed and became "white." One way for an ethnic group to prove their "whiteness" is to persecute blacks. Reeve, P. W. (2015). *Religion of a different color: Race and the Mormon struggle for whiteness*. New York: Oxford University Press.

78. Smith, D. T. (2011, Fall). Dirty hands and unclean practice: How medical neglect and the preponderance of stress illustrates how medicine harms rather than helps. In D. T. Smith (Guest Ed.), *Journal of Black Masculinity—Special Issue: African Americans and Public Health,* 2(1), 11–34.

2. THE ORIGINS OF RACISM AND FRAMING

1. Rhoden, W. C. (2006). *Forty million dollar slaves: The rise, fall, and redemption of the Black athlete*. New York: Three Rivers Press, p. 6.

2. Mudimbe, V. Y. (1988). *The invention of Africa: Gnosis, philosophy and the order of knowledge*. Bloomington and Indianapolis: Indiana University Press.

3. Rodney, W. (1972). *How Europe underdeveloped Africa*. Washington, DC: Howard University Press, p. 22.

4. Montagu, A. (1997). *Man's most dangerous myth*. Walnut Creek, CA: AltaMira Press.

5. Fredrickson, G. M. (1971). *The Black image in the White mind: The debate on Afro-American character and destiny 1817–1914*. Wesleyan, MA: Wesleyan University Press.

6. Gould, S. J. (1996). *The mismeasure of man*. New York: W. W. Norton & Company.

7. Feagin, J. (2006). *Systemic racism: A theory of oppression*. New York: Routledge.

8. Cartwright, S. A. (1851). The disease and physical peculiarities of the Negro race (continued). *New Orleans Medical and Surgical Journal, 8*(1), 187–94.

9. Crais, C., and Scully, P. (2009). *Sara Baartman and the Hottentot Venus: A ghost story and a biography*. Princeton, NJ: Princeton University Press.

10. Witzig, R. (1996). The medicalization of race: Scientific legitimization of a flawed social construct. *Annals of Internal Medicine, 125*(8), 675–79.

11. Washington, H. A. (2006). *Medical apartheid: The dark history of medical experimentation on Black Americans from colonial times to the present*. New York: Harlem Moon.

12. Jordan, W. D. (1974). *The white man's burden*. New York: Oxford University Press, p. 6.

13. Jordan, *The white man's burden*, p. 33.

14. Smedley, A., and Smedley, B. D. (2012). *Races in North America: Origin and evolution of a worldview* (4th ed.). Boulder, CO: Westview Press.

15. Lovejoy, A. O. (1973). *The great chain of being: A study of the history of an idea*. Cambridge, MA: Harvard University Press. (Originally published in 1936.)

16. Bennett, L. J. (1993). *Before the Mayflower: A history of Black America* (6th ed.). New York: Penguin Books.

17. Stannard, E. D. (1992). *American holocaust: The conquest of the New World*. Oxford: Oxford University Press.

18. Mills, C. W. (1997). *The racial contract.* Ithaca, NY: Cornell University Press, p. 27.

19. Kelley, R. (1997). *Yo mama's disfunktional!* Boston: Beacon Press, p. 106.

20. Feagin, *Systemic racism*, p. 23.

21. Williams, C. (1987). *The destruction of Black civilization: Great issues of race from 4500 B.C. to 2000 A.D.* Chicago: Third World Press.

22. Marable, M. (2000). *How capitalism underdeveloped Black America.* Cambridge, MA: South End Press.

23. Stannard, *American holocaust.*

24. Johnson-Laird, P. N. (1986). *Mental models: Toward a cognitive science of language, inference, and consciousness.* Cambridge, MA: Harvard University Press.

25. In other words, we make sense of our external reality based in part on European and European American history as it has been presented and taught to us in public education. But we neglect to recognize that the history that we know has been orchestrated by the country's elites—historically, white male elites—who have chosen what is deemed "official knowledge" to be written down in the history books.

26. Harrison. L. (2001). Understanding the influence of stereotypes: Implications for the African American in sport and physical activity. *Quest, 53*(1).

27. Frijda, N. H. (1993). Moods, emotion episodes, and emotions. In M. Lewis and I. M. Haviland (Eds.), *Handbook of emotions* (pp. 381–403). New York: Guilford Press.

28. Burgdorf, J., Panksepp, J. (2006). The neurobiology of positive emotions. *Neuroscience & Biobehavioral Reviews, 30*(2), 173–87.

29. Ortony, A., and Turner, T. J. (1990). What's basic about basic emotions? *Psychological Review, 3,* 315–31.

30. Lakoff, G., and Johnson, M. (1999). *Philosophy in the flesh: The embodied mind and its challenges to western thought.* New York: Basic Books, p. 13.

31. hooks, b. (1992). Representing Whiteness in the Black imagination. In L. Grossberg, C. Nelson, and P.A. Treichler (Eds.), *Cultural studies* (pp. 338–46). New York: Routledge.

32. In Susan Harris O'Connor's book, *The Harris Narratives*, she eloquently illustrates one's various identity constructions and how they engage one another in what she describes as "converging mind constructs." Harris O'Connor, S. (2012). *The Harris narratives: An introspective study of a transracial adoptee.* Arlington, MA: The Pumping Station.

33. Feagin, J. R. (2010). *The white racial frame: Centuries of racial framing and counterframing.* New York: Routledge.

34. Feagin, *Systemic racism*, p. 25.

35. Blumenfeld, W. J. (2006). Christian privilege and the promotion of "secular" and not-so "secular" mainline Christianity in public schooling and in the larger society. *Equity & Excellence in Education, 39*, 195–200.

36. Lakoff, G., and Johnson, M. (1980). *Metaphors we live by*. Chicago and London: University of Chicago Press.

37. The probability of jumping social classes is extremely low. If it were more common, society would see poverty levels dropping and the percentage of middle-class people rising.

38. Hughes, R. T. (2003). *Myths America lives by*. Urbana and Chicago: University of Illinois Press.

39. Hargreaves, S. (2013). The myth of the American dream. *CNN Money*. Retrieved from http://money.cnn.com/2013/12/09/news/economy/america-economic-mobility/

40. Shapiro, T., Meschede, T., and Osoro, S. (2013). The roots of the widening racial wealth gap: Explaining the Black-White economic divide. *Institute on Assets and Social Policy*.

41. Voborníková, P. (2014). Divided we live: Racial and ethnic segregation in housing in the US. *Scientific Journal of Humanistic Studies, 6*(10).

42. Goldberg, D. T. (1993). *Racist culture: Philosophy and the politics of meaning*. Cambridge: Blackwell, p. 5.

43. Quoted in Pager, D. (2007). *Marked: Race, crime, and finding work in an era of mass incarceration*. Chicago: University of Chicago Press, p. 17.

44. Alexander, M. (2010). *The new Jim Crow: Mass incarceration in the age of colorblindness* . New York: The New Press.

45. Lovejoy, *The great chain of being*.

46. Honour, H. (1989). *The image of the Black in western art*, Vol. 4: From the American Revolution to World War I, part 1: Slaves and liberators. Cambridge, MA: Harvard University Press.

47. Gladwell, M. (2005). *Blink*. New York: Little Brown and Company.

48. Waytz, A., Hoffman, K. M., and Trawalter, S. (2014). A superhumanization bias in Whites' perceptions of Blacks. *Social Psychological and Personality Science*. doi:10.1177/1948550614553642.

49. Smith, D. T. (2011, Fall). Dirty hands and unclean practice: How medical neglect and the preponderance of stress illustrates how medicine harms rather than helps. In D. T. Smith (Guest Ed.), *Journal of Black Masculinity—Special Issue: African Americans and Public Health, 2*(1), 11–34.

50. Entman, R. M., and Rojecki, A. (2000). *The Black image in the White mind: Media and race in America*. Chicago: University of Chicago Press.

51. Witzig, The medicalization of race.

52. Waytz, Hoffman, and Trawalter, A superhumanization bias.

53. Smith D. T. (2004). Unpacking Whiteness in Zion: Some personal reflections and general observations. In N. G. Bringhurst, and D. T. Smith (Eds.), *Black and Mormon* (pp. 148–66). Urbana and Chicago: University of Illinois Press.

54. Smith, D. T. (2005, July). These house-Negroes still think we're cursed: Struggling against racism in the classroom. *Cultural Studies, 19*(4), 439–54.

55. Feagin, *Systemic racism.*

56. McIntosh, P. (1989, July/August). White privilege: Unpacking the invisible knapsack, *Peace and Freedom*, 10–12.

57. Picca, L. H., and Feagin, J. (2007). *Two-faced racism: Whites in the backstage and frontstage.* New York: Routledge, p. 9.

58. Feagin, J. R. (2012). *White party, the White government: Race, class and U.S. politics.* New York: Routledge, p. 6.

59. Picca and Feagin, *Two-faced racism*, pp. 12–13.

60. Feagin, *Systemic racism.*

61. Carmichael, S. and Hamilton, C. V. (1967). *Black power: The politics of liberation in America.* New York: Vintage Books, p. 3.

62. Domhoff, G. W. (2009). *Who rules America? Challenges to corporate and class dominance* (6th ed.). New York: McGraw-Hill.

63. Reed, E., Lawrence, D. A., Santana, M. C., Welles, C. S., Horsburgh, C. R., Silverman, J. G., Raj, A. (2014, February). Adolescent experiences of violence and relation to violence perpetration beyond young adulthood among an urban sample of Black and African American males. *Journal of Urban Health, 91*(1), 96–106.

64. Wines, M. (2014). Are police bigoted? Race and police shootings: Are Blacks targeted more? *New York Times*. Retrieved from http://www.nytimes.com/2014/08/31/sunday-review/race-and-police-shootings-are-blacks-targeted-more.html?_r=0

65. Wiggins, D. (1997). *Glory bound: Black athletes in White America*. Syracuse, NY: Syracuse University Press.

66. Zinn, D. (2008). *A people's history of sports in the United States: 250 years of politics, protest, people, and play*. New York and London: The New Press.

67. This book employs Feagin's eloquently written discussion on black, anti-racist counter-frames (see his book *The White Racial Frame*), which developed in part as a coping strategy against the realities of living in a hostile and racist context. The black counter-frame is a combination of received wisdoms handed down from rich generations of enslaved black Africans and their descendants (the Yorubas, Akans, Ibos, and many other tribes) on how to best resist white supremacy and survive. In other words, a best-practice guide for surviving centuries-old racism lodged within the collective memories of con-

temporary African Americans in which blacks learn to redirect and reframe white-racist thoughts, beliefs, and stereotypes to more accurate and productive frames. Black Americans have developed an expressive style found in music, language, poetry, and other endeavors as a way to redefine themselves and the limits placed on blackness. A classic example of counter-framing black radical tradition can be found in *David Walker's Appeal*.

68. Wiggins, D. K., and Miller, P. B. (2005). *The unlevel playing field: A documentary history of African American experiences in sport*. Urbana and Chicago: University of Illinois Press.

69. Mooney, K. (2014). *Race horse men: How slavery and freedom were made at the racetrack*. Cambridge, MA: Harvard University Press.

70. Hotaling, E. (1999). *The great Black jockeys: The lives and times of the men who dominated America's first national sport*. New York: Crown Publishing Group.

71. Reese, R. (1998, Spring). The socio-political context of the integration of sport in America. *Journal of African American Men, 3*(4), 5–22. Retrieved from https://www.csupomona.edu/~rrreese/integration.html

72. Stewart, C. (1884, June–November). My life as a slave. *Harper's New Monthly Magazine, LXIX* (413), 730–38. Retrieved from http://matrix.msu.edu/hst/hst324/media/stewart.pdf

73. Edwards, H. (1970). *The revolt of the Black athlete*. New York: Free Press.

74. Edwards, H. (2010). Social change and popular culture: Seminal developments at the interface of race, sport and society. *Sport in Society, 13*(1), 59–71.

75. Winkler, L. K. (2009). The Kentucky Derby's forgotten jockeys. *Smithsonian Magazine*. Retrieved from: www.smithsonianmag.com/history/the-kentucky-derbys-forgotten-jockeys-128781428/. Accessed on January 27, 2014.

76. Ashe, A. R., Jr. (1988). *A hard road to glory: A history of the African-*American athlete 1619–1918 (Vol. 1). New York: Amistad.

77. Bryant, H. (2002). *Shut out: A story of race and baseball in Boston*. New York: Routledge.

78. Ashe, *A hard road*.

79. Voogd, J. (2008). *Race, riots & resistance: The red summer of 1919*. New York: Peter Lang.

80. Rhoden, *Forty million dollar slaves*.

81. Foster, F. (2012). *The forgotten league: A history of Negro League Baseball*. CreateSpace Independent Publishing Platform.

82. Wiggins, D. K. (1983, Summer). Wendell Smith, the *Pittsburgh Courier-Journal* and the campaign to include Blacks in organized baseball, 1933–1945. *Journal of Sport History, 10*(2), 5–29.

83. Everson, D. (2009, December 4). The game that changed Alabama. *Wall Street Journal*, p. 8. Retrieved from http://online.wsj.com/articles/SB10001424052748704107104574572340901355488

84. Buffington, D., and Fraley, T. (2011). Racetalk and sport: The color consciousness discourse on basketball. *Sociological Inquiry, 81*(3), 333–52.

85. According to Göran Therborn (2013), existential inequality is the "unequal allocation of personhood, i.e., of autonomy, dignity, degrees of freedom, and of rights to respect and self-development" (p. 49). Racism is one such construct that limits human capability. Therborn, G. (2013). *The killing fields of inequality*. Cambridge, UK: Polity Press.

86. Therborn, *The killing fields of inequality*.

3. THE WHITE RACIAL FRAMING OF BLACKS IN MORMON THEOLOGY

1. Young, B. (1863, March 8). The persecutions of the Saints—Their loyalty to the constitution—The Mormon Battalion—The Laws of God relative to the African Race: Remarks by President Brigham Young, made in the Tabernacle, Great Salt Lake City. In G. D. Watt (Ed.), *Journal of Discourses, 10*, 104–11. Liverpool: Orson Pratt, p.110.

2. Morning, A. (2011). *The Nature of race: How scientists think and teach about human difference.* Berkeley and Los Angeles, CA: University of California Press.

3. Feagin, J. R. (2013). *The White racial frame: Centuries of racial framing and counterframing.* New York, NY: Routledge.

4. Feagin, J. R. (2006). *Systemic racism: A theory of oppression.* New York, NY: Routledge.

5. Zafirovski, M. (2007). The most cherished myth: Puritanism and liberty reconsidered and revised. *American Sociologist, 38*, 53–59.

6. Jefferson, T. (1787). *Notes on the State of Virginia*. London: John Stockdale, p. 261.

7. In 2007, the responsibility for church governance became shared with the Quorum of the Twelve Apostles, http://www.mormonnewsroom.org/article/approaching-mormon-doctrine

8. Benson, E. T. (1976, September 17). *The Gospel teacher and his message : Given to religious educators*, p. 8. Retrieved from http://zackc.files.wordpress.com/2008/09/the-gospel-teacher-and-his-message-benson.pdf

9. Romney, M. G. (1945, April 7). *Living prophets as guides*. Presented at the One hundred fifteenth Annual Conference of the Church of Jesus Christ of Latter-day Saints, pp. 86–91 (p. 90). Salt Lake City: The Church of Jesus

Christ of Latter-day Saints. Retrieved from http://scriptures.byu.edu/gc-historical/1945-A.pdf

10. Feagin, J. (2012). *White party, White government: Race, class, and U.S. politics*. New York: Routledge.

11. Altemeyer, B. (2006). *The Authoritarians.* Winnipeg: Department of Psychology, University of Manitoba, p. 2.

12. Genesis 9:18–27, King James Version.

13. The Curse of Ham was applied to any person that Mormons denoted were of African lineage, particularly African Americans. Those of nonwhite, nonblack origins such as the people of Fiji (subgroup of Polynesians) were included in the initial priesthood ban until they were later reclassified in 1952 by Mormon leader Harold B. Lee as "Israelites." They were then considered to be of white descent and, thus, were allowed full access to the priesthood and the Church's higher authority.

14. Barnes, T. (2011). *Constantine: Dynasty, religion and power in the later Roman Empire*. Chichester, UK: Blackwell.

15. Haynes, S. R. (2002). *Noah's curse: The biblical justification of American slavery*. New York: Oxford University Press, p. 7.

16. Feagin, J. R. (2014). *Racist America: Roots, current realities, and future reparations* (3rd ed.). New York: Routledge.

17. Kidd, C. (2006). *The forging of races: Race and scripture in the protestant Atlantic world, 1600–2000*. New York: Cambridge University Press.

18. Quoted in Goldenberg, D. (2003). *The Curse of Ham: Race and slavery in early Judaism, Christianity, and Islam.* Princeton, NJ: Princeton University Press, p. 143.

19. Blyden, E. (1869, January). The Negro in ancient history. *Methodist Quarterly Review*, p. 75.

20. Eastman, H. P. (1905). *The Negro, his origin, history and destiny: Containing a reply to "the Negro a beast."* Boston: Eastern Publishing Company.

21. Flournoy, J. J. (1838). *A reply, to a pamphlet, entitled "Bondage, a moral institution, sanctioned by the Scriptures and the Savior."* Athens, GA, p. 16.

22. See Pieterse, J. N. (1995). *White on Black: Images of Africa and Blacks in western popular culture.* New Haven, CT: Yale University Press.

23. Marable, M. (2000). *How capitalism underdeveloped Black America*. Cambridge, MA: South End Press.

24. Peterson, T. V. (1978). *Ham and Japeth: The mythic world of Whiteness in the antebellum south*. Metuchen, NJ: American Theological Library Association.

25. Douglass, F. (1969). *My bondage and my freedom,* 1855 Edition. Dover Publications, p. 258.

26. Douglass, *My bondage and my freedom*.

27. Thiemann, R. (1996). *Religion in public life: A dilemma for democracy*. Washington, DC: Georgetown University Press.

28. Noll, M. (2002). *The old religion: The history of North American Christianity in a new world*. Grand Rapids, MI: Wm. B. Eerdmans.

29. Meacham, J. (2006). *American gospel: God, the founding fathers, and the making of a nation*. New York: Random House Trade Paperbacks.

30. Emerson, M. O., and Smith, C. (2000). *Divided by faith: Evangelical religion and the problem of race in America*. New York: Oxford Press.

31. Manifest Destiny is a nineteenth-century frame that espoused that the idea of westward expansion of the United States from the Atlantic to Pacific Ocean was divinely sanctioned. American settlers thought the land was ripe for building wealth and wealth-generating opportunities at the expense of the native inhabitants who, like Africans, were anthropomorphized into soulless beings. The idea was to overspread the continent with Americans who would expand and share their unique from of government.

32. Horsman, R. (1986). *Race and manifest destiny: The origins of American Anglo-Saxonism*. Cambridge, MA: Harvard University Press.

33. Smith, J., and Roberts, B. H. (1902). *History of the Church of Jesus Christ of Latter-day Saints* (Vol. 7). Salt Lake City: Church of Jesus Christ of Latter-day Saints.

34. Jackson, W. K. (2013). *Elijah Abel: The life and times of a black priesthood.* Springville, UT: Holder.

35. Bringhurst, N. G. (2006). The "Missouri Thesis" revisited: Early Mormonism, slavery, and the status of black people. In N. G. Bringhurst and D. T. Smith (Eds.), *Black and Mormon* (p. 13-33). Urbana, IL: University of Illinois Press.

36. O'Donovan, C. (2006). The Mormon priesthood ban & Elder Q. Walker Lewis: An example for his more whiter brethren to follow. *John Whitmer Historical Association Journal, 26*, 48-100.

37. Bushman, R.L. (2005). Joseph Smith Rough Stone Rolling: A Cultural biography of Mormonism's founder. Vintage Books: New York.

38. Newell, Q. D. (2013): The autobiography and interview of Jane Elizabeth Manning James. *Journal of Africana Religions, 1* (2), 251-252.

39. Young, B. (1855, February 18). The constitution and government of the United States—rights and policy of the Latter-day Saints: A discourse by President Brigham Young, delivered in the Tabernacle. In G. D. Watt (Ed.), *Journal of Discourses* (Vol. 2), (pp. 170–78). Liverpool: Orson Pratt, p. 172.

40. Nibley, H. (1981). *Collected works of Hugh Nibley, Vol. 14: Abraham in Egypt*. Salt Lake City: Deseret Book.

41. Rhodes, M. D. (1977, Spring). A translation and commentary on the Joseph Smith Hypocephalus. *BYU Studies Quarterly, 17*(3), 259–74.

42. Interestingly, LDS theology believes strongly that no one shall bear the sins of Adam. "We believe that men will be punished for their own sins, and not for Adam's transgressions," 13 Articles of Faith, #2, http://mormon.org/articles-of-faith. Yet this did not seem to apply to the assumed "sins" of Cain and his progeny. This is evidence that Mormons did not see blacks as spiritual equals from the very beginning.

43. Smith, G. A. (1855, September 23). The history of Mahomedanism: A discourse of by Elder G. A. Smith, delivered in the Bowery, Great Salt Lake City. In G. D. Watt (Ed.), *Journal of Discourses* (Vol. 3), (pp. 28–37). Liverpool: Orson Pratt, p. 29.

44. Smith, J. F. (1931). *The way to perfection: Short discourses on gospel themes*. Salt Lake City,: Genealogical Society of Utah, p. 107.

45. Hyde, O. (1845, April 25). Speech given before the High Priests Quorum in Nauvoo. Liverpool, England.

46. Smith, *The way to perfection*.

47. McConkie, B. R. (1966). *Mormon doctrine*. Salt Lake City: Deseret Book, p. 527.

48. Bush, L. E., Jr. (1973, Spring). Mormonism's Negro doctrine: An historical overview. *Dialogue: A Journal of Mormon Thought, 8*, 11–68.

49. Bringhurst, N. G. (1981). *Saints, slaves, and Blacks: The changing place of Black people within Mormonism*. Westport, CT: Greenwood Press.

50. Allred, A. (2004). The traditions of their fathers: Myth versus reality in LDS scriptural writings. In N. G. Bringhurst, and D. T. Smith (Eds.), *Black and Mormon* (p. 34–49). Urbana and Chicago: University of Illinois Press.

51. The Catholic Church and other Protestant-based faiths—Episcopal Church, United Methodist Church, Southern Baptist, Lutheran—have since made peace with their racist past and issued public apologies for their role in slavery, Jim Crow racism, and their participation in the mistreatment of African Americans at the hands of misguided Christians. Still holding onto the belief that, for reasons unknown to us humans on earth, it was "God's will" that blacks were discriminated against, Mormons have yet to issue any such apology. Hence, this idea of "God's will" and its looming ambiguity is still strongly present throughout the LDS faith.

52. Minutes of the Quorum of the Twelve. (1847, December 3). pp. 6–7.

53. Botham, F. (2009). *Almighty God created the races: Christianity, interracial marriage, and American law*. Chapel Hill, NC: University of North Carolina Press.

54. Kennedy, R. (2004). *Interracial intimacies: Sex, marriage, identity, and adoption*. New York: Pantheon Books.

55. Minutes of the Quorum of the Twelve.

56. Young, The persecution of the Saints.

57. Lee, H. B. (1973). *Decisions for successful living*. Salt Lake City: Deseret Book, p. 168
58. Lee, H. B. (1955). *Youth of a noble birthright*. Salt Lake City: Deseret Book.
59. Harris, M. L. (2013, March). Mormonism's problematic racial past and the evolution of the divine-curse doctrine. *John Whitmer Historical Association Journal, 33*(1), 90.
60. Clark, J. R., Jr. (1946, August). *Improvement Era, 49*, p. 492.
61. Petersen, M. E. (1954, August 27). *Race problems as they affect the Church* [transcription]. Delivered at The Convention of Teachers of Religion on the College Level. Brigham Young University, Provo, UT.
62. Correspondence Between First Presidency and Lowry Nelson. (1947, July 17). G. A. Smith Letter to Dr. Lowry Nelson. Salt Lake City. Retrieved from https://archive.org/stream/LowryNelson1stPresidencyExchange/Lowry_Nelson_1st_Presidency_Exchange#page/n5/mode/1up
63. Wilkinson, E. L. (1949, June). Tribute to Christen Jensen. *BYU, 2*, 476.
64. Oaks, D. H. (1999, May). The ordinances of the Aaronic Priesthood are vital to all of us. How well do you understand them? *New Era*, 4–7.
65. Quinn, D. M. (1997). *The Mormon hierarchy: Extensions of power*. Salt Lake City: Signature Books.
66. Nelson, R. M. (2010, January). The New Gospel Principles Manual. *Ensign*, 28–31.
67. Hales, R. D. (1995, November). Blessings of the Priesthood. *Ensign*, 32.
68. Harrison, J. F. C. (1979). *The second coming: Popular millenarianism, 1780–1850*. New Brunswick, NJ: Rutgers University Press.
69. Sandeen, E. R. (1970). *The roots of fundamentalism: British and American millenarianism, 1800–1930*. Chicago: University of Chicago Press.
70. Underwood, G. (1982). Millenarianism and the early Mormon mind. *Journal of Mormon History, 9*, 41–51.
71. Backman, M. V. (1971). *Joseph Smith's first vision: The First Vision in its historical context*. Salt Lake City: Bookcraft.
72. Marquardt, H. M., and Walters, W. P. (1994). *Inventing Mormonism: Tradition and the historical record*. San Francisco: Smith Research Associates.
73. Smith, J. (1832). Letterbook 1. *The Joseph Smith Papers*. Church Archives, p. 2.
74. James 1:5, King James Version.
75. For an exhaustive and thorough review of visions and dreams during the nineteenth century, see D. Michael Quinn's book on early Mormon mysticism, particularly his notes on the subject. Quinn, D. M. (1998) *Early Mormonism and the magic world view.* Salt Lake City: Signature Books.

76. Porter, L. (1996, December). The restoration of the Aaronic and Melchizedek priesthoods. *Ensign: The Ensign of the Church of Jesus Christ of Latter-day Saints*.

77. John 10:16, King James Version. Mormons use this scripture as part of its theology to teach that their concept of Christ extends beyond the Old World and into the New World—the Americas.

78. The notion that Native American populations in the Western Hemisphere are the ancestors of ancient Israelites has been largely debunked from the scientific community through genealogical tracing.

79. Givens, T. L. (2002). *By the hand of Mormon: The American scripture that launched a new world religion*. Oxford and New York: Oxford University Press.

80. Palmer, G. H. (2002). *An insider's view of Mormon origins*. Salt Lake City: Signature Books.

81. William, J. A. (1994). Lehi's Jerusalem and writing on metal plates. *Journal of Book of Mormon Studies*, *3*(1), 204–6

82. The irony here is that historical record has confirmed that Jesus would have had "dark skin" and "wooly hair." The all-white male leadership, then, are unknowingly calling on a black Jesus and invoking his name to ostracize and denigrate other blacks.

83. Blum, E. J., and Harvey, P. (2012). *The color of Christ: The son of God and the saga of race in America*. Chapel Hill, NC: University of North Carolina Press, p. 15.

84. Richard Wright introduction in Drake, S., and Cayton, H. R. (1993). *Black metropolis: A study of Negro life in a northern city*. Chicago: University of Chicago Press, p. xxi.

85. The First Presidency represents the highest authorities of leadership in the LDS Church. The triad consists of the president of the Church and his two counselors, all selected from among fifteen men called to serve for life as apostles of Jesus Christ. The remaining twelve apostles are called the Quorum of the Twelve, and they are the second highest ruling elite behind the First Presidency. The current president of the church is Thomas S. Monson, and his two counselors are Henry B. Erying and Dieter F. Uchtdorf, who together advance causes of their faith worldwide.

86. Correspondence between First Presidency and Lowry Nelson. (1947, June 20). H. Meeks Letter to Dr. Lowry Nelson. Atlanta, GA. Retrieved from https://archive.org/stream/LowryNelson1stPresidencyExchange/Lowry_Nelson_1st_Presidency_Exchange#page/n5/mode/1up

87. Nelson, L. (1986). *In the direction of his dreams: Memoirs*. New York: Philosophical Library.

88. Nelson, *In the direction of his dreams*.

89. Nelson, *In the direction of his dreams.*

90. The Brethren is used as a synonym of the highest Mormon authorities on earth. Refer to note 73.

91. Mormon Newsroom. (2007). Elder Oaks interview transcripts from PBS documentary, para 141. Retrieved fromhttp://www.mormonnewsroom.org/article/elder-oaks-interview-transcript-from-pbs-documentary

92. Bush, L. E., Jr., and Mauss, A. L. (1984). *Neither White nor Black: Mormon scholars confront the race issue in a universal church.* Midvale, UT: Signature Books, appendix.

93. Young, B. (1866, August 19). Delegate Hooper—Beneficial effects of polygamy—Final redemption of Cain: Remarks by President Brigham Young, in the Bowery, G.S.L. City. In G. D. Watt (Ed.), *Journal of Discourses, 11,* 266–72. Liverpool: Orson Pratt, p. 272.

94. Prince, G. A., and Wright, W. R. (2005). *David O. McKay and the rise of modern Mormonism.* Salt Lake City: University of Utah Press, p. 70.

95. Following the June 1978 priesthood announcement in which the ban was lifted, Bruce R. McConkie also amended his prior declarations in his book *Mormon Doctrine.* On August 18, 1978, McConkie delivered remarks at a Church Educational Symposium. In his address, he directed those in attendance to "forget everything that I have said, or what President Brigham Young or President George Q. Cannon or whomsoever has said in days past that is contrary to the present revelation. We spoke with a limited understanding and without the light and knowledge that has now come into the world." McConkie, B. R. (1978, August 18). *All are alike unto God.* Delivered at The Second Annual Church Educational System Religious Educators Symposium. Brigham Young University, Provo, UT. Retrieved from http://https://si.lds.org/bc/seminary/content/library/talks/ces-symposium-addresses/all-are-alike-unto-god_eng.pdf

96. Theodore G. Bilbo was a sensational Mississippi senator who worked to deny blacks the right to vote, while openly and proudly embracing white supremacy through his membership in the Klan even as an elected official. His racism was so extensive and his beliefs in the separation of races (for all eternity) so obdurate that he liked to use and often shouted the word "nigger" from the floor of the Senate for the purpose of purely entertaining himself, much to the chagrin of Representative Adam Clayton Powell, Jr., the first African American elected to Congress from New York City in 1945. (See Powell, A. C. 1971. *The Autobiography of Adam Clayton Powell, Jr.* New York: Kensington Publishing.) His push to round up all the blacks and ship them to Liberia came to a head with his Greater Liberia Act of 1939, in which he tried to show his openness to blacks by siding with black nationalists. Fitzgerald, M. W. (1997,

May). "We have found a Moses": Theodore Bilbo, black nationalism, and the Greater Liberia Bill of 1939. *The Journal of Southern History, 63*(2), 293–320.

97. Bilbo, T. G. (1947). *Take your choice: Separation or mongrelization*. Poplarville, MS: Dream House Publishing, p. 105. Retrieved from http://archive.org/stream/TakeYourChoice/TakeYourChoice_djvu

98. Cone, J. H. (1990). *Black theology & Black power* (2nd ed.). Maryknoll, NY: Orbis Books.

99. Cone, J. H. (2004). Theology's great sin: Silence in the face of White supremacy. *Black Theology: An International Journal, 2*(2).

100. Blum and Harvey. *The color of Christ*.

101. Smith, D. T. (2004). Unpacking Whiteness in Zion: Some personal reflections and general observations. In N. G. Bringhurst and D. T. Smith (Eds.), *Black and Mormon* (p. 148–66). Urbana, IL: University of Illinois Press.

102. Jefferson, T. (1785). *Notes on the State of Virginia*. New York: Penguin Books.

103. Wilson, W. J. (1987). *The truly disadvantaged: The inner city, the underclass, and public policy*. Chicago: University of Chicago Press, p. 12.

4. POLITICAL UPRISING IN THE LATE SIXTIES AND EARLY SEVENTIES

1. Whitfield, M. (1964, March). Let's boycott the Olympics: Olympic champ asks Negro athletes to act. *Ebony*, 95–96, 98–100 (p. 95).

2. Domhoff, G. W. (2009). *Who rules America? Challenges to corporate and class dominance* (6th ed.). New York: McGraw-Hill.

3. Winters, J. A., and Page, B. I. Oligarchy in the United States? *Perspectives on Politics, 7*(4), 731–51.

4. Stannard, E. D. (1992). *American Holocaust: The conquest of the new world.* Oxford, England: Oxford University Press.

5. Brown, D. (1970). *Bury my heart at Wounded Knee: An Indian history of the American West*. New York: Holt, Rinehart, & Winston.

6. Washington, H. A. (2006). *Medical apartheid: The dark history of medical experimentation on Black Americans from colonial times to the present*. New York: Harlem Moon.

7. Alesina, A., and La Ferrara E. 2002. Who trusts others? *Journal of Public Economics, 85*, 207–34.

8. Biafora, F. A., Taylor, D. L., Warheit, G. J., Zimmerman, R. S., and Vega, W. A. (1993). Cultural mistrust and racial awareness among ethnically diverse black adolescent boys. *Journal of Black Psychology, 19*(3), 266–81.

9. Smith, S. S. (2010). Race and trust. *Annual Review of Sociology, 36*, 453–75.

10. Spigel, L. (1992). *Make room for TV: Television and the family ideal in postwar America*. Chicago: University of Chicago Press.

11. Dittmer, J. (1994). *Local people: The struggle for Civil Rights in Mississippi*. Chicago: University of Illinois Press.

12. Bell, D., Jr. (1980). *Brown v. Board of Education* and the interest convergence dilemma. *Harvard Law Review, 518*, 93.

13. Allen, J., Lewis, J., Litwack, L. F., and Als, H. (2000). *Without sanctuary: Lynching photography in America*. Santa Fe, NM: Twin Palms Publishers.

14. Dudziak, M. L. (2000). *Cold War civil rights: Race and image of American democracy*. Princeton, NJ: Princeton University Press.

15. European colonization consisted of three crucial elements: 1) stripping indigenious peoples of their native languages and dialects; 2) changing their concept of diety; 3) and finally, changing the perception of the indigenious self as people belonging to a community to one of free-thinking, autonomous individuals.

16. Melamed, J. (2011). *Represent and destroy: Rationalizing violence in the new racial capitalism*. Minneapolis: University of Minnesota Press.

17. Feagin, J. R. (2006). *Systemic racism: A theory of oppression*. New York: Routledge.

18. Feagin, J. R. (2010). *Racist America* (Rev. ed.). New York: Routledge.

19. Feagin, J. R., and Vera, H. (1995). *White racism: The basics*. New York: Routledge

20. Bonilla-Silva, E. (1997). Rethinking racism: Toward a structural interpretation. *American Sociological Review, 62*(3), 465–80.

21. Condit, C. M., and Lucaites, J. L. 1993. *Crafting equality: America's Anglo-African word.* Chicago: University of Chicago Press.

22. Fischer, L. (1998). *The Life of Mahatma Gandhi* (7th ed.). India: Bhavan.

23. Lewis, J., and D'Orso, M. (1998). *Walking in the wind: A memoir of the movement*. New York: Simon and Schuster.

24. Arsenault, R. (2011). *Freedom riders: 1961 and the struggle for racial justice*. New York: Oxford Press.

25. Farmer, J. (1985). *Lay bare the heart: An autobiography of the Civil Rights Movement*. New York: New American Library.

26. Andrews, K. T., and Biggs, M. (2006, October). The dynamics of protest diffusion: Movement organization, social networks, and news media in the 1960 sit-ins. *American Sociological Review, 71*, 752–77.

27. The end of segregation in interstate transportation resulted from the *Boynton v. Virginia* case. Bruce Boynton, a law student attending the historically black Howard University Law School in Washington, D.C., was on a bus bound for Montgomery, Alabama, when, during the trip, the bus stopped to allow passengers to dine and freshen up. Boynton sat in the white section and refused to move. He was arrested and fined $10 for violating the law by not sitting in the "colored section." With the help of Thurgood Marshall, the Supreme Court weighed in on the matter and determined that the student's rights had been violated. This case determined that the Constitution gave the young man the right to equal protection under the law and, therefore, the right to service.

28. Pearson, H. (1994). *The shadow of the panther: Huey Newton and the price of Black power in America*. New York: Perseus Publishing.

29. This act ended Jim Crow laws, which mandated racial segregation in all public spaces throughout the South. These laws were created following the 1896 case, *Plessy v. Ferguson*, in which the Supreme Court declared "separate but equal" to be constitutional. Lovey, R. D. (1997). *The Civil Rights Act of 1964: The passage of the law that ended racial segregation*. Albany, NY: State University of New York Press.

30. May, G. (2013). *Bending toward justice: The Voting Rights Act and the transformation of American democracy*. New York: Basic Books.

31. Guterl, M. P. (2002). *The color of race in America, 1900–1940*. Cambridge, MA: Harvard University Press.

32. Hochschild, J. L., and Weaver, V. (2007, December). The skin color paradox and the American racial order. *Social Forces, 86*, 1–28.

33. Johnson, W. (2000, June). The slave trader, the White slave, and the politics of racial determination in the 1850s. *Journal of American History, 87*, 13–38.

34. Kotz, N. (2005). *Judgment days: Lyndon Baines Johnson, Martin Luther King, Jr., and the laws that changed America*. Boston: Houghton Mifflin.

35. Two years after the infamous Watts Riots, as many as 159 cities all across America engaged in race riots during the summer of 1967 that historians dubbed the "long hot summer." Olzak, S., Shanahan, S., and McEneaney, E. H. (1996, August). Poverty, segregation, and race riots: 1960 to 1993. *American Sociological Review, 61*(4).

36. Dudziak, *Cold War civil rights*.

37. Thornton, J. M., III. (2002). *Dividing lines: Municipal politics and the struggle for civil rights in Montgomery, Birmingham, and Selma*. Tuscaloosa, AL: University of Alabama Press.

38. Feagin, J. R. (2013). *The White racial frame: Centuries of racial framing and counter-framing* (2nd ed.). New York: Routledge.

39. Lew Alcindor, who later became Kareem Adbul Jabbar, was a bona fide college basketball star when he attended and played at UCLA in 1966. Discouraged by the racial prejudice he experienced on campus, he later reflected on why he joined the protest movement. "I got more and more lonely and more and more hurt by all the prejudice, and finally I made a decision. . . . I pushed to the back of my mind all the normalcies of college life . . . and I dug down deep into my black studies and religious studies. I withdrew into myself to find myself. I made no further attempts to integrate. I was consumed and obsessed by my interest in the black man, in Black Power, black pride, black courage. That, for me, would suffice." Alcindor, L. and Olsen, J. (1969, November 3). UCLA was a mistake: The basketball was fine, says Lew, but campus conditions almost impelled him to quit school. *Sports Illustrated*, 35. Retrieved from http://www.si.com/vault/1969/11/03/611046/ucla-was-a-mistake

40. Henderson, S. (2009). Crossing the line: Sport and the limits of Civil Rights Protest. *The International Journal of the History of Sport, 26*(1).

41. Ashe, A. R., Jr. (1993). *A hard road to glory: A history of the African American athlete, 1619–1918* (Vol. 1). New York: John Wiley and Sons.

42. Prugh, J. (1967, November 25). Alcindor says Olympic boycott doesn't bind him personally. *Los Angeles Times*, p. 21.

43. Smith, J. (2009, Summer). It's not really my country: Lew Alcindor and the revolt of the Black athlete. *Journal of Sport History, 36*(2).

44. Western Athletic Conference. (2013). History of the WAC. Retrieved from http://www.wacsports.com/ViewArticle.dbml?DB_OEM_ID=10100&ATCLID=537066

45. Thomas, A. J., and Speight, S. L. (1999). Racial identity and racial socialization attitudes of African American parents. *Journal of Black Psychology, 25*(2), 152–70.

46. Smith, D. T., Jacobson, C., and Juarez, B. G. (2011). *White parents, Black children: Experiencing transracial adoption.* Lanham, MD: Rowman & Littlefield Publishers, Inc.

47. Forman, J. (1972). *The making of Black revolutionaries: A personal account*. New York: Macmillan.

48. Found in the February 1967 *FBI Law Information Bulletin*, J. Edgar Hoover attributes campus unrest to communism.

49. Sugrue, T. J. (2008). *Sweet land of liberty: The forgotten struggle for civil rights in the North*. New York: Random House Publishing Group, p. 336.

50. Carmichael, S. (1966, Autumn). Toward Black Liberation. *Massachusetts Review* , 7, 639–51.

51. Edwards, H. (1980). *The struggle that must be: An autobiography*. New York: Macmillan.

52. Bullock, C. (1996). Fired by conscience: The "Black 14" incident at the University of Wyoming and Black protest in the Western Athletic Conference, 1968–1970. *Wyoming History Journal, 68*(1), 9–10 (p. 5).

53. Edwards, H. (1979). The Olympic Project for Human Rights: An assessment ten years later. *Black Scholar, 10* (6–7), 2.

54. Fraser, C. G. (1968, February 16). Black athletes are cautioned not to cross picket lines. *New York Times*. Retrieved from http://www.nytimes.com/specials/olympics/history/1968–lines.html

55. Considine, B., and Jarvis, F. R. (1969). *The first hundred years: A portrait of NYAC*. New York: Macmillan.

56. Leonard, D. (1998, June 10). What happened to the revolt of the Black athlete?: An interview with Harry Edwards. *Colorlines*. Retrieved from http://colorlines.com/archives/1998/06/what_happened_to_the_revolt_of_the_black_athlete.html

57. Edwards, H. (1969). *The revolt of the Black athlete.* New York: Free Press.

58. Edwards, *The revolt of the Black athlete* .

59. Hartmann, D. (2003). *Race, culture, and the revolt of the Black athlete: The 1968 Olympic protests and their aftermath.* Chicago: University of Chicago Press.

60. Olsen, J. (1968). *The Black athlete: A shameful story*. New York: Time-Life Books, p. 66.

61. Halftime protest erupts; seven people arrested. (1970, February 6). *CSU Collegian*, p. 1.

62. Horn, C. (1981). *The university in turmoil and transition: Crises decades at the University of New Mexico*. Albuquerque, NM: Rocky Mountain Publishing.

63. Bergera, G. J., and Priddis, R. (1985). *Brigham Young University: A house of faith*. Salt Lake City: Signature Books.

64. Bullock, Fired by conscience.

65. Horn, *The university in turmoil and transition*.

66. Flying bricks heighten tension on eve of UNM-BYU court battle. (1970, February 28). *Laramie Daily Boomerang*, p. 11.

67. Thorburn, R. (2009). *Black 14: The rise, fall, and rebirth of Wyoming football* . Boulder, CO: Burning Daylight.

68. Olsen, *The Black athlete*.

69. Bullock, Fired by conscience .

70. McElreath, M., Coker, N., Pedersen, T., Costin, S., and Bobo, M. (Producers). (2007). *The Black 14* [DVD]. Laramie, WY: University of Wyoming Television.

71. Hardy, D. (1986). *Wyoming University: The first 100 years 1886–1986.* Laramie, WY: University of Wyoming.

72. Wiggins, D., and Miller, P. (2005). *The unlevel playing field: A documentary history of the African American experience in sport*. Champaign, IL: University of Illinois Press.

73. Demas, L. (2010). *Integrating the gridiron: Black civil rights and American college football*. New Brunswick, NJ: Rutgers University Press.

74. Cooper, T. (1969, November 26). Irate reaction to BYU stand. *The Stanford Daily, 156*(43), 1.

75. Bergera and Priddis, *Brigham Young University*.

76. Bergera, G. J. & Priddis, R. (1985). Brigham Young University: A house of faith. Salt Lake City, UT: Signature Books.

77. Dole, A. A. (1995). Why not drop race as a term? *American Psychologist, 54*, 40.

5. MORMON ATTITUDES TOWARD CIVIL RIGHTS

1. First Presidency statement, December 15, 1969.

2. Prince, G. A., and Wright, W. R. (2005). *David O. McKay and the rise of modern Mormonism*. Salt Lake City: University of Utah Press.

3. Bringhurst, N. G. (1981). *Saints, slaves, and Blacks: The changing place of Black people within Mormonism*. Westport, CT: Greenwood Press, p. 231.

4. Geisler, J. (1968, November 27). The way it is. *Daily Universe*.

5. Benson, E. T. (1968). *Civil Rights: Tool of communist deception*. Salt Lake City: Deseret Book, p. 3.

6. The lone exception to this was Hugh B. Brown, who served as a First Counselor in the First Presidency under David O. McKay. In 1969 Brown worked toward rescinding the LDS priesthood ban on black males that many members of the Quorum of the Twelve Apostles endorsed. Because Harold B. Lee was not in attendance at the same meeting, and upon his return from church duties elsewhere, Lee was able to secure a reversal of the proposed change on black priesthood ordination. For his work on bringing the LDS Church into the twentieth century with human equality, and after the death of McKay, Brown was not retained (as tradition would have) as a counselor under Joseph Fielding Smith. Never before had a new president of the Mormon faith not called upon the service and experience of a trusted and reliable counselor such as Brown. It is suspected this move under Smith had much to do with his advocacy of social justice. (*The Mormon Hierarchy: Extensions of Power*, D. Michael Quinn, Signature Books, 1997, p. 14)

7. David O. McKay papers, (1954). Ms 668, Box 32, Folder 3, pp. 7–9. Special Collections and Archives, University of Utah, J. Willard Marriott, Salt Lake City, UT.

8. McConkie, B. (1958). *Mormon doctrine*. Salt Lake City: Bookcraft, p. 477.

9. Turner, W. (1966). *The Mormon establishment.* New York: Houghton Mifflin, pp. 218–19.

10. Smith, J. F. (1963, October 22). Memo from a Mormon. *Look*, 79.

11. Edmund Burke is known as the father of modern conservatism. His ideas on conservative ideology can be summed up as follows: "a deep suspicion of the power of the state; a preference for liberty over equality; patriotism; a belief in established institutions and hierarchies; skepticism about the idea of progress; and elitism." Micklethwait, J., and Wooldridge, A. (2004). *The right nation: Conservative power in America*. New York: Penguin Press, p. 13.

12. Quoted in Bergera, G. J., and Priddis, R. (1985). *Brigham Young University: A house of faith*. Salt Lake City: Signature Books.

13. Wilkinson, E. L. (1965, May 28). The decline and possible fall of the American Republic: Commencement Address. [Transcript]. Retrieved from http://www.stoutner.org/government/republic/republic.pdf

14. Bergera and Priddis, *Brigham Young University*.

15. Blake, J. D. (1995, Spring). Ernest L. Wilkinson and the 1966 BYU spy ring: A response to D. Michael Quinn. *Dialogue: A Journal of Mormon Thought*, *28*(1), 163–72.

16. Waterman, B., and Kagel, B. (1998). *The Lord's university: Freedom and authority at BYU*. Salt Lake City: Signature Books.

17. Quoted in Bergera, G. J. (2012, Spring). The Richard D. Poll and J. Kenneth Davies cases: Politics and religion at BYU during the Wilkinson years. *Dialogue: A Journal of Mormon Thought*, *45*(1), 43–73 (p. 45).

18. Bergera and Priddis, *Brigham Young University*.

19. Brown, H. B., and Tanner, N. E. (1969, December 15). 1969 First Presidency statement. Retrieved from http://www.blacklds.org/1969-first-presidency-statement

20. Feagin, J. (2010). *The White racial frame: Centuries of racial framing and counter-framing*. New York: Routledge, p. 16.

21. Brigham Young was quoted as saying, "Any man having one drop of the seed of Cain in him cannot hold the priesthood and if no other Prophet ever spake it before I will say it now in the name of Jesus Christ" (Wilford Woodruff's Journal, Vol. 4, p. 97).

22. Entman, R., and Rojecki, A. (2000). *The Black image in the White mind*. Chicago: University of Chicago Press.

23. Smith, D. T. (2013, March 14). Images of Black males in popular media. *Huffington Post*. Retrieved from http://www.huffingtonpost.com/darron-t-smith-phd/Black-men-media_b_2844990.html

24. Pres. Wilkinson lays riots squarely on revolutionaries. (1969, April 18). *Daily Universe*.

25. Waterman and Kagel, *The Lord's university*, p. 77.

26. Wheelwright, L. F. (1969, June 27). *Memo to Wilkinson: Regarding recommended policies and organizations for publishing the Daily Universe* (Series 3, Box 33, Folder 5). Brigham Young University archives. Provo, UT.

27. Waterman and Kagel, *The Lord's university*.

28. Smith, A. (2009, March 19). CRM, the Daily Universe, and the 1950s—Part one. The *Juvenile Instructor*. Retreived from http://www.juvenileinstructor.org/crm-the-daily-universe-and-the-1950s-part-one/

29. Young, B. (1863, March 8). The persecutions of the saints—their loyalty to the constitution—the Mormon battalion—the Laws of God relative to the African Race: Remarks by President Brigham Young, delivered in the Tabernacle, Great Salt Lake City. *Journal of Discourses, 10*, 104–11 (p. 110). Liverpool: Orson Pratt.

30. Some twenty years later, Peterson denied having given this statement. Furthermore, he threatened to sue anyone who quoted him as doing so. See Peterson, Mark. Mark E. Peterson to Jerald and Sandra Tanner, Salt Lake City, UT, February 13, 1965.

31. Mason, P. Q. (2008, Spring). The prohibition of interracial marriage in Utah, 1888–1963. *Utah Historical Quarterly*, 76, 108–31.

32. Wilkinson, E. L. (1960, November 10). *Wilkinson Diaries*.

33. Hudspeth talks about interracial marriage at BYU. (1970, February 16). *Daily Herald*.

34. Bergera and Priddis, *Brigham Young University*.

35. Gross, A. J. (2008). *What blood won't tell: A history of race on trial in America*. Cambridge, MA: Harvard University Press.

36. Pascoe, P. (2009). *What comes naturally: Miscegenation Law and the making of race in America*. New York: Oxford University Press.

37. Drew, J. (2009, November 6). BYU football: Remembering the Black 14 protest. *Salt Lake Tribune*.

38. Wyoming 14 players removed. (1969, November 30). *Salt Lake Tribune*.

39. Quinn, D. M. (2002). *Elder statesman: A biography of J. Reuben Clark*. Salt Lake City: Signature Books.

40. Horowitz, J. (2012, February 29). Former ban on Black priests still reverberates through Mormon faith. *Salt Lake Tribune*. Retrieved from http://www.sltrib.com/sltrib/world/53618680-68/church-romney-ban-mormon.html.csp

41. Horowitz, Former ban on Black priests still reverberates, para 12.

42. Horowitz, Former ban on Black priests still reverberates, para 13.

43. Horowitz, Former ban on Black priests still reverberates, para 13.

44. Tanner, J. and Tanner, S. (2004). *Curse of Cain? Racism in the Mormon Church* (p. 64). Utah Lighthouse Ministry.

45. Walton, B. (1971, Spring). A university dilemma: BYU and Blacks. *Dialogue: A Journal of Mormon Thought* , *6*, 31–36, (p. 31).

46. Ostling, R. N., and Ostling, J. K. (1999). *Mormon America*. San Francisco: Harper.

47. Wyoming 14 players removed. (1969, November 30). *Salt Lake Tribune*.

48. Kranish, M., and Helman, S. (2012). *The real Romney*. New York: HarperCollins, pp. 114–15.

49. Horowitz, Former ban on Black priests still reverberates, para 14.

50. Tanner and Tanner, *Curse of Cain?*, p. 64.

51. Worst race problem: Negroes in Utah are told they bear a curse. (1963, October 27). *Daytona Beach Sunday News-Journal*, p. 5D. Retrieved from http://news.google.com/newspapers?nid=1873&dat=19631027&id=yX4eAAAAIBAJ&sjid=RcoEAAAAIBAJ&pg=692,5136112

52. Prince and Wright, *David O. McKay and the rise of modern Mormonism*, p. 70.

53. Bennett, W. (1953, Spring). The Negro in Utah. *Utah Law Review*.

54. Collisson, Craig. The fight to legitimize blackness: How black students changed the university [Dissertation], p. 78. ProQuest, 2008.

55. Drake, W. F. (1979). Tax status of private segregated schools: The new revenue procedure. *William & Mary Law Review*, *20*(3), 463–512 (p. 480).

56. Asaki, D., Jacobs, M. A., and Scott, S. Y. (1982). Racial segregation and the tax-exempt status of private educational and religious institutions. *Howard Law Journal*, *25*(7), 545.

57. Joe R. Feagin and Leslie Houts Picca coined the terms "frontstage" and "backstage" racism to describe how white racial conversations play out publicly and behind closed doors. As a general rule, most whites know that it is inappropriate to express and perform acts of racial contempt for people of color in public settings. Backstage interactions with other whites allow a space where whites can bond with one another in the telling of racist jokes, free from scrutiny and charges of racism. Picca, L. H., and Feagin, J. H. (2007). *Two-faced racism: Whites in the backstage and frontstage*. New York: Routledge.

58. Proposed letter to be used for non-L.D.S. Negro students who inquire about attendance at Brigham Young University. (1969). *Lester Bush Papers* (Box 4, Folder 4, pp. 296–300). University of Utah J. Willard Marriot Library, Special Collections.

59. Bergera and Priddis, *Brigham Young University*.

60. Wilkinson, 1960.

61. Johnson, O. (2010, March 11). The story of Bob Jones University v. United States: Race, religion, and Congress' extraordinary acquiescence. *Columbia Public Law & Legal Theory Working Papers*.

62. After the Church statement by the First Presidency regarding the lifting of the priesthood ban, it was printed in the *Deseret News* and later printed as Official Declaration No. 2, dated June 8, 1978, in *The Doctrine and Covenants of the Church of Jesus Christ of Latter-day Saints* (Salt Lake City: Church of Jesus Christ of Latter day Saints, 1981).

63. LDS church extends priesthood to all worthy male members. (1978, June 9). *Deseret News*.

64. Van Leer, T. (1978, June 12). Black LDS Priesthood Holder. *Deseret News*, p. A-1.

65. Martin, B. F. (Executive Producer). (2007, December 16). Meet the Press with moderator Tim Russert [Television broadcast]. Washington, DC: National Broadcasting Company. Transcript retrieved from http://www.presidency.ucsb.edu/ws/index.php?pid=77749

66. Kranish and Helman, *The real Romney*.

67. Carter praises LDS Church action. (1978, June 10). *Deseret News*, p. A-1.

68. A burden is lifted (Editorial),(1978, June 11) *Salt Lake Tribune*.

69. Woodward, K. L. (1978, June 19). Race revelations. *Newsweek*, p. 56.

70. Ward Teachers' message: "Sustaining the General Authorities of the Church." (1945, June). *The Improvement Era,* p.1.

71. The Church of Jesus Christ of Latter-day Saints. (2014). Race and the Priesthood. Retrieved from https://www.lds.org/topics/race-and-the-priesthood

6. NO HONOR IN THE HONOR CODE

1. Horowitz, J. (2012, February 28). The genesis of a church's stand on race. *Washington Post*. Retrieved from http://www.washingtonpost.com/politics/the-genesis-of-a-churchs-stand-on-race/2012/02/22/gIQAQZXyfR_story.html

2. Drew, J. (2011, March 3). BYU's Brandon Davies apologies to teammates. *Salt Lake Tribune*.

3. The Church of Jesus Christ of Latter-day Saints. (2014). Word of Wisdom. Retrieved from https://www.lds.org/topics/word-of-wisdom?lang=eng

4. Western thought normalizes binary language. Reality is demonstrated in the binary language such as man/woman, white/black, and straight/gay. Binary

oppositions are unstable structures within language as discourse that amounts to oppressive formations and social arrangements.

5. Derrida, J. (1978). *Writing and difference.* London: Routledge.

6. Weedon, C. (1999). *Feminism, theory, and the politics of difference.* New York: Blackwell Publishers.

7. Haws, J. B. (2013). *The Mormon image in the American mind: Fifty years of public perception*. Oxford University Press.

8. Bergera, G. J., and Priddis, R. (1985). *Brigham Young University: A house of faith*. Salt Lake City, UT: Signature Books.

9. *Ibid.*

10. Waterman, B., and Kagel, B. (1998). *The Lord's university: Freedom and authority at BYU.* Salt Lake City: Signature Books.

11. Wilkinson, E. L. (Ed.). (1975). *Brigham Young University: The first 100 years*. Provo, UT: BYU Press, p. 331–32.

12. The Church of Jesus Christ of Latter-day Saints. (2014).

13. Christofferson, T. D. (2012, April). The doctrine of Christ. *The Church of Jesus Christ of Latter-day Saints.* Retrieved from http://www.lds.org/general-conference/2012/04/the-doctrine-of-christ?lang=eng

14. Stack, P. F. (2012). Apostle says key to LDS beliefs is divine revelation. *Salt Lake Tribune.* Retrieved from http://www.sltrib.com/sltrib/news/53833402-78/uchtdorf-members-someone-mormon.html.csp

15. An endowed member of the LDS church is someone who has gone through the Mormon Temple and received special rituals considered sacred to Mormons.

16. Hassan McCullough, telephone interview with author, May 3, 2014.

17. Bonilla-Silva, E. (2003). *Racism without racists: Color-blind racism and the persistence of racial inequality in the United States.* New York: Rowman & Littlefield.

18. Smith, D. T. (2005, July). These house-Negroes still think we're cursed: Struggling against racism in the classroom. *Cultural Studies, 19*(4), 439–54.

19. Currently at the helm of this initiative is a Mormon university administrator who lacks the formal religious training that a traditional chaplain typically receives.

20. Harrison, C. K., Lawrence, S. M., Plecha, M., Bukstein, S. J., and Janson, N. K. (2009). Stereotypes and stigmas of college athletes in Tank McNamara's cartoon strip: Fact or fiction? *Journal of Issues in Intercollegiate Athletics, 1*, 1–18.

21. Ronney Jenkins, telephone interview with author, May 26, 2014.

22. Jenkins, telephone interview with author.

23. Hassan McCullough, telephone interview with author, May 3, 2014.

24. DeCourcy, M. (2011). Jimmer Fredette, BYU guard: "Player of the year is a great thing." *Sporting News*. Retrieved from http://www.sportingnews.com/ncaa-basketball/story/2011-03-22/jimmer-fredette-byu-guard-player-of-the-year-is-a-great-thing

25. Owens, S. J. (2011, March 5). Tim Tebow says BYU's Brandon Davies may deserve second chance. *Orlando Sentinel*, para 4. Retrieved from http://articles.orlandosentinel.com/2011-03-05/sports/os-tim-tebow-byu-brandon-davies-second-chance-honor-code_1_tim-tebow-tebow-talks-honor-code

26. Soshnick, S. (2011). Sex suspension at BYU is reason for celebration. *Bloomberg.com*. Retrieved from http://www.bloomberg.com/news/2011-03-07/sex-suspension-at-byu-is-cause-to-celebrate-commentary-by-scott-soshnick.html

27. Askar, J. G. (2011, March 5). BYU praised for Honor Code enforcement in Brandon Davies case. *Deseret News*, para 3.

28. Forde, P. (2011). BYU puts principle over performance. *ESPN Men's Basketball*, para 24. Retrieved from http://sports.espn.go.com/ncb/columns/story?id=6175251

29. Other athletes, black and white, who remained in good faith with the school were unwilling to engage in discussion/answer questions with respect to this topic.

30. O'Brien, L., and Smith, D. T. (2011, April 13). The truth about race, religion, and the honor code at BYU. *Deadspin*, para 27. Retrieved from http://deadspin.com/5791461/the-truth-about-race-religion-and-the-honor-code-at-byu

31. Entman, R., and Rojecki A. (2000). *The Black image in the White mind*. Chicago: University of Chicago Press.

32. Branch, J. (2011). Kept off court, but welcomed by B.Y.U. fans and teammates. *New York Times*. Retrieved from http://www.nytimes.com/2011/03/13/sports/ncaabasketball/13byu.html?pagewanted=all&_r=1&

33. Jacobson, C. K. and Smith, D. T. (2013). Emotion work in Black and White: Transracial adoption and process of racial socialization. In P. N. Claster and S. L. Blair (Eds.), *Visions of the 21st century family: Transforming structures and identities*. Contemporary Perspectives in Family Research. Bingley, UK: Emerald Group Publishing.

34. Smith, D. T., and Juarez, B. G. (2014). Race lessons in Black and White: How do White adoptive parents socialize Black adoptees in predominately White communities? *Adoption Quarterly*. doi:10.1080/10926755.2014.895465

35. Smith, D. T. (2014, Jan 2). Keiran Romney and the paradox of transracial adoption. *Huffington Post*. Retrieved from http://www.huffingtonpost.com/darron-t-smith-phd/kieran-romney_b_4531158.html

36. Branch, Kept off court.

37. It is widely accepted in the social and behavioral sciences that the concept of race is socially engineered rather than biologically determined. Europeans and European Americans created discourse (talk and text) about the nature and disposition of black people as less human. The white power structure would later institutionalize these beliefs within U.S. structures like education, health care, and law enforcement, for example, to the detriment of black Americans and other Americans of color.

38. Smith, D. T., Jacobson, C. K., and Juarez, B. G. (2011). *White parents, black children: Experiencing transracial adoption*. Lanham, MD: Rowman & Littlefield.

39. Smith, D. T. (2015). The emotional labor of playing cool: How Black male transracial adoptees find ways to cope within predominantly white settings. In R. A. Javier, G. A. Pantoja, J. Raible, and A. Baden (Eds.), Race, religion, and rescue in adoption: Part II [Special issue]. *Journal of Social Distress and the Homeless, 25* (1).

40. Majors, R., and Billson, J. M. (1992). *Cool pose: The dilemmas of Black manhood in America.* New York: Lexington Books.

41. Edwards, H. (1984). The Black "dumb jock": An American sports tragedy. *The College Board Review, 131*, 8–13.

42. Harper, S. R. (2014, January 20). Black men as college athletes: The real win-loss record. *The Chronicle of Higher Education*. Retrieved from http://chronicle.com/article/Black-Men-as-College-Athletes-/144095/

43. Sailes, G. A. (1993). An investigation of campus stereotypes: The myth of Black athletic superiority and the dumb jock stereotype. *Sociology of Sport Journal, 10*, 88–97.

44. Y Facts: Brigham Young University. (2014). Enrollment by ethnicity (not including Caucasion). Retrieved from http://yfacts.byu.edu/Article?id=265

45. Aud, S., Fox, M., and KewalRamani, A. (2010). Status and trends in the education of racial and ethnic groups (NCES 2010-015). *U.S. Department of Education, National Center for Education Statistics.* Washington, DC: U.S. Government Printing Office.

46. Knowlton, R. (November 28, 1978). Recruiting problems common. *Daily Universe*.

47. Schwenke, L. R. (2004). An end to negative "race card" recruiting for BYU. *Total Blue Sports*. Retrieved from http://byu.scout.com/story/231165-an-end-to-negative-race-card-recruiting-for-byu

48. Nielsen, C. (2005, May 2). BYU confidential. *Salt Lake Magazine, 16*(3).

49. Nielsen, BYU confidential.

50. Oler, D. (2001). Five BYU football players have brush with the law. *The Digital Universe*. Retrieved from http://universe.byu.edu/2001/06/15/five-byu-football-players-have-brush-with-the-law/

51. Waterman, B. (1998). Ernest Wilkinson and the transformation of BYU's honor code, 1965–71. *Dialogue: A Journal of Mormon Thought, 31*, 85–112.

52. Waterman and Kagel, *The Lord's university*.

53. Nielsen, BYU confidential

54. Romboy, D. (2004). Bearded man a BYU oddity: Only a few exempt from university's clean-shaven rule. *Deseret News*. Retrieved from http://www.deseretnews.com/article/595067258/Bearded-man-a-BYU-oddity.html?pg=all

55. Nielsen, BYU confidential .

56. Israelsen, S. (2005, September 3). Ex-Y. players not guilty of charges. *Deseret News*. Retrieved from http://www.deseretnews.com/article/600160674/Former-Y-players-acquitted-on-rape-charges.html?pg=all

57. Nielsen, BYU confidential, para 8.

58. Killion, A. (2011, March 24). By sticking to guns, persevering, could BYU become America's team? *Sports Illustrated*, para 7. Retrieved from http://www.si.com/more-sports/2011/03/24/byu

59. Hudson was not the first player to acknowledge the lack of transparency. Bennie Smith, lettering in the sport of football in 1971, was one of the first African Americans on campus and was also the first black player to acknowledge his perceptions of a "bait-and-switch" approach to recruiting that afflicts BYU to the present day. Smith told Don Smurthwaite, a sportswriter for BYU's school newspaper, the *Daily Universe*, that he felt BYU was not completely transparent during his recruiting trip: "After you get here, it's a whole different story." Smith likewise expressed the social life at BYU as "so conservative . . . it's like if they told you to wear a tie to class you wouldn't do it because you feel like you've already got one on." Other black athletes have raised similar allegations over the past forty years.

60. O'Brien and Smith, The truth about race, para 27.

61. Associated Press. (2014, October 3). BYU Retires Jim McMahon's No. 9. *USA Today*. Retrieved from http://www.usatoday.com/story/sports/ncaaf/2014/10/03/byu-retires-jim-mcmahons-no-9/16693439/

62. Kragthorpe, K. (2014, October 1). Jim McMahon is No. 1 among BYU quarterbacks. *Salt Lake Tribune*. Retrieved from http://www.sltrib.com/sltrib/cougars/58475337-88/mcmahon-byu-utah-hall.html.csp

63. Call, J. (2014). BYU confirms Jim McMahon will be inducted into school's Athletic Hall of Fame, have jersey retired. *Deseret News*. Retrieved from http://www.deseretnews.com/article/865611202/BYU-confirms-Jim-McMahon-will-be-inducted-into-schools-Athletic-Hall-of-Fame-have-jersey-retired.html?pg=all

64. Oler, Five BYU football players have brush with the law.

65. O'Brien and Smith, The truth about race.

66. Hinnen, J. (2014). BYU WR Devon Blackmon tweets he has been suspended over earrings. CBSsports.com. Retrieved at: http://www.cbssports.com/collegefootball/eye-on-college-football/24657887/byu-wr-devon-blackmon-tweets-hes-been-suspended-over-earrings

67. Devon Blackmon was publically lambasted, not only by his coach for publicly admitting his honor code offenses, but also by a former player who questioned his integrity—further underscoring the stereotype that blacks are deviant and should not be trusted if left to their own devices. Yet, this is the entire point of this book, as this has been the consistent pattern. (http://www.deseretnews.com/article/865610178/BYU-receiver-Devon-Blackmon-excited-to-make-a-big-2nd-impression.html?pg=all)

68. Burke, J. (2004). BYU says tattoos were not "erased." *Deseret News*, para 21. Retrieved from http://www.deseretnews.com/article/585037887/BYU-says-tattoos-were-not-erased.html?pg=all

69. Neilsen, C. (2009, April 15). A question of faith. *ESPN the Magazine*, para 22. Retrieved from http://sports.espn.go.com/espnmag/story?id=3717470

70. Baird, J. (1995, June 4). Cougar honor: Some BYU athletes struggle with the code. *Salt Lake Tribune*.

71. Nielsen, BYU confidential.

72. O'Brien and Smith, The truth about race.

73. Drew, J. (2014, March 31). Why BYU is going silent on honor code violation. *Salt Lake Tribune*. Retrieved from http://www.sltrib.com/sltrib/mobile3/57714167-219/byu-honor-code-jenkins.html.csp

74. Taylor, S. (2010). BYU football: Former recruit Karland Bennett arrested, charged in Dallas killing. *Deseret News*. Retrieved from http://www.deseretnews.com/article/700026289/BYU-football-Former-recruit-Karland-Bennett-arrested-charged-in-Dallas-killing.html?pg=all

75. DelVecchio, S. (2011, April 11). Jim McMahon on BYU honor code: Find girls who keep their mouths shut. *Larry Brown Sports*, para 3. Retrieved from http://larrybrownsports.com/football/jim-mcmahon-on-byu-honor-code-find-girls-who-keep-their-mouths-shut/62933

76. Martin, B. E. (2009). Redefining championship in college sports: Enhancing outcomes and increasing student-athlete engagement. In S. R. Harper and S. J. Quaye (Eds.), *Student engagement in higher education: Theoretical perspectives and practical approaches for diverse populations* (pp. 283–93). New York: Routledge.

77. Harrison, C. K., Comeaux, E., and Plecha, M. (2006). Faculty and male football and basketball players on university campuses: An empirical investigation of the "intellectual" as mentor to the student athlete. *Research Quarterly for Exercise and Sport*, 77(2), 277–83.

78. McCullough, telephone interview with author.

79. Matthew 19:24, King James Version.
80. Nielsen, BYU confidential, para 16.
81. Rashaun Broadus, telephone interview with author, November 4, 2014.
82. Broadus, telephone interview with author.
83. McCullough, telephone interview with author.
84. John 8:7, King James Version.

7. COLORBLINDNESS AND THE HEALTH CONSEQUENCES TO BLACK MALE STUDENT-ATHLETES THROUGH THE ILLUSION OF A FREE EDUCATION

1. Rhoden, W. C. (2006). *Forty million dollar slaves: The rise, fall, and redemption of the Black athlete*. New York: Three Rivers Press.

2. Harwood, S. A., Huntt, M. B., Mendenhall, R., and Lewis, J. A. (2012, September). Racial microaggressions in the residence halls: Experiences of students of color at a predominantly White university. *Journal of Diversity in Higher Education, 5*(3), 159–73. http://dx.doi.org/10.1037/a0028956

3. Norton, M. I., and Sommers, S. R. (2011). Whites see racism as a zero-sum game that they are now losing. *Perspectives on Psychological Science, 6*(3), 215–18.

4. Brunker, M., Alba, M., and Dedman, B. (2014). Snapshot: Hate crime in America, by the numbers. NBC News. Retrieved from http://www.nbcnews.com/storyline/jewish-center-shootings/snapshot-hate-crime-america-numbers-n81521

5. Potok, M. (2015). The year in hate and extremism. *Southern Poverty Law Center*. Retrieved from http://www.splcenter.org/Year-in-Hate-and-Extremism

6. Kingkade, T. (2015, March 8). Oklahoma frat boys caught singing "there will never be a n***** in SAE." *Huff Post College*. Retrieved from http://www.huffingtonpost.com/2015/03/08/frat-racist-sae-oklahoma_n_6828212.html

7. Strachan, M. (2015, March 10). Oklahoma linebacker Eric Striker shares his thoughts on fraternity's racist chant. *The Huffington Post*. Retrieved from http://www.huffingtonpost.com/2015/03/10/eric-striker-oklahoma-football-racism_n_6838804.html

8. Smith, W. A., Yosso, T. J., and Solórzano, D. G. (2007). Racial primes and Black misandry on historically White campuses: Toward critical race accountability in educational administration. *The Journal of Leadership Effective and Equitable Organizations, 43*(5), 559–85.

9. Feagin, J. R., Vera, H., and Imani, N. (1996). *The agony of education: Black students at white colleges and universities*. New York: Routledge.

10. Fleming, J. (1984). *Blacks in college: A comparative study of students' success in Black and in White institutions*. San Francisco: Jossey-Bass.

11. Robert Foster, telephone interview with author, November 2013.

12. Smith, D. T. (2012, February 9). Are you serious? BYU Black face and the meaning of race in America. Retrieved from http://www.darronsmith.com/2012/02/are-you-serious-byu-black-face-and-the-meaning-of-race-in-america/

13. Maffly, B. (2012). Video made at BYU about Black culture sparks controversy. *Salt Lake Tribune*. Retrieved from http://www.sltrib.com/sltrib/news/53482773-78/black-ackerman-history-students.html.csp

14. Bloome, D. (2014). Income inequality and intergenerational income mobility in the United States. *Social Forces*. doi:10.1093/sf/sou092.

15. Krieger, N. (2014). Discrimination and health inequalities. *International Journal of Health Services, 44*(4), 643–710.

16. Dee, T. S. (2014). Stereotype threat and the student-athlete. *Economic Inquiry, 52*(1), 173–82.

17. Chae, D. H. et al. (2014). Discrimination, racial bias, and telomere length in African-American men. *American Journal of Preventive Medicine, 46*(2), 103–11.

18. Dovidio, J. F., and Gaertner, S. L. (1998). On the nature of contemporary prejudice: The causes, consequences, and challenges of aversive racism. In J. L. Eberhardt and S. T. Fisk (Eds.), *Confronting racism: The problem and the response*. Thousand Oaks, CA: Sage Publications.

19. Smith, D. T. (2005). These house-Negroes still think we cursed: Struggling against racism in the classroom. *Cultural Studies, 19*(4), 439–54.

20. Bobo, L. D., Kluegel, J. R., and Smith, R. A. (1997). Laissez-faire racism: The crystallization of "kinder, gentler" anti-black ideology. In S. A. Tuch and J. K. Martin (Eds.), *Racial attitudes in the 1990s: Continuity and change*. Westport, CT: Praeger.

21. Schuman, H. (Ed.). *Racial attitudes in America: Trends and interpretations*. Cambridge, MA: Harvard University Press, 1997.

22. McConahay, J. B. (1983). Modern racism and modern discrimination. *Personality and Social Psychology Bulletin, 9*(4), 551–58.

23. Sears, D. O., and Kinder, D. R. (1971). Racial tensions and voting in Los Angeles. In W. Z. Hirsch (Ed.), *Los Angeles: Viability and prospects for metropolitan leadership*. New York: Praeger.

24. Sears, David O. (1988). Symbolic racism. In P. A. Katz, and D. A. Taylor, (Eds.), *Eliminating racism: Profiles in controversy*. New York: Plenum.

25. Feagin, J. R. (2010). *The white racial frame: Centuries of racial framing and counter-framing*. New York: Routledge.

26. Greenwald, A. G., McGhee, D. E., and Schwartz, J. L., (1998). Measuring individual differences in implicit cognition: The Implicit Association Test. *Journal of Personality and Social Psychology, 74*, 1464–80.

27. To explain further, the IAT will flash positive and negative adjectives (love, peace, joy versus terrible, criminal, failure) one at a time on the screen, and the test-taker is tasked with placing it in the appropriate column labeled "positive" or "negative." In addition, the test will either pair the words "white" with the positive column and "black" with the negative column or vice versa ("white" with "negative," "black" with "positive"). The test-taker will perform the activity with both combinations. What the IAT found was that subjects had a harder time linking positive words into the "positive or black" column than "positive or white" column and an easier time linking negative words into a column labeled "negative or black" than into a column labeled "negative or white." This was determined by the speed in which they answered. Just the same, IAT found comparable results when flashing black or white faces or names on the screen for placement into a column.https://implicit.harvard.edu/implicit/education.html

28. Smith-McLallen, A., Johnson, B. T., Dovidio, J. F., and Pearson, A. R. (2006). Black and white: The role of color bias in implicit race bias. *Social Cognition, 24*(1), 46–73, quoted on p. 47.

29. Lee, C. (2013). Making race salient: Trayvon Martin and implicit bias in a not yet post-racial society. *North Carolina Law Review, 91*(5), 1555–1612, quoted on p. 1577.

30. Kang, J. (2012). Communications law: Bits of bias. In J. D. Levinson and R. J. Smith (Eds.), *Implicit racial bias across the law* (pp. 132–45). Cambridge: Cambridge University Press.

31. Telzer, E. H., Humphreys, K. L., Shapiro, M., and Tottenham, N. (2013). Amygdala sensitivity to race is not present in childhood but emerges over adolescence. *Journal of Cognitive Neuroscience, 25*(2), 234–44.

32. Frankenburg, R. (1993). *White women, race matters*. Minneapolis: University of Minnesota Press, p. 142.

33. Ferguson, Missouri, was a hotbed for protest and civil unrest in the wake of the shooting of an unarmed black teen, Michael Brown, in the summer of 2014. His death symbolized the brutality of conditions that black Americans endure at the hand of white police officers. These protests have continued through 2015, calling for change. Despite controversy over what actually happened between Officer Darren Wilson and Mike Brown, his death was a tipping point in the unjustness that black Ferguson residents (and blacks across the country) faced at the hands of white authority. And this was validated in the Justice Department report that found widespread racism and racial targeting

throughout the Ferguson Police Department. Not much has changed in fifty years.

34. Rothstein, B., and Uslaner, E. (2005). All for all: Equality, corruption and social trust. *World Politics*, *58*, 41–72.

35. Uslaner, E. M. (2002). The moral foundations of trust. Cambridge: Cambridge University Press.

36. Kang, Communications law.

37. Rooth, D.-O. (2007). Implicit discrimination in hiring: Real world evidence (Discussion Paper No. 2764). Bonn, Germany: Forschungsinstitut zur Zukunft/der Arbeit/Institute for the Study of Labor.

38. Sullivan, S. (2014). *Good white people: The problem with middle-class white anti-racism*. New York: State University of New York Press.

39. Volk, P. (2015, January 30). Richard Sherman on the NCAA: You're not on scholarship for school. *SBNation*. Retrieved from http://www.sbnation.com/college-football/2015/1/30/7951529/seahawks-richard-sherman-michael-bennett-slam-ncaa

40. Harper, S. R., Williams, C. D., and Blackman, H. (2013). *Black male student-athletes and racial inequities in NCAA Division I revenue-generating college sports*. Philadelphia: University of Pennsylvania, Center for the Study of Race and Equity in Education.

41. Smith, D. T. (2014, May 9). Emancipate the players. *The Chronicle Review*. Retrieved from http://chronicle.com/article/Emancipate-the-Black-College/146273/

42. Volk, Richard Sherman.

43. Harper, Williams, and Blackman, *Black male student-athletes*.

44. Huma, R., and Staurowsky, E. J. (n.d.). The price of poverty in big time college sport. National College Players Association. Retrieved from http://www.ncpanow.org/research/body/The-Price-of-Poverty-in-Big-Time-College-Sport.pdf

45. Northwestern Athletic Department, Academic Services and Student Development. (n.d.). Student-athlete employment guidelines. Retrieved from http://www.northwestern.edu/academicservices/cats-lifeskills/career-development/employment-guidelines.html

46. Adelson, E. (2015, March 24). Getting a shot at NFL could mean taking out a loan. *Yahoo! Sports*. Retrieved from http://sports.yahoo.com/news/getting-shot-at-nfl-could-mean-taking-out-a-loan-064043953.html

47. Huma and Staurowsky, The price of poverty.

48. McNeil, M., Blad, E. (2014, March 21). Nation falls short on educational equity, data show: Disparities seen from pre-K to high school. *Education Week*. Retrieved from: http://www.edweek.org/ew/articles/2014/03/21/26ocr.h33.html

49. Harper, S. R. (2014). Black men as college athletes: The real win-loss record. *Chronicle of Higher Education, LX*(19), A60.

50. Lleras, C. (2008). Race, racial concentration, and the dynamics of educational inequality across urban and suburban schools. *American Educational Research Journal, 45*(4), 886–912.

51. Ganim, S. (2014, January 8). CNN analysis: Some college athletes play like adults, read like 5th graders. CNN. Retrieved from http://www.cnn.com/2014/01/07/us/ncaa-athletes-reading-scores

52. LaForge, L., Hodge, J. (2011). NCAA academic performance metrics: Implications for institutional policy and practice. *Journal of Higher Education, 62*(2), 217–35.

53. Johnon, J. E., Wessel, R. D., Piece, D. A. (2012). The influence of selected variables on NCAA Academic Progress Rate. *Journal of Issues in Intercollegiate Athletics, 5*, 149–71.

54. Barrett, P. M. (2014). In fake classes scandal, UNC fails its athletes—and whistle-blower. *Bloomberg Business*. Retrieved from http://www.bloomberg.com/bw/articles/2014-02-27/in-fake-classes-scandal-unc-fails-its-athletes-whistle-blower

55. Payne, M. (2015, January 21). NCAA is reportedly investigating 20 universities for academic fraud. *Washington Post*. Retrieved from http://www.washingtonpost.com/blogs/early-lead/wp/2015/01/21/ncaa-is-reportedly-investigating-20-universities-for-academic-fraud/

56. Ganim, S. (2015, January 23). Lawsuit claims UNC and NCAA broke promises in spectacular fashion. CNN. Retrieved from: http://www.cnn.com/2015/01/22/us/unc-paper-classes-lawsuit/index.html

57. Guskiewicz, K. M., Weaver, N. L., Padua, D. A., and Garrett, W. E. (2000). Epidemiology of concussion in collegiate and high school football players. *American Journal of Sports Medicine, 28*, 643–50.

58. Lapchick, R., Sanders, D., Fox, J., and Van Berlo, V. (2015). *Keeping score when it counts: Assessing the academic records of the 2014–2015 bowl-bound college football teams*. Orlando: University of Central Florida, The Institute for Diversity and Ethics in Sport.

59. Lapchick et al., *Keeping score when it counts*.

60. Christian started his career as a redshirt freshman at BYU-Hawaii prior to his two-year LDS mission. He later transferred to the University of Washington for two years following his year at SCI junior college.

61. Christian Parker, telephone interview with author, February 4, 2015.

62. Christian Parker, electronic messaging interview with author, August 24, 2014.

63. Parker, electronic messaging interview.

64. Heaton, T. B., Jacobson, C. K. (2015). The social life of Mormons. Forthcoming in *Oxford Handbook on Mormonism*. Oxford: Oxford University Press.

65. Smith, D. (2015). The emotional labor of playing cool: How black male transracial adoptees find ways to cope within predominantly white settings. In R. A. Javier, G. A. Pantoja, J. Raible, and A. Baden (Eds.), Race, religion, and rescue in adoption: Part II [Special issue]. *Journal of Social Distress and the Homeless, 25*(1).

66. Parker, electronic messaging interview.

67. Kochanek, K. D., Xu, J., Murphy, S. L., Minino, A. M., and Kung, H. (2011). Deaths: Final data for 2009. *National Vital Statistics Reports: From the Centers for Disease Control and Prevention, National Center for Health Statistics, National Vital Statistics System, 60*(3), 1–116.

68. Harper, S. R. (2013). Am I my brother's teacher? Black undergraduates, racial socialization, and peer pedagogies in predominately white postsecondary contexts. *Review of Research in Education, 37*(1), 183–211.

69. Edwards, H. (1984). The Black 'dumb jock': An American sports tragedy. *The College Board Review, 131*, 8–13, quoted on p. 8.

70. Hodge, S. R., Burden, J. W., Robinson, L. E., and Bennett III, R. A. (2008). Theorizing on the stereotyping of black male student-athletes: Issues and implications. *Journal for the Study of Sports and Athletes in Education, 2*(2), 203–26.

71. Hughes, R. L., Satterfield, J. W., and Giles, M. S. (2007). Athletisizing black male student-athletes: The social construction of race, sports, myths, and realities. *NASAP Journal, 10*(1), 112–27.

72. Harper, Am I my brother's.

73. Fleming, *Blacks in college*, p. 130.

74. Smith, W. A. (2004). Black faculty coping with racial battle fatigue: The campus racial climate in a post-civil rights era. In D. Cleveland (Ed.), *A long way to go: Conversations about race by African American faculty and graduate students* (pp. 171–90). New York: Peter Lang.

75. Smith, Black faculty coping with racial battle fatigue.

76. Fleming, *Blacks in college*.

77. Berger, J. B., and Milem, J. F. (2000). Exploring the impact of historically black colleges in promoting the development of undergraduates' self-concept. *Journal of College Student Development, 41*, 381–94.

78. Smith, D. T. (2014). The effects of living with race-based discrimination and stress: The impact on the body and mental health. In D. T. Smith and T. E. Sabino, *The impact of social factors on health: A critical reader for the physician assistant*. San Diego: Cognella Academic Publishing.

79. DeSantis, A. S., Adam, E. K., Doane, L. D., Mineka, S., Zinbarg, R. E., and Craske, M. G. (2007). Racial/ethnic differences in cortisol diurnal rhythms in a community sample of adolescents. *Journal of Adolescent Health, 41*, 3–13.

80. Evans, G. W., and English, K. (2002). The environment of poverty: Multiple stressor exposure, psychophysiological stress, and socioemotional adjustment. *Child Development, 73*, 1238–48.

81. McEwen, B. S. (1998). Protective and damaging effects of stress mediators. *New England Journal of Medicine, 338*, 171–79. doi:10.1056/NEJM199801153380307.

82. Telomeres are repetitive sequences of DNA at the ends of chromosomes that protect against DNA degradation. Think of telomeres as caps to the tips of chromosomes to protect the cellular matrix and DNA. Telomeres are important in providing stability to the human chromosome—the longer the telomere, the less chance of chromosomal death. With each cell made up of forty-six chromosomes, the cell life depends on the life of the chromosome, in essence, the length of the telomere. Believed to be impacted by elevated levels of cortisol and oxidative stress, critically shortened telomeres are associated with cellular senescence (death). Hence, telomere length is thought to be a marker of replicative history and aging at the cellular level. Research suggests there are health consequences to prolonged exposure to stress-inducing situations and environments (e.g., financial difficulties, noise, conditions of poverty, mental and physical abuse, discrimination), which can shorten telomere length, causing them to become difficult to repair. The life expectancy of the chromosome, then, enters into a state of arrest and the cell eventually dies. Repeated exposure to the harmful physiological effects of oxidative stress has been linked with biological pathways associated with aging, overactive stress response (HPA axis system) increasing the risk of the development of certain chronic disease. Following other scientific research, it is believed telomeres may serve as a potent, novel biomarker of overall health and well-being as they are responsive to the environmental changes in the human condition. Chae, Discrimination.

83. Paradies Y. (2006). A systematic review of empirical research on self-reported racism and health. *International Journal of Epidemiology, 35*, 888–901.

84. Fuller-Rowell, T. E., Doan, S. N., and Eccles, J. S. (2012). Differential effects of perceived discrimination on the diurnal cortisol rhythm of African Americans and whites. *Psychoneuroendocrinology, 37*, 107–18.

85. Mays, V. M., Cochran, S. D., and Barnes, N. W. (2007). Race, race-based discrimination, and health outcomes among African Americans. *Annual Review of Psychology, 58*, 201–25

86. Sellers, R. M., Caldwell, C. H., Schmeelk-Cone, K., H., and Zimmerman, M. A. (2003). Racial identity, racial discrimination, perceived stress, and psychological distress among African American young adults. *Journal of Health and Social Behavior, 44*, 302–17.

87. Paige, J. M. (1970). Changing patterns of anti-white attitudes among blacks. *Journal of Social Issues, 26*, 69–86.

88. Citrin, J., Green, D. P., & Sears, D. O. (1990). White reactions to black candidates: When does race matter? *Public Opinion Quarterly, 54*(1), 74–96.

89. Highton, B. (2004). White voters and African American candidates for congress. *Political Behavior, 26*(1), 1–25.

90. Tesler, M. (2014). The return of old-fashioned racism to white Americans' partisan preferences in the early Obama era. *The Journal of Politics, 75*(1), 110–23.

91. Noguera, P. A. (2003). The trouble with black boys: The role and influence of environmental and cultural factors on the academic performance of African-American males. *Urban Education, 38*(4), 431–59.

92. Alexander, M. (2010). *The new Jim Crow: Mass incarceration in the age of colorblindness*. New York: The New Press.

93. Pager, D. (2007). *Marked: Race, crime, and finding work in an era of mass incarceration*. Chicago: University of Chicago Press.

94. Williamson, J. A. (2003). *Black power on campus: The University of Illinois, 1965–75*. Champaign, IL: University of Illinois Press.

8. PIPELINE TO A PIPEDREAM

1. Newton, H. P. (1973). *Revolutionary suicide*. San Diego: Harcourt Brace Jovanovich, p. 22.

2. O'Connor, W. (2014, May 6). Speed read: The juiciest bits of a new Michael Jordan biography. *The Daily Beast*. Retrieved from http://www.thedailybeast.com/articles/2014/05/06/speed-read-the-juiciest-bits-of-a-new-michael-jordan-biography.html

3. Rhoden, W. C. (2006). *Forty million dollar slaves: The rise, fall, and redemption of the black athlete*. New York: Three Rivers Press.

4. Rhoden, *Forty million dollar slaves.*

5. Haq, H. (2014, December 8). LeBron James and the return of the activist athlete. *Christian Science Monitor*. Retrieved from http://www.csmonitor.com/USA/Society/2014/1208/LeBron-James-and-the-return-of-the-activist-athlete-video

6. Parker, D. (2014, December 1). Protests around the country mark the moment of Ferguson shooting. *New York Times*. Retrieved from http://www.

nytimes.com/2014/12/02/us/protests-around-the-country-mark-the-moment-of-ferguson-shooting.html?_r=0

7. Almasy, S., and Yan, H. (2014, November 26). Protestors fill streets across country as Ferguson protests spread coast to coast. CNN. Retrieved from http://www.cnn.com/2014/11/25/us/national-ferguson-protests/

8. Associated Press. (2014, December 2). Did Rams apologize to police for hands-up gesture? CBS News. Retrieved from http://www.cbsnews.com/news/st-louis-rams-apologize-for-players-ferguson-hands-up-dont-shoot/

9. Zirin, D. (2014, December 1). St. Louis Rams players tell the world that #BlackLivesMatter. *The Nation*. Retrieved from http://www.thenation.com/blog/191697/st-louis-rams-players-tell-world-blacklivesmatter#

10. BET-Staff. (2014, December 8). Reggie Bush, Derrick Rose wear "I can't breathe" t-shirts for Eric Garner. *BET Sports*. Retrieved from http://www.bet.com/news/sports/2014/12/08/reggie-bush-derrick-rose-wear-i-can-t-breathe-t-shirts-for-eric-garner.html

11. Zirin, D. (2014, December 8). #BlackLivesMatter takes the field: A weekend of athletes speaking out. *The Nation*. Retrieved from http://www.thenation.com/blog/192121/blacklivesmatter-takes-field-weekend-athletes-speaking-out

12. Associated Press. (2014, December 18). Jaguars' receivers wear "I can't breathe" shirts during warm-ups. *Fox Sports NFL*. Retrieved from http://www.foxsports.com/nfl/story/jacksonville-jaguars-players-wear-i-can-t-breathe-t-shirts-during-warm-ups-121814

13. Bieler, D. (December 4, 2014). Terps wide receiver Deon Long joined #BlackLivesMatter protest outside Xfinity Center. *Washington Post*. Retrieved from: http://www.washingtonpost.com/blogs/dc-sports-bog/wp/2014/12/04/terps-wide-receiver-deon-long-joined-blacklivesmatter-protest-outside-xfinity-center/

14. Jamieson, D. (2015, March 21). Obama calls on NCAA to rethink the way it protects and punishes athletes. *Huffington Post Politics*. Retrieved from http://www.huffingtonpost.com/2015/03/21/obama-ncaa-scholarships_n_6911804.html

15. McCune, C. (2013, April 8). NCAA policies for student-athlete medical insurance breakdown. *Bleacher Report*. Retrieved from http://bleacherreport.com/articles/1595326-ncaa-policies-for-student-athlete-medical-insurance-breakdown

16. Sinha, S. (2014, November 5). The NCAA's shameful failure to insure its athletes. *Vice Sports*. Retrieved from https://sports.vice.com/article/the-ncaas-shameful-failure-to-insure-its-athletes

17. Jamieson, Obama calls on NCAA.

18. *O'Bannon v. Nat. Collegiate Athletic Association*, 7 F. Supp. 3d 955 (N.D. Cal. 2014); p.2

19. The full grant-in-aid value is set by each institution and "consists of tuition and fees, room and board, and required course-related books." Money earned from students' grant-in-aid is solely limited to their athletic scholarship based on the current rule. The *O'Bannon* ruling would allow students to earn money from commercials, magazines, etc. Up until this ruling, the NCAA prohibited its student-athletes from receiving any monies above the cost of attendance without exception. This included income they earn from a place of employment. Now some schools are able to offer up to an additional $2,000 to cover the cost of attendance, which includes "supplies, transportation, and other expenses related to attendance"; hence, cost of attendance is higher than the full grant-in-aid.

20. *O'Bannon v. Nat. Collegiate Athletic Association*, p.95.

21. *O'Bannon v. Nat. Collegiate Athletic Association*, p.95.

22. Associated Press. (2015, Jan 17). NCAA Big 5 pass athletic scholarship value increases, concussion protocol. Fox Sports. Retrieved from http://www.foxsports.com/college-football/story/ncaa-big-ten-big-12-acc-pac-12-sec-concussion-athletic-scholarship-011715.

23. Fornelli, T. (2014, March 26). NLRB rules in favor of College Athletes Players Association. CBS Sports. Retrieved from http://www.cbssports.com/collegefootball/eye-on-college-football/24501646/college-athletes-players-association-wins-case-at-nlrb.

24. Huguenin, M. (2014, February 18). Northwestern's Kain Colter: Playing football "truly is a job." NFL.com. Retrieved from http://www.nfl.com/news/story/0ap2000000326397/article/northwesterns-kain-colter-playing-football-truly-is-a-job.

25. Strauss, B. (2015, August 17). N.L.R.B. rejects Northwestern football players' union bid. *The New York Times*. Retrieved from http://www.nytimes.com/2015/08/18/sports/ncaafootball/nlrb-says-northwestern-football-players-cannot-unionize.html?_r=0.

26. Remy, D. (n.d.). NCAA responds to union proposal. NCAA. http://www.ncaa.org/about/resources/media-center/press-releases/ncaa-responds-union-proposal

27. "CBS Sports, Turner Broadcasting, NCAA reach 14-year agreement." (2010, April 22). NCAA. Retrieved from http://www.ncaa.com/news/basketball-men/2010-04-21/cbs-sports-turner-broadcasting-ncaa-reach-14-year-agreement

28. Solomon, J. (2014, January 14). UNC academic whistleblower supports Ed O'Bannon plaintiffs' goal of paying players. *AL.com*. Retrieved from http://www.al.com/sports/index.ssf/2014/01/post_568.html

29. Ganim, S. (January 8, 2014). CNN analysis: Some college athletes play like adults, read like 5th graders. CNN. Retrieved from: http://www.cnn.com/2014/01/07/us/ncaa-athletes-reading-scores

30. Noguera, P. A. (2003). The trouble with black boys: The role and influence of environmental and cultural factors on the academic performance of African-American males. *Urban Education, 38*(4), 431–59.

31. Kunjufu, J. (1995). *Countering the conspiracy to destroy black boys*. Chicago: African American Images.

32. Toldson, I. A. (2008). *Breaking barriers: Plotting the path to academic success for school-age African-American males*. Washington, DC: Congressional Black Caucus Foundation.

33. Juarez, B., and Hayes, C. (2012). An endarkened learning and transformative education for freedom dreams. *The Journal of Educational Controversy, 6*(1), 1–17.

34. Beamon, K. K., and Bell, P. A. (2006). Academics versus athletics: An examination of the effects of background and socialization on African American male student-athletes. *Social Science Journal, 43*(3), 393–403.

35. Fleming, J. (1984). Blacks in college: A comparative study of students' success in Black and in White institutions. San Francisco: Jossey-Bass.

36. Zirin, St. Louis Rams players.

37. Lapchick, R., Sanders, D., Fox, J., and Van Berlo, V. (2015). *Keeping score when it counts: Assessing the academic records of the 2014–2015 bowl-bound college football teams*. Orlando: University of Central Florida, The Institute for Diversity and Ethics in Sport.

38. Uchtdorf, D. F. (March 7, 2014). Seeing beyond the Leaf. *The Church of Jesus Christ of Latter-Day Saints*. Retrieved from https://www.lds.org/prophets-and-apostles/unto-all-the-world/seeing-beyond-the-leaf?lang=eng

39. Marlon Terrell, telephone interview with author, March 2015.

40. The U.S. Naval Academy is an animal unto itself. The athletes at the academy are truly students and midshipmen first, as they must receive a letter of recommendation from a member of Congress before consideration for admission. That said, they are athletes second. Because of their exchange in service to the country, *all* midshipment at the U.S. Naval Academy not only obtain a "free ride," but they actually get paid to attend the academy with a monthly stipend. Hence, the NCAA guidelines do not entirely apply to them. However, a sponsor program is still possible for the typical college and university, and it would be permissible within NCAA guidelines under NCAA rule 16.11.1.5. See http://byucougars.com/files/handbook_0.pdf

41. Milkman, K. L., Akinola, M., and Chugh, D. (2014, December 13). What happens before? A field experiment exploring how pay and representa-

tion differentially shape bias on the pathway into organizations. *Social Science Research Network*. Retrieved from http://dx.doi.org/10.2139/ssrn.2063742

42. The Church of Jesus Christ of Latter-day Saints. (2015). General authorities and general officers. Retrieved from https://www.lds.org/church/leaders?lang=eng

43. Stack, P. F. (March 3, 2015). With average age of 80, Mormon church has never had older top leaders. *Salt Lake Tribune.* Retrieved from http://www.sltrib.com/home/2245029-155/with-average-age-of-80-mormon

44. Associated Press. (2014, December 22). Brawl erupts after Memphis beats BYU in 2OT in Miami Beach Bowl. *Fox Sports*. Retrieved from http://www.foxsports.com/college-football/story/memphis-tigers-byu-cougars-fight-punches-miami-beach-bowl-122214

45. Harper, S. R., Patton, L. D., and Wooden, O. S. (2009). Access and equity for African American students in higher education: A critical race historical analysis of policy efforts. *Journal of Higher Education, 80*, 389–414.

46. Harper, S. R., Williams, C. D., Jr. and Blackman, H. W. (2013). Black male student-athletes and racial inequities in NCAA Division I college sports. Center for the Study of Race & Equity in Education.

INDEX

ABOUT THE AUTHOR

Darron T. Smith is an adjunct faculty member in the Department of Sociology at the University of Memphis. He has lectured and published widely in the fields of healthcare disparities, religious studies, and transracial adoption and the black family. Dr. Smith is coauthor of *White Parents, Black Children: Experiencing Transracial Adoption* as well as coeditor of *Black and Mormon* and *The Impact of Social Factors on Health*. He is a frequent political and cultural commentator for the *Huffington Post* on various issues of U.S.-based oppression and has contributed to various media, including *Religion Dispatches* and ESPN's *Outside the Lines*.